Strategy and the Second World War

JEREMY BLACK

ROBINSON

ROBINSON

First published in Great Britain in 2021 by Robinson

1 3 5 7 9 10 8 6 4 2

ISBN: 978-1-47214-510-9

Typeset in Scala by Hewer Text UK Ltd, Edinburgh
Printed and bound in Great Britain by Clays Ltd, Elcograf S.p.A.

Papers used by Robinson are from well-managed forests and other responsible sources.
[Typesetters: please add FSC responsible sources logo, Cert no: FSC® C104740]

Robinson
An imprint of
Little, Brown Book Group
Carmelite House
50 Victoria Embankment
London EC4Y 0DZ

An Hachette UK Company
www.hachette.co.uk

www.littlebrown.co.uk

For Robert Crowcroft

Contents

Preface

In relaxed poses, Churchill and Roosevelt amiably share a bench on New Bond Street in London, or at least they have done so since the life-size sculpture *Allies* by Lawrence Holofcener was erected there in 1995. Commissioned to commemorate fifty years of peace, and largely paid for by the luxury businesses on the street that serve many foreign tourists, prominently Americans, the sculpture testifies to the strong desire to propagate and celebrate a memory of wartime cooperation, and a wish to humanise it, as well as to focus on the role of the leaders who are presented as equals.

This cooperation is a memory much used today by both Americans and, far more, Britons who emphasise the value of the frequently proclaimed 'Special Relationship' between the two powers. In doing so, they see this wartime alliance as an important lesson for modern Britain and, indeed, the United States. The reality, then and now, however, was of a different relationship; one, largely born of necessity, that was very much transactional and, at times, extremely troubled. Which is not surprising between allies. Indeed, Roosevelt could be very harsh to Churchill, notably at the Tehran conference of Allied war leaders in November–December 1943. He carefully avoided visiting London during the war and was a persistent and vigorous critic of the British Empire. At the governmental and popular levels, the British were keener on the Americans than vice versa.

In practice, indeed, the interplay of impression and reality, both then and subsequently, captures much of the politics of strategy. This interplay needs to be pushed to the fore. This is not least because the political dimension undermines the idea that there was an optimal choice of strategy, whether in intention or in implementation; and this undermining is correct. Indeed, strategy, an all-encompassing phenomenon and practice, has integral ideological, political, social and cultural elements, all of which are of great consequence; and each of which affects the conception, formulation, implementation and assessment of strategy.

Moreover, it is necessary to unpick the idea of national strategy and to emphasise, instead, the variety of strategies on offer at the national level. In large part, this situation, as far as military strategy was concerned, reflected the very different perspective of the individual services – although far more was entailed, including divisions within the services and, at the level of government, very different assessments of national interests and goals. This tension is generally underplayed due to the emphasis, instead, on national leaders. While that emphasis is valuable, it suggests a misleading degree of coherence.

A short, accessible and, in particular, very lightly footnoted public- and student-friendly account of strategy and the Second World War is missing from the literature. There is a need for one promptly as we have just had the eightieth anniversaries of its start in Europe (1939) and the Fall of France (1940), which left Germany in an apparently dominant position. These will be followed, in 2021, by the eightieth anniversary of the war becoming global, with the German attack on the Soviet Union, that of Japan on Britain and the United States, and the German declaration of war on the United States. American participation helped lead much of Latin America into the war against Germany.

That the anniversaries accentuate longstanding 'history wars' about the causes, course, consequences and meaning of the world war, both as a whole and for particular countries, underlines the need for such a concise book. It is particularly necessary to be alive to these present-day controversies and their undoubted significance, both for the understanding of the world war and for that of the present day. Linked to this, it is important to engage explicitly not only with the strategic issues of the time (and as they developed chronologically and also how they interacted), but also to relate those to subsequent debates about the choices made. The continued political contexts and resonances of these debates require discussion. Chapters seven and eight explicitly address this issue. The continuing need for such discussion is illustrated by the renewed controversy over strategic bombing that was pushed to the fore in February 2020 at the time of the seventy-fifth anniversary of the bombing of Dresden.

Underlying these points comes the understanding of strategy. I build on the conceptual and methodological perspectives offered in my existing works on strategy: *Plotting Power. Strategy in the Eighteenth Century* (2017) and *Military Strategy. A Global History* (2020). As a result of this approach, there will be a wide-ranging treatment of strategy, and not one framed by a tight definition. The book focuses on strategy as the integration of long-term political, economic and military planning; but strategy also relates to military doctrine, as with the Soviet 'deep battle' concept. Strategy, moreover, focuses on the level where theoretical doctrine meets practical operational planning, which is crucial to the strategic level of military planning. The key stance in this book will be, first, to emphasise strategic culture, secondly, to collapse the questionable distinction between policy and strategy, and, thirdly, to stress the dynamic impact of contexts, the continual significance of prioritisation and the significance of the unfixed nature of alliance systems. Bringing dynamic, fluid and chaotic factors into the examination of strategy is helpful. Hindsight gives us knowledge of the whole story, so that we tend to impose order when none may have existed.

Thanks to an emphasis on strategic culture, strategy encompasses not only conflict but also domestic goals, and economic and ideological means. These were understood by contemporaries as intertwined, which, indeed, helps explain the use by all powers of the vocabulary of battle and war to discuss the domestic situation. The Holocaust was as much part of Hitler's strategy as war at all levels with communism. It is also useful to see how ideology and circumstances each played a role in the interplay between the longer-term factors discussed in terms of strategic culture and, on the other hand, the more specific nature of the strategy pursued, and the strategies implemented to that end.

In thinking about, researching and writing this work, an overview for the general reader, I benefited greatly from teaching a Second World War special subject at the University of Exeter, and profited much from the excellent existing scholarship on the subject, to which my book is intended as a contribution. I have also benefited from the opportunity to speak publicly on aspects of this subject, including, in 2019–20 at the National WWII Museum in New Orleans, at the Second World War Research Group Annual Conference in Wolverhampton, to the New York Military Affairs Symposium, at the universities of South-East Louisiana, Southern Mississippi, Ohio, Louisiana–Shreveport and Westminster, to the Royal Artillery Historical Society at Larkhill, at the Chalke Valley History Festival, to the Exeter branch of the Historical Association, at Radley College and at Torquay Museum; but most memorably for me on earlier occasions, notably on the deck of the USS *Missouri* in Pearl Harbor in 2005, on the cliff overlooking Omaha Beach, and at Sebastopol and St Petersburg. I was also fortunate in 2019 to be able to visit Pacific war sites, notably Guadalcanal and Rabaul, and European war sites, including Dresden and Potsdam. Touring the Sudetenland made clear its defensive possibilities.

I have been helped greatly by the comments of Pete Brown, Stan Carpenter, Enrico Cernuschi, Jonathan Fennell, Heiko Werner Henning, Steve Minor, Ciro Paoletti, Bill Purdue, Alexander Querengässer, Mark Stevens, Ulf Sundberg, David Ulbrich and Tony Wells, on all or part of an earlier draft of this book, and from discussing the subject with John Brobst, Andrew Buchanan, Roger Moorhouse, Jeremy Noakes and Barnett Singer. Their kindness is much appreciated. None is responsible for any errors that remain. Duncan Proudfoot has again proved a most supportive publisher and Howard Watson an exemplary copy editor. It is a great pleasure to dedicate this book to Robert Crowcroft, an important scholar on the period, a rising talent, and a friend.

1

Projecting War

World domination, that was the strategy attributed to Hitler by his opponents. An American film, *The Nazi Strike* (1943), depicted what it claimed were German geopolitical plans: 'Conquer Eastern Europe and you dominate the Heartland. Conquer the Heartland and you dominate the World Island. Conquer the World Island and you dominate the World.' That was propaganda, intended to energise and direct the American public, once the world war was at full charge. Prior to the German attack on the Soviet Union in June 1941, the situation was far less open to this apparent clarity.

Strategic consideration and engagement are particularly significant in the run-up to wars. Once conflict has begun, strategy has to share this position with the biting immediacies of operational and tactical considerations, and the incessant pressures of resource factors. These are all present in the earlier stage of the run-up; but strategy is more to the fore. It both helps to frame, just as it is framed by, the central questions of the identity and goals of the protagonists, and the timing of their conflicts. Thus, Appeasement and the Soviet–German pact of 1939 can both be seen as key strategic means that were important to the initial circumstances of the struggle and, indeed, thereby helped play a major role in its subsequent course, as well as the retrospective discussion of the war.

We have the benefit of hindsight, so it is difficult to appreciate the degree to which a major, and continuing, element for contemporaries was strategic uncertainty, a factor that greatly encouraged emphasis on espionage. This uncertainty repeatedly linked the pre-conflict years to their wartime sequel, just as it acted as a point of tension when considering the possible relationship between the war and the post-war world. In particular, up to the end of 1941, it was unclear which powers would be involved, and on what side or, given the variety of conflicts involved, sides. This element, in practice, went on being significant until the end of the war, with the Soviet Union not attacking Japan until August 1945. This was far more important than Argentina and Turkey joining the Allies in 1945 as the war neared its close, or Ireland, Sweden and Switzerland remaining neutral.

This uncertainty, however, was most significant until the end of 1941, during which time the powers had to plan in a context of constant unpredictability. The uncertainty was accentuated by a greater lack of clarity as to the broader situation beyond that of bilateral relations. The outbreak of war did not lessen this element, because the outbreak itself proved far more drawn-out than in the First World War, as did the conflict itself. In the First World War, Austria-Hungary (often referred to as Austria), Russia, Germany, France and Britain were all at war within a month, and with no neutralities confusing what were clearly two sides. Each of these powers declared war on all of those on the other side.

The situation was very different in the Second World War. Although Japan did not present it as such, China and Japan were at full-scale war from 1937, but with no other power involved on either side, and indeed with far less international intervention than in the Spanish Civil War of 1936–9. On 3 September

1939, Britain and France went to war with Germany in response to the latter's invasion of Poland on 1 September. However, when Germany's ally, the Soviet Union (the successor to Russia), also attacked Poland on 17 September, Britain and France did not extend the war to include it. In this decision, there was not the extent and immediacy of alliance systems seen in 1914; rather, it was informed by prudence or what may be termed 'the cartography of concern'.

In each world war, Italy (1915, 1940) and the United States (1917, 1941) were later entrants, but in the Second World War there was generally more delay before nations committed completely to the fray. Germany and the Soviet Union did not begin fighting each other until the German attack on 22 June 1941. Furthermore, the linkage was not complete as Japan and the Soviet Union did not go to war until 9 August 1945. There had been delays in the First World War – Italy, for example, waiting until after its declaration of war on Austria-Hungary before going to war with Germany, and the United States not declaring war on Austria-Hungary until December 1917; but none on the scale comparable to what was seen in the Second World War.

Moreover, the Asian war was not really linked to the European one until the Japanese attacks of 7 December 1941 and Germany's declaration of war on the United States on behalf of its ally Japan on 11 December; a declaration that was not reciprocated by Japan declaring war on the Soviet Union. The Japanese attacks put greater pressure on Britain than it faced from Germany and Italy alone, and the German declaration of war led to the United States playing a role in both the Asian and European conflicts. In contrast, while the conflict in the Far East was far less significant in the First World War, the timing then was very different, with Japan rapidly coming in on the Allied side in 1914 and swiftly capturing the local German bases in China and the north-west Pacific. These bases were not as heavily defended as comparable Japanese ones were in 1943–5.

The far more complex and protracted beginning thus made the Second World War different to the previous world war. So did its greater geographical range: the first war did not have an Asian dimension on anywhere near the scale seen in the second. In part, this was because the Russo-Japanese War of 1904–5 was very separate both chronologically and in terms of the alignment to the First World War, in which the two had been on the same side; whereas the conflict between them was part of the Second World War, although not until 1945.

From the early 1930s, powers strategised over likely international combinations in a situation made more volatile by the growing aggressiveness of those pursuing expansion, notably Japan from 1931, Italy from 1935 and Germany from 1936. Each was a year when significant acts of aggression occurred, in the shape of the invasion of Manchuria, the attack on Abyssinia (Ethiopia) and the occupation of the Rhineland.

Yet, that aggressiveness in itself did not make strategy clear, for these powers, for their potential opponents or for the possible allies of both. The relationships between expansionism, aggression and conflict were in practice complex, and certainly far from obvious. Indeed, strategies were in part a matter of taskings in a context in which it was unclear when limited peace would become limited war; and, in each case, for whom; and with what consequences for other powers. What limited war would mean, and how it would be conducted, were uncertain.

The new international order created in 1917 had involved American participation in the global system. This order was achieved in 1918 through victory and the overthrow of the ruling élites in Austria-Hungary and Germany, which had been primarily responsible for the world war. The subsequent peace treaties of 1919–20, collectively known as the Peace of Versailles, however, brought new commitments to the victorious powers, but with the United States choosing not to be fully involved. These commitments were underlined both by the failure to defeat the communists who had seized control in Russia in 1917, and, in contrast, by the subsequent containment of communism and the Soviet Union.

The resulting international order had a novel format in the League of Nations, but it essentially rested on the example of having defeated Austro-Hungarian and German expansionism. As such, there was a parallel with the European system after the defeat in 1812–15 of Napoleonic expansionism, with the Congress of Vienna (1814–15) then followed by the 'Congress System' of the major powers. The example of defeating expansionism was underlined when, after initial success that took their forces close to Warsaw, the Soviet attempt to conquer Poland was, with French help, totally quashed in 1920, and the Soviets then driven back. Thanks in part to British naval intervention, the Soviets also failed to conquer the Baltic states (Estonia, Latvia, Lithuania), all formerly part of Russia, but they did reconquer Ukraine and the Caucasus republics of Armenia, Georgia and Azerbaijan. By 1925, the political situation had been largely stabilised, even if the United States did not guarantee it by becoming, as had been envisaged by President Woodrow Wilson, a member of the League of Nations with the consequent obligation to maintain the Versailles agreement. Nor was there ever a League army.

As a result of this stabilisation, military activity for the major powers became less consequential and, indeed, focused on maintaining control or defending interests in areas of formal or informal imperial interest: for Britain in the Middle East; for France in Morocco and Syria; and for the United States in Central America and the Caribbean. This theme remained important in the 1930s, with Britain, in particular, devoting significant military resources in the late 1930s to suppressing, successfully, both the Arab Rising in Palestine and opposition in Waziristan on the North-West Frontier of British India (now part of Pakistan). In the meantime, both the revolts repressed and British failures, notably in Ireland (1919–21) and Turkey (1922), as well as issues in Britain, not least the Invergordon naval mutiny of 1931, demonstrated to many others that Britain's position had weaknesses. This opened up windows of opportunity for other states and for opponents within the British Empire.

The imperial commitment was a key aspect of strategic planning, that of the protection of existing possessions. The prime threat could be from within empires, as in these cases, but challenges from without were also significant. Thus, in the 1920s, the British were worried about territorial disputes with Turkey over their new position in oil-rich northern Iraq, a League of Nations mandate given to Britain. There was no agreed frontier between Turkey and Iraq, which, indeed, had been part of the Turkish-ruled Ottoman Empire since the early sixteenth century.

The security of possessions had a wider-ranging meaning in light of the developing weapons technologies of the period, and notably those of aircraft and of aircraft carriers. The belief that the bomber would 'get through' – the contemporary phrase used in the House of Commons in 1932 by Stanley Baldwin, a former and future Prime Minister – and would get through to deadly effect for civilian casualties and morale, dramatically altered the parameters of security and, moreover, did so in a highly destabilising fashion. This instability was enhanced by concerns, political and popular, about the possible use of gas weapons by bombers.

Baldwin had told the Commons that 'the only defence is in offence, which means that you will have to kill more women and children more quickly than the enemy'. This point captured the extent to which it was not clear how best to reconcile offensive and defensive tasks and capabilities, with the strategic goal of defence in this case requiring the operational and tactical tools for attack. So also with the protection of trade against submarine attacks.

The question of how best to protect against threats, notably air attack, was made more difficult by a lack of clarity as to their severity. The relevant experience was lacking. The previous world war had left only suggestions about the potency of bombing, although they had then been magnified by enthusiasts for air power, alongside those fearful of an airborne cataclysm.

Separately, the protection of existing possessions took on a different meaning when the latter were understood in terms of existing interests. These could include the territorial integrity of trading partners, for example China for Britain, freedom of navigation and, indeed, the existing situation as a whole. For the 'liberal' trading powers, among which Britain was the foremost, that element was important to their understanding of the world order and to their particular prosperity. This situation also helped explain Britain's emphasis on the navy.

If defence was both task and strategy, that left unclear how best to prepare, and, also, how to prioritise between different challenges, both real and apparent. The commitments that could, and should, be entered into were unclear, as were the parameters within which governments could operate, not least acceptance by public opinion. Moreover, this situation was exacerbated by uncertainty about the role of other powers, by a lack of sufficient resources to meet all tasks, and by an absence of certainty as to the effectiveness of particular weapons systems, both those of opponents and those that might be adopted to thwart them. True of the 1920s, this situation remained the case in the subsequent years. In a sense, it continued throughout the world war, with new weapons brought into use both in order to address existing problems and uncertainties, and so as to impose risk on opponents.

Britain was a key victor of the recent world war, the leading naval power and a major air power, but it was under challenge. It had the most wide-ranging of imperial networks, both political and commercial, an empire particularly dependent on the navy and, due in part to the major commitments coming with this range, its resources were particularly stretched. The First World War had left Britain with a degree of exhaustion as well as a significant national debt, but also a prudence about the consequences of another world war; although, as with other aspects of strategic tone, the consequences stemming from that prudence were unclear. In 1934, a Defence Requirements Sub-Committee report noted:

> The complete mechanisation of the army is not today, or in the near future, a possible or desirable measure. It would demand a highly specialised army trained and equipped for one contingency only, vis. war in a European theatre and on ground suitable for its employment . . . it would not be possible to organise a larger mechanised force than the one we recommend below without upsetting the whole system by which our forces overseas are maintained by the Home Army.

The sub-committee proposed a tank brigade as part of the expeditionary force, but argued that imperial commitments could not 'be met by the creation of a highly specialised "robot" army at home, even if that were the best system for a continental war, itself a matter far from certain.'[1] 'Robot army' meant a force light in infantry and emphasising tanks. However, in September 1935, the prediction that Germany would outflank France's defences by advancing through Belgium, as indeed was to happen in 1940, underlined the needed for British armour to help resist this.[2]

Yet, there were also strategic challenges to other powers such as the Soviet Union. To Joseph Stalin, its paranoid dictator from 1924, Britain, Germany, Japan and Poland all appeared major threats and, in addition, the extent to which they might cooperate, including against the Soviet Union as many powers had done in the Russian Civil War, was unclear. Thus, winning the alliance or neutrality of other powers was a key element of the strategic equation. The Soviet Union did so with Germany in 1939 and Japan in 1941. Germany did better at winning allies or the acceptance of its aggression by neutrals in 1939–40 than Britain, only to change the situation totally in 1941 by invading the Soviet Union and declaring war on the United States. Earlier, the extent to which Germany, Italy, Japan and the Soviet Union might be willing to ally with or against Britain, and to what ends, were fundamental to the strategic situation for these and other powers.

Threat-based assessments dominated strategy to a degree that later discussions, which focus on developments in weaponry, can underplay. Thus, German strategists considered challenges, real or potential, from the west (France) as well as the east (France's allies Czechoslovakia, Poland and/or the Soviet Union). The *panzer* divisions established by Germany in 1935, after a staff exercise involving three notional divisions, at first served as a mobile means to counter strategic vulnerability, indeed as providing a defensive capability. This only changed into consideration as an offensive capability as German aspirations altered.

The alteration was the crucial element, not the specifications of the tanks themselves. Indeed, at this point, their specifications were limited by the standards of the tanks of 1944. The point about flexibility was less the case with bombers, but they could serve as a deterrent and thus have a defensive capability. Tanks also served to restore mobility to the battlefield as opposed to the static fixed-trench fortifications of the previous world war on the Western Front.

The nature of military capability was clearly a factor. Whereas Japan was a land challenger to China and (in the Far East) the Soviet Union, it was increasingly a naval and air challenger to Britain and the United States in the shape of their empires. This contrast between Japanese challenges had major implications in terms of the strategic profile of the possible combatants and the measure of their strategic capability. For Britain and the United States, the relevant needs were warships, aircraft and bases capable of matching Japanese capabilities and defending relevant interests, notably territorial ones. Thus, American and British expansion over the previous century into the western Pacific and East Asia had produced strategic commitments for these powers that were in practice encumbrances, notably the vulnerable Philippines for the United States.

The British development of Singapore as a key base was a strategic decision with far-reaching consequences as, in practice, it increased British vulnerability to Japan. On the naval side, but not that of the army, the end of the Anglo-Japanese alliance in 1923, as a result in particular of the Washington Naval Treaty of 1922, was significant: it encouraged the Japanese navy to see Britain as a challenge. The Royal Navy, however, was exposed to Japanese attack. From 1919, the navy's 1st Battle Squadron, the full-strength battleships in commission, was in the Mediterranean, leaving only a small carrier, cruisers, destroyers and submarines in the Far East. As a result, London could only bargain for time, and Admiralty planning focused on how long Singapore could resist attack while the navy sailed to its relief from European waters. There was no consistent and effective plan for the defence of Singapore.[3]

For Britain and France, there was the challenge posed to Mediterranean imperial interests, for both were Mediterranean powers to an extent that is not always appreciated today. France was dependent on its links with its North African colonies, notably that between Marseille and Algiers, the garrison in North Africa being a major source of troops; the British empire was reliant on the link from Gibraltar to the Suez Canal via Malta. During the 1920s and until 1934, the Mediterranean and Middle East parade of essential naval British strength was more a tribute to old memories of the traditional rivalry with France than a reply to any real menace. Notably in 1923, the British popular press emphasised the size of the French air force and the threat it posed to Britain. This echo of the German raids during the First World War confirmed the scars British public opinions had suffered then, but it was not a realistic response to the situation.

Italy, except for a brief crisis in 1923 during its invasion of the Greek island of Corfu, was considered by the British government not as a danger but as a helpful power which indeed, from late 1926 until 1931, acted as a counterweight to France. In return, Britain supported Italian interests in Albania in 1925 and on the Kenyan–Somali frontier in 1926, as well as backing Italy for a seat on the international body running Tangier and supporting modest oil concessions in Romania and Iraq. However, Italian competition in imperial matters became more significant in the 1930s, notably with Italy supporting opposition to Britain in the Islamic world and also acting as a rival source of arms supplies, as in Afghanistan and Yemen. More generally, there was a petty teasing worldwide between the colonial powers as they competed for influence, but no war. That situation changed, totally, in June 1940 when Italy attacked Britain and France, and in December 1941 with the Japanese attack on Britain, the Netherlands and the United States.

When Italy moved towards Germany, the prime threat it posed to Britain and France was naval, although there were also concerns about its army and air force. Germany, in contrast, appeared to be a challenge to Britain mostly as an air power after Hitler announced in 1935 the creation of a new air force, the *Luftwaffe*. German naval construction threatened both Britain and France, but Britain discounted this threat with a unilateral Anglo-German naval treaty of June 1935. This treaty did not please France or Italy. Breaking with the Treaty of Versailles, Britain allowed Germany a fleet as large as a third of the Royal Navy, with a submarine force of the same tonnage. This proved a bad bargain. As the French were concerned about the Italian navy, which menaced France's position in the western Mediterranean, so the increase in the German navy, while also challenging France, in practice increased the pressure on Britain. This was especially so as German warships were deliberately designed with a fuel capacity giving them a cruising range to threaten British oceanic links. This capability was enhanced by building long-distance tankers to refuel the warships at sea, as spectacularly happened with the *Graf Spee* in the South Atlantic in 1939.

There were no correct strategic analyses for Britain or other powers because the situation moved in a highly dynamic fashion. The chronology and sequencing of threats were uncertain, and unsurprisingly so due to the degree of opportunism involved in the devising and implementation of strategy. That Britain did not have the strength capable to fight Germany, Italy and Japan simultaneously, and certainly in a manner that would protect the empire, was not a surprise. Indeed, it was in line with Britain's historical experience of trying to separate threats, albeit failing to do so in 1778–83 when France backed the American Revolutionaries, which proved an existential challenge for the empire.

This inability to fight all three Axis powers became the strategic fact from December 1941 able to redress the situation. To have expected the navy to do battle with all three states was to anticipate a margin of superiority that was unreasonable given the state of Britain and the fact that the potential enemies were well apart. Moreover, diplomacy sought to avoid this need.

British naval strategy planned that, if necessary, operations against threats arising simultaneously would be conducted sequentially in separate theatres; as, indeed, the United States sought to do from 1941 with the 'Germany First' policy. This British strategy, which aimed for a superiority in resources in the key theatre, assumed an ability to seize the initiative, and also that operational flexibility could help lessen the constraints posed by tough fiscal limits, and would overcome the strategic challenge posed by simultaneous threats. In addition, war, it was hoped, was likely to bring Britain the support of allies, notably France against Germany and Italy, and the United States against Japan.

In practice, the United States did not engage in the early years of the war as it remained on the defensive, and French support was completely lost in June 1940, as the Free French who fought on against Germany only enjoyed limited support in the French Empire at this stage, and, even more, had only minor naval and air strength. However, because Japan did not attack Britain until December 1941, there was no simultaneous naval challenge to

Britain until after the German and Italian navies had been weakened by conflict with Britain. Alongside the retention of major warships, important German naval surface units had been sunk by December 1941, notably at the hands of the British Royal Navy and Norwegian defences in the conquest of Norway in April 1940, but also with the battleship *Bismarck*, the most formidable German warship, sunk by the Royal Navy on 26–7 May 1941 about 350 miles (560 km) west of Brest. This was a clash that President Roosevelt followed with great attention, not least as the *Bismarck* was seen as a threat to the anchorage of the American Atlantic fleet at Norfolk, Virginia.

For the United States, Japan was to the fore as a challenger in the 1920s and 1930s. The United States was not acting aggressively, though, as it was primarily concerned with sustaining the existing situation. The bellicose 'atmosphere of gun-grease' that a British diplomat discerned in Japan in 1932[4] was the case for both the United States and Britain in the 1890s, but not for these powers in the 1930s as the nature of their imperialism had changed greatly. The imperialism of those who had 'got there first' was different from that of the imperial pretenders who sought to break into the existing situation, as with Japan in the Asia-Pacific, or to reverse earlier losses, as with Germany. Moreover, the economic development of Japan had been compromised by the Chinese boycott of Tokyo's products and services, as well as by the British Imperial Preference (based on the trade principle: British and empire producers first, the rest of the world last) declared in 1931, and confirmed at the Ottawa Conference the next year.

The rise of militarism as the dominant element in Japanese strategy owed much in practice to specific political episodes in which those taking a different view were assassinated, intimidated or circumvented. Leadership greatly affected strategy and the willingness to persist with it. As a consequence, the Japanese occupation of Manchuria in 1931–2 was followed by further expansionism in northern China. The unwillingness of the Soviet Union to intervene, in spite of many border incidents, was important to this expansionism, and contrasted with the Soviet willingness to fight the Manchurian warlord Zhang Xueliang in 1929.

Japanese strategy was predicated, however, on the basis that large-scale war with the Soviet Union was probably unavoidable. The two powers, indeed, had competed in the late nineteenth century and fought in 1904–5, while Japan provided the largest contingent among those who intervened (unsuccessfully) in the Russian Civil War (1919–21) and retained a presence in the Soviet Far East until 1922. This assumption led to pressure in Japan for the strengthening of the military, the state and society, with the latter two seen in an authoritarian and militaristic perspective.

China, more particularly Manchuria, was regarded as a base for vital resources necessary to Japan for preparing for this conflict, as well as offering territory, especially agricultural land, for settlement by Japan's growing population. There was therefore an equivalent to German interest in *lebensraum* (living space), and to the accompanying fusion of ideology and strategy that can be described in terms of strategic culture. Japan's hostility to the Soviets – the principal geopolitical threat to Manchuria – was an aspect of its China policy, and a continuation of pre-First World War Russo-Japanese rivalry, as well as being a product of more recent Japanese ideological hostility towards communism.

Similarly, an ordering of strategic priorities and a sequencing in implementation were involved in Chinese policy. Jiang Jieshi (Chiang Kai Shek), China's dictator and the leader of the

Guomindang (Nationalists) from 1925, proved willing to accommodate Japanese demands in 1933–5. This was in large part because he wished to strengthen and unify China, not least by destroying the Communists, a step that Jiang saw as necessary before confronting Japan. Indeed, the *Guomindang* campaigns against the Communists were some of the largest campaigns of the early 1930s and are unduly underplayed in military histories of the 1930s. Sequencing was also seen with Hitler's view that it was important for Germany to 'deal' with Austria, Czechoslovakia and, he hoped, Poland, before confronting Britain and France.

Strategy, therefore, was centrally involved for all powers in the timing of challenges designed to create opportunities and to overcome problems. This timing was a matter of the prioritisation that, in practice, provided a force-enabler and multiplier. Conversely, it was necessary to force on one's opponent a poor choice of priorities; a poor choice, moreover, in military, diplomatic and, even, domestic political terms.

These equations involved both specific readings of particular conjunctures and the more general issues of strategic culture. The latter played a significant role in guiding individual strategic choices. Thus, in the case of Japan, there was a confidence in a sense of innate superiority over China. This confidence was linked to a belief in Japan's divine providential purpose. Racism was also important, such that there were parallels with Germany in Europe, although the Japanese emphasis was not genocidal but, rather, a stress on racial purity and superiority.[5] These beliefs affected the perception of the determination and fighting quality of the Chinese. At the same time, there was a hope that China could be persuaded to act as a junior partner of Japan against the Soviet Union. This was misleading. Nevertheless, the hope captured a needs-must approach to strategy that was understandably prevalent in the adversarial attitudes of the period; a form of enforced transactional character to strategy. Such an enforcement was important within alliances, as well as in treating opponents. Indeed, the character and tone of Allied strategy in 1941–5 can also be approached in these terms.

Given that the full-scale war between China and Japan lasted from July 1937 to September 1945, and was a central aspect of the strategic equation for Japan and, therefore, significant for Japan's potential opponents – the Soviet Union, Britain, and the United States – it is surprising that it is treated as far less consequential than the move towards war in Europe. This is even more the case because, although the Sino-Japanese war did not initially widen out in order to involve other powers, it did, in effect, eventually do so. Moreover, the scale of the casualties was extraordinary.

At the same time, as a reminder of the difficulty of analysing developments, the sequence from 1937 to 1941 can be seen in very different terms, and the 1941 Pacific war can be traced to other causes and with a largely separate trajectory at stake. If the focus on the cause of this war is to be on East Asia, more particularly Japanese hostility to American pressure, one can consider that the establishment of Japanese bases in northern Indo-China (the French colonies of Vietnam, Laos, Cambodia) following the Fall of France in 1940 was more significant than the conflict in China in itself. Stemming from the successful military intimidation of the French in September 1940, these bases were important to a southward projection of Japanese power, as much as to any cutting off of China from foreign assistance. On 28 July 1941, the Japanese pressed on to invade southern Indo-China.

Concerns about China, nevertheless, were highly significant to the widening out of the war in 1941, as both Japan and the United States manoeuvred and prepared in a context made more unstable by the failure of Japan's China strategy. In the Rainbow

5 plan revision in November 1941, the Americans prepared to undertake a more vigorous position. The revision upgraded the defence of the Philippines from one restricted to that of the entrance to Manila Bay to a defence of the entire archipelago, as well as more offensive attacks on Japanese forces. This change was made possible by the larger forces available, including new assets such as the B-17 'Flying Fortress' bombers flying in from Hamilton Field, California. In the event, these aircraft flew en route into Hawai'i at the time of the Japanese attack on Pearl Harbor and were eventually redeployed to Australia.

American pressure on Japan failed in 1941, and led to a situation in which the Americans, by cutting off Japanese oil supplies, forced Japan to choose (or to think that there was a choice) between going to war with the Western powers or giving up the possibility of being able to go to war. Germany, in turn, declared war on the United States. The link from the outbreak of the Sino-Japanese War to that step was indirect. Yet, there was a relationship in the strategic escalation of the period, and one that cannot be adequately explained by an account of the war that begins with German expansionism in Europe.

In terms of strategic parameters, the Japanese showed in China that it was not necessary to introduce mass mechanisation in order to conquer large tracts of territory. Lacking raw materials and industrial capability, which helped explain the strategic importance of Manchuria, Japan, which was in a very different position of that of today, was technologically behind the Western powers and/or the Soviet Union in some aspects of military innovation, such as radar, self-sealing aircraft fuel tanks and, compared to the Soviets in 1939, the use of tanks. On the other hand, Japanese aircraft and torpedoes proved highly effective against the USA and Britain in December 1941. Japanese air crew had excellent training, but were mostly dead by

December 1942, notably as a result of defeat at Midway that June, and were replaced by less trained personnel.

Relative advantage, however, is not easy to evaluate. Armoured carrier decks might appear to be a clear British advantage but they could also be seen as a problem, putting too much weight high in the ship, and risking the distortion of the hull after a direct hit, as happened with HMS *Illustrious* at the hands of German dive-bombers in January 1941. She was out of service for a year.

There was also a congruence, at least on land, in the character of strategic, operational and tactical elements of Japanese war making; a congruence that strengthened this character. At the tactical level, a lack of materiel, and the limited use that could be made of what was available, led to a greater stress on 'spirit' over resources, for example with an emphasis on the use of bayonets in attack. 'Spirit' and offensive tactics were combined by the Japanese at operational levels, in order to ensure success, and thus to provide confidence in the strategy followed. Other powers did the same, but the Japanese reliance, when engaging on land, was particularly on the attack.

However, the strategy Japan chose to follow was flawed because it underrated the extent of nationalist determination in China, because the value of Japanese willpower was exaggerated, and because the impracticality for Japan of readily sustaining a protracted war strategy was not appreciated. There were insufficient troops in what was a very large space, and inadequate logistics. The attrition of a long war was, by late 1939, very much working against Japan. This was increasingly understood both in Japan and elsewhere; the latter being a key element of the sense of capability that was an important strategic resource. That December, the British Chiefs of Staff noted 'Japanese authority in China is limited to certain main centres and to lines of communication, and Chinese guerrilla forces continue to take considerable toll of Japanese garrison posts.'[6] Japanese military leaders were surprised and frustrated by their failure.

The western provinces of China were totally beyond the Japanese, while much of the area in the Japanese zone of occupation was not in fact under control. Both of these points prefigured the situation for Germany on the Eastern Front against the Soviet Union from late 1941. In a stalemated strategy, thirty-four Japanese divisions were bogged down by 1939. This situation made any large-scale Japanese conflict with the Soviet Union unlikely, and therefore left Japan with far fewer options when there were border clashes with the Soviet Union in 1938 and, more seriously and less successfully for Japan, 1939.

Moreover, this commitment meant only a limited availability of troops for the war with Britain, the United States, the Dutch and Australia, launched in December 1941. At the same time, resources could not always be readily redeployed. Indeed, Japan lacked sufficient merchant shipping to transport and supply another division in the Pacific, a factor that would have affected any attempted invasion of Australia. However, that limited availability was in large part to be overcome in 1941–2 by the skill of Japanese operations, which permitted, as in Malaya against the British, the defeat of larger forces; by the sequential nature of these Japanese operations; and by the importance to them of significant naval and air strength, both in gaining superiority and then in using it.

The problem of translating output, in the shape of conquests, into outcomes, in the form of obliging the opponent to accept the will of the victor, was abundantly on display in China. Indeed, Japanese campaigning in China indicated a lesson that Hitler would have done well to consider before attacking the

Soviet Union in 1941: that high-visibility gains did not necessarily lead to overall victory, and that conflicts could develop an
insuperable complexity. On the pattern of its conduct of the
First World War, the German military leadership as a whole
shared Hitler's reluctance to engage with these points. So, for
example, with the German navy and air force.

In terms of embedding successes, the Japanese failed to implement either of the strategies that might have worked, let alone
combine both. This prefigured Germany's comparable failure
against the Soviet Union. First, across occupied China, the
Japanese failed to win over sufficient Chinese support. They
established client states: in the shape of Manchukuo, the
Provisional Government of the Republic of China, formed in
1937, and the Reformed Government of the Republic of China,
formed in 1938. Founded in 1932, the first was nominally
placed by the Japanese under the formal rule of Aisin-Gioro
Puyi, the last Qing (Manchu) emperor, first as chief executive
and from 1934 as emperor, but he was very much a Japanese
client. Further south, in 1940, the Provisional Government and
the Reformed Government were merged into the Nanjing-based
'Reorganised National Government', which was placed under
Wang Ching-wei, a longstanding rival of Jiang Jieshi for the
leadership of the Nationalists. However, the Japanese could not
decide how much power to allow Wang: caught between accusa-
tions of betrayal and ineffectiveness, his government was quickly
discredited. More generally, the Japanese, like the Germans,
found the client states and their forces of limited value, and
treated them with suspicion.

In China, neither these forces nor those of the Japanese could
control the conquered areas. Indeed, Japanese control outside the
cities was limited and episodic, and they lacked both a strategy
and an operational means to respond. In rural areas, the ratio of

strength and space told against the Japanese, especially when their opponents, employing guerrilla tactics, hit Japanese communications, and thus their logistics and sense of confidence.

The alternative strategy for embedment, that of negotiation with Japan's opponents, was not followed. Ishiwara Kanji, the Chief of the Operations Section of the General Staff, had warned of the risk of an intractable commitment and encouraged an attempt to secure German mediation. The latter was abandoned in January 1938 when the Japanese announced that the *Guomindang* was not an acceptable participant in peace talks. This pushed Japan to try to create a new puppet government in China in the shape of the 'Reorganised National Government', as a basis for a Japanese-dominated strategic and economic 'new order' in Asia. Wang was encouraged to defect later that year.

However, aside from the lack of a grounding in China for such a 'new order', there was an absence of agreement within Japan on policy towards China, let alone its implementation. This was a troubling background for the effectiveness of strategic planning by Japan, and indeed across the world, as a whole during the subsequent world war. The Japanese never really overcame this problem. The lack of agreement on policy towards China prefigured major divisions within German strategy, including towards Britain.

It has been argued that Japanese strategy failed because it returned to a *samurai* (warrior) culture of emphasis on the land, rather than adopting the strategy of a maritime power such as the United States.[7] However, this approach is problematic, as Britain (notably in India) and the United States, like Japan, were continental as well as maritime powers. The real problem for Japan was that, in fighting China, it took on the task of conquest with no ally, and despite the task being implausible. As such, there was a contrast with the more limited Sino-Japanese

(1894–5), Russo-Japanese (1904–5), Sino-Soviet (1929) and Soviet-Japanese (episodically 1938–9) conflicts, in each of which the determination was to conquer, or control, essentially peripheral areas as far as China and Russia/the Soviet Union were concerned. Even so, and despite important victories, the most significant of these conflicts, the Russo-Japanese War of 1904–5, had placed a very heavy burden on Japan. In 1937–8, towards China, there was an incremental drift in strategy by Japan that reflected a 'victory fever' of a loss of perspective stemming from success.

Germany was to do the same in 1940–1, and, again, in contrast with the far more limited wars of 1864–71. In the case of Germany, however, there was a similarity to the situation in the First World War, at least in so far as the unwillingness to consider a peace unless the gains made in 1914–16 were retained was concerned. In the case of Japan and Germany in the early stages of the Second World War, the effect of 'victory fever' was to crowd out the bigger perspective by focusing on shorter term options for success, and, in doing so, foolishly to seek to 'de-risk' the future or to underplay the issue.

In contrast, due to a lack of initial success, there was no equivalent move on the part of the Allies. Nevertheless, in the context of success, a failure to appreciate limitations and constraints, as well as to understand the situation, could lead to unrealistic expectations. This was particularly the case on the part of Stalin in early 1942, and by Britain and America, both over the fall of Italy in 1943 and again, at the expense of Germany, in the late summer of 1944.

Strategic viability for all powers was also affected, although it was unclear by how much, by the related issues of weapon procurement and prioritisation. These issues indicate that, far from capability flowing automatically, or semi-automatically, from new developments, it is necessary to appreciate the degree to which, at any one time, there was a range of military options available for investment.

At sea in the 1930s, for example, it was possible to emphasise the role of gunnery in future ship-to-ship clashes, or of air power, or of amphibious capability, or of submarines; but the likely tactical, operational and strategic relations between them was unclear. In hindsight, the battleship, the focus in ship-to-ship clashes, appears clearly redundant, but that was not how it seemed to contemporaries, including Hitler and Stalin, as well as Britain, the United States, Japan, France and Italy. Instead, it was believed that battleships could be protected against air attack (like bombers from fighter interception), while aircraft carriers appeared vulnerable to gunnery; and the First World War had shown that submarine campaigns could be defeated. Battleships were also crucial for shore bombardment, providing more impact than air attack, a lesson learned by Britain and the United States in 1943 and employed in 1944. Aircraft lacked the equipment to attack ground targets. Battleships could also operate at night, as carriers could not.

In theory, strategy should have set procurement through the process of tasking and related planning. In practice, however, there was a more complex interaction with the tasks defined or reconceptualised, at least in part, in terms of apparent capabilities. Thus, in the *Zengen Sakusen* (Attritional Campaign), the Japanese focused, in their pre-war planning, on the successive use of submarines, long-range shore-based bombers, carrier-based dive-bombers and destroyer night-time torpedo attacks against the advancing American fleet, leading up to an engagement by the Japanese warships. This strategy encouraged the resource-draining construction of the two battleships of the *Yamato* class, the largest ever built, and the rebuilding in

1939–40 of the four heavy cruisers of the *Takao* class (although their shells could not pierce battleship armour). It also led to a policy of seizing Pacific islands, such as Guam and Wake from the Americans, so as to deny these to their opponent in the event of war. As the Japanese had plenty of islands and airbases in the region, they were less in need of these potential bases themselves than of depriving their opponents.

Claims about the potential for change provided by weapons offered a prospectus that combined futurology with counterfactuals and threat environments. These claims became a key aspect in bidding wars. In these, the military-industrial complex in each major state was not a monolith, but rather a sphere of competing interests, each advancing its case through bold claims. Thus, procurement and strategy, far from being determined by strategic culture, were contested through different interpretations, both of this culture and of how best to implement it.

The past offered very different approaches to understanding strategic culture. For example, for Britain, there was the 'indirect' approach, focusing on amphibious attacks and on not engaging the main army of the opponent, as opposed to that of seeking such an engagement. This approach looked back to British successes against France in the Peninsular War of 1808–13 and drew on concern about the very heavy losses of the First World War. Alongside the powerful exigencies of the moment and related factors, this element of strategic preference played a role in British hesitation about launching a 'Second Front' in 1942–3.

From the modern perspective, in addition to the fundamental question of strategic culture, there was that of implementation, which introduced a greater element of choice. Indeed, a key element of military training, war games, accepted the fluidity of strategies in terms of goals, means and outcomes. Again, these issues of implementation fed back into the formulation of strategy.

The varied meanings and implications of strategy to contemporaries can be seen in a letter of 2 August 1944 from Field Marshal Sir Alan Brooke (later Lord Alanbrooke), Chief of the British Imperial General Staff, to Sir Henry Maitland Wilson, Supreme Commander, Mediterranean, referring to Lieutenant-General Sir Harold Alexander's advance in Italy:

> I am rather disappointed that Alex did not make a more definite attempt to smash Kesselring's forces up whilst they are south of the Apennines. He has planned a battle on the Apennine position and seems to be deliberately driving the Germans back onto that position instead of breaking them up in the more favourable country. I cannot feel that this policy of small pushes all along the line and driving the Boche [Germans] like partridges can be right. I should have liked to see one concentrated attack with sufficient depth to it, put in at a suitable spot with a view to breaking through and smashing up German divisions by swinging with right and left. However it is a bit late for that now . . . very hard to get old Alex to grasp the real requirements of any strategic situation.[8]

To a degree, Brooke was writing about operational issues, but the wider context was there in the failure to achieve a strategic outcome, in terms of the shattering of the German force, comparable to that which the Soviets, over far easier terrain, with more manpower and tanks and with more space for manoeuvre, were achieving at that moment over Army Group Centre in Belarus. Moreover, for the Americans and British to take appreciable casualties in Italy without achieving strategic results or the fixing of much of the German army was of limited overall value. Certainly this situation did not help greatly with the timeline of the conflict, in the sense of obtaining major achievements not least before the unexpected might occur, including the tensions between the Allies that Hitler hoped for and, indeed, anticipated.

Alongside questions of alliances and of military capabilities came uncertainties about the domestic dimension. What would be the social implications of modern warfare, and how could they be successfully managed? And what if a lengthy war posed issues of labour mobilisation and civilian morale that could not be readily confronted? Such issues and choices did not end with the outbreak of the war. They were also set in the competitive context of being unclear what other powers had learned or would learn. Moreover, learning in a competitive context could both enhance the uncertainty of developments and, yet, also limit it by delivering an answer that set a pattern. How, furthermore, would the fortunes of war, and the inroads of enemy propaganda, affect the situation? They appeared to do so dramatically with the Fall of France in 1940. The collapses of Russia in 1917, and of Austria-Hungary and Germany in 1918, offered precedents for such developments, and Hitler was very mindful of the last.

In addition to the more general problem of assessing the impact of changing weapon systems, one already apparent before the recent world war but far less to the fore then, there was also the contrast offered by the situation in 1939 compared to the more clear-cut alliance systems that took effect in 1914. These elements ensured that pre-war military planning was both more significant for the first of the world wars, and longer lasting in the strategic culture on which it drew. There were common features in the planning for both world wars; and, in particular, the German strategies for both were not nearly as impressive as people frequently assume. Moreover, in each war, the survival of empires was a factor, as was the pressure from revisionist powers. Nevertheless, the differences between the two world wars were to be more apparent.

2

Strategic Shocks

Japan in 1938–9 was not alone in finding that strategic assumptions proved misleading in a context of anxiety and uncertainty.
So did other powers in the 1930s. Moreover, this was true in a
fashion that bridged the essentially limited wars of the 1930s to
the fuller-scale counterparts of the early 1940s. That distinction,
however, would have meant nothing in China where war was
anything but limited, and notably so as a result of the harsh
Japanese treatment of Chinese civilians, most prominently in
Nanjing in December 1937 to January 1938. Involving the bulk
of the Japanese army and part of the navy, conflict in China was
very much full-scale from 7 July 1937. Indeed, the scale of
conflict was greater in 1937–9 than it was to be thereafter until
Japan, after a more limited offensive in 1942, attacked again on
a major scale, and with great success, in 1944, an offensive that
lasted into 1945.

Concerns about vulnerabilities, and the need to respond to
them, drove strategic culture and planning for all powers. It is
usual to begin this discussion with Britain and France, and to
assess how their attempt to respond to Germany was accompa-
nied by diplomatic shocks in March–August 1939, leading to
war, followed by military shocks for Britain and France the

following May to June. That then opens a perspective that is broadened out to present 1941 as offering unpredictable solutions for Britain, in the case of Hitler's attacks on the Soviet Union and declaration of war on the United States, in June and December respectively. However, it is more appropriate to begin with the Soviet Union, as the unexpected choice for alliance with Germany it made in 1939 turned the profound and accelerating European crisis – caused by German expansionism and aggression that was greater in scale than that prior to the First World War – into a major opportunity for Hitler.

Sir Halford Mackinder, the leading British geopolitician and, in 1920, the British High Commissioner in South Russia, had pressed the British cabinet then on the danger of 'a new Russian czardom of the Proletariat' and of 'Bolshevism, sweeping forward like a prairie fire' towards India and 'lower Asia'.[1] Mackinder was certain that Russia represented a geopolitical threat in the shape of a determination and ability to dominate Eurasia. The very assumptions and core strategies of the Soviet Union certainly posed a major and continuing challenge to the international system. However, after the heavy defeat of its invasion of Poland in 1920, the Soviet Union later in that decade came, for tactical reasons, to accept a degree of *realpolitik* and normalisation in international relations.

Only, however, to a degree. With Stalin, there is a parallel with Hitler's more frenetic counterpointing of long-term drives with tactical opportunism. Stalin regarded powerful military force as a way to defend the Soviet revolution against what he consistently saw as the implacably hostile capitalist states, a group in which, to him, Britain was foremost. Continual conflict and inevitable war were part of an ideology of hostility to foreign powers that dominated strategy, helped Stalin extend his domestic power, and provided self-justification.

Rather than Europe being the sole strategic crux initially for the Soviet Union under Stalin, it was the Far East that to a degree took this position. Historical rivalry with Japan, looking back to the 1850s when Russia had expanded into the Amur Valley region and the founding of Vladivostok as a Pacific naval base in 1860, had been underlined by major defeat on land and at sea for Russia in the Russo-Japanese War of 1904–5. In an instance of the continuity of strategic culture, this rivalry had been exacerbated by the clash of ideologies following the Russian Revolution, and had been greatly strengthened by revived competition over China. The catalyst for full Soviet militarisation, indeed, was Japan's successful invasion of Manchuria from September 1931 to February 1932. This major territorial gain focused Soviet concerns on Japanese strength, the fate of China and Japanese intentions towards the Soviets, who now had a much longer common frontier. Stalin's interest in these concerns led to an expansion of Soviet military preparedness in the Far East, a measure pushed by the Committee of Defence in January 1932, and also to a massive rise in armaments production, one that continued into the Second World War. Aside from deploying more army units near Manchuria, the Soviet Union developed a long-range bomber force able to attack Japan.

Japanese strategy continued to encourage Soviet preparedness because, alongside persisting in expansionism in China, Japan came to look to Germany for a strategic partnership. This was designed to counter both the clear hostility of Britain and the United States to Japanese expansion against China, and the challenge posed by the Soviet Union to both Japanese and German ambitions and ideologies, as well as to Japan's position in the Far East. Moreover, this partnership meant that Germany would not continue to help China modernise its army, help that had been important from 1927, but that largely came to an end when war between China and Japan began in July 1937, with the German military advisors recalled in May 1938. Reports in late 1935 about an Anti-Comintern Pact with Germany, which Japan, in fact, was to sign on 25 November 1936, led Soviet strategists to fear a war on two fronts, as opposed to their previous confidence that they would be able to fight on only one front at a time.

This element requires underlining due to a tendency by some commentators to emphasise Hitler's hostility to Britain, France and the United States. In practice, Germany was more threatening to the Soviet Union, not only on ideological grounds but also because of its alignment with Japan, an alignment advocated by Karl Haushofer, the leading German geopolitician, not that his recommendation was crucial. In January 1936, Marshal Mikhail Tukhachevsky, the Soviet First Deputy Commissar for Defence, pressed the Central Committee of the Communist Party on the need to confront the danger of simultaneous war with Germany and Japan. For Stalin, this issue was increasingly urgent, not only due to Japan, but also because of German rearmament which, after Hitler came to power in 1933, gathered pace from 1934.[2] The German Four-Year Plan, initiated in 1936, was designed to ensure self-sufficiency and readiness to go to war in four years. The experience of the First World War was a grim warning of potential German strength and the threat posed to the Soviet Union.

Tukhachevsky was committed to 'deep battle' in the form of large armoured formations able to mount rapid and far-flung operational exploitation of tactical success. This strategy might be regarded as vindicated by posterity in the shape of the Soviet successes of 1944–5 against, first, Germany and, then, Japan. Accordingly, a bold, offensive strategy might appear to have been well within Soviet capabilities and therefore to have been the appropriate consequence. That approach, however, downplays the dynamics arising from international alignments, and the related pressures of the threat alignment. Moreover, the Tukhachevsky doctrine exaggerated the economic potential of the Soviet Union in the late 1930s, the strength of Soviet armour and the friction that an effective defence could engender for armour attacks. The 1936 manoeuvres had revealed design problems in the tank models available, as well as serious tactical and operational flaws in their use. The large-scale purges of the military leadership and officer corps that began in May 1937, with Tukhachevsky tortured, convicted and then executed for treason the following month, certainly did not help. Nevertheless, the Soviet military was affected by more systemic issues including the problem of matching improved effectiveness to increased size. These issues indicate the problems posed by a confidence in offensive strategic capability.

As a result of concern about Japan, the Soviets further built up their forces in the Far East, which, in turn, strengthened the Japanese case for cooperation with Germany. Moreover, signing a non-aggression pact with China on 21 August 1937 and supplying Jiang Jieshi with arms and advisors were steps of strategic direction taken by Stalin that were intended to weaken and distract Japan, as well as to support China. In the event, in contrast to failure in a border clash at Lake Khasan on 29 July–11 August 1938, Soviet success against Japan in fighting on the Manchurian–Mongolian border at Khalkin Gol (also known as the Battle of Nomonhan) in August 1939 had strategic impact. The Soviets used combined arms effectively, while the Japanese found that tactics that had been employed more successfully against the Chinese proved unsuccessful. In that sense, the Japanese army was not fit for purpose. This instructive defeat led

Japan to prepare for peace with the Soviet Union, which enabled the latter to focus on relations with Germany.

Appeasement, the strategy towards Germany, Italy and Japan adopted by Britain and France, was an important part of the geopolitical and military landscape. In practice, Appeasement was both in line with the historical (and present-day) decision to limit commitments,[3] and the norm in this period, for example characterising American and French strategies towards Germany, Japan and Italy. Moreover, Appeasement was also seen in other contexts, as with France ceding to Turkey the part of Syria around Alexandretta in 1938–9 in order to foster good relations against Italy, and, possibly, Britain transferring naval bases to Ireland in 1938.

However, just as conflict was unpredictable, so also with diplomacy. An effort to sway Germany towards better behaviour (successful in the 1920s), and a sense that compromise with Germany was possible, combined with a lack of British interest in the areas in Eastern Europe threatened by German expansionism, encouraged a conciliatory search for a settlement. So also did the extent of denial about what Nazism was really like, both in domestic and international policy. In practice, Hitler had clearly written in *Mein Kampf* about what he saw as the need to expand to the east, and *lebensraum* (living space) was a key idea that he fostered, one, moreover, in line with German geopolitical ideas from before the First World War.

The devastation and disruption caused by the First World War were a key factor in the strategic landscape for Britain and France. So also was the knowledge of limited domestic support for rearmament, let alone war. In addition, the British government's fear that war would wreck both domestic policy and the British Empire was in practice well-grounded. Military and political factors were entwined in this analysis. Thus, British ministers assumed that, if conflict broke out with Germany, then Japan might be encouraged to attack Britain's Asian territories, which were correctly seen as militarily and politically vulnerable, and notably so to the Japanese navy. Japan, indeed, did so from December 1941 and to devastating effect, although this element of the war tends to be overshadowed by the contemporaneous Japanese war with the United States.

The force profile pursued by Britain matched the strategy adopted: the focus in the late 1930s was on deterrence of Germany by means of a stronger navy and, in particular, air force, each of which was to be based in Britain, rather than through an army that was to be sent to the Continent. Numbers for the latter were lacking due to British military commitments in the empire, the extent to which Australian and Canadian forces were not available to help suppress imperial insurgencies, and the absence of conscription in Britain until 1939. Moreover, British control over any army to be sent to the Continent would be compromised by cooperation with France.

British diplomacy helped ensure the avoidance of war in Europe in 1938. The range of British commitments, and the many political hotspots, meant that Germany was not yet the major and immediate threat dictating war which it became for the British government by the autumn of 1939, and which possibly it should earlier have been, at least in retrospect. Peace in Europe was a key part of Britain's global strategy, a part separately pursued by non-intervention in the Spanish Civil War of 1936–9. The Munich agreement of 29 September 1938 brought a settlement of German–Czech border issues essentially on German terms, a fatal strategic shock for Czechoslovakia. However, as a result of this agreement, Hitler did not get the short war he wanted. The caution of his European ally, Benito Mussolini, the Fascist dictator of Italy from 1922, had undercut

Hitler's wish for war; and the outcome of the 1938 crisis demonstrated the interaction of diplomatic and military factors in overall strategy.

Economics also played a role. Hitler sought a new economic order in which Germany would become the leader of Europe, with Britain and Italy allied, as outlined in *Mein Kampf*, and France and Poland destroyed. To that end, he wanted an economically stronger Germany, and therefore a weakening in Europe of the major international economies, Britain and the United States. The goals and terms of a planned rationalisation and specialisation of the economy of mainland Europe were to be set in Berlin. By early 1939, for example, Germany, a key ally of the victorious Nationalists in the Spanish Civil War, was taking three-quarters of Spain's exports, so that Spain was brought into an informal *Reichsmark* sphere. The sectors of Spanish production targeted were iron ore, pyrites, copper, tungsten and foodstuffs. This economic strategy was pursued also when Germany conquered territory from 1939 and expanded its alliance network.

The Western strategies for maintaining peace failed. Alongside criticism, the Munich Settlement had been widely acclaimed in Britain and was widely assumed to have ensured peace. As a result, there was another strategic shock on 15 March 1939 when Germany occupied Bohemia and Moravia, and renounced the guarantees made at Munich. On 28 April, Hitler also renounced the 1934 German–Polish Non-Aggression Pact and the 1935 Anglo-German Naval Agreement.

On 22 May 1939, the Pact of Steel with Italy followed. This might not appear significant, given that, in the subsequent war, Italy was to be badly defeated, and rapidly so, but that outcome was less predictable in May 1939. Instead, Italy was the power that had stopped Germany when it sought to seize Austria in July 1934, that had conquered Ethiopia (1935–6) and Albania

(April 1939), and that had played a key role in the Spanish Civil War on behalf of the Nationalists. The Pact of Steel was designed to stop Italy being part of an anti-German pact.

On 23 May 1939, Hitler informed his army commanders that it was necessary to seize France, Belgium and the Netherlands in order to provide the navy and air force with bases from which to attack Britain. The strength of Britain's economy, its ability to blockade Germany and the capacity to bomb Germany's leading industrial zone, the Ruhr, which was vulnerable to aircraft based in France, all worried Hitler at this stage. Given the then capabilities of bombers, he was overly impressed with the threat of air attack, as were most leaders and commentators at the time, although not many admirals, who, instead, often remained committed to battle-ships. The prospect of war with Britain led Hitler to take a greater interest in the build-up of the German navy. In practice, with its aircraft having limited bombloads, the Royal Air Force was unable to deliver the sort of bombing attacks that were to be powerfully seen from 1943. Moreover, the French could not offer a capability comparable to that which the Americans were able to provide in the Combined Bomber Offensive.

Hitler did not wish to go to war with Britain, and did not expect Britain to start it in the summer of 1939. Indeed, he was undecided whether to go to war with Poland, a more formidable military challenge than Czechoslovakia, let alone Austria; and a key element in his decision was the assurance by his foreign minister, Joachim von Ribbentrop, that Britain would never declare war to protect Poland. On 5 April 1939, Wilhelm Keitel, the head of the *Wehrmacht* High Command, told the Italian Chief of Staff that no war was to be expected for 'three or four years', which accorded with Ribbentrop's approach to Mussolini in late 1938, offering an alliance and promising no war for two or three years, which lessened the risk posed by the alliance.

On land, Germany's principal opponent in Western Europe was France, which had borne the bulk of the struggle there with Germany in the First World War, and certainly so in 1914–15 before the relative significance of the British deployment increased. French strategy sought to inhibit German attack with the modern fixed fortifications of the well-developed Maginot Line, while also adding a mobile defence to protect neutral Belgium, which was unwilling to commit to the French system. The development of mechanised and motorised divisions by the French was intended to provide a mobility capable of countering any German advance via Belgium, as had been mounted in 1914, and as a prelude to an engagement by the slower-moving mass French army with its infantry and artillery.

With the benefit of hindsight, French investment in the Maginot Line is generally treated as both foolish and anachronistic, indeed as a strategy made redundant by technological development in the shape of the tank. However, as indicated above, French strategy was more nuanced and flexible, for the fortifications were regarded, not as the definition, indeed determinant, of a defensive stance but as a crucial aspect of a force structure and strategy of place that could support both a defensive and an offensive course, the two being linked. The French were committed to a methodical battle. The Maginot Line was intended to constrain German options (as indeed happened), to channel the Germans into Belgium (as indeed happened) and to advance to fight them there (which the Germans circumvented by striking successfully through a different part of Belgium).

The French approach was seriously hindered by Belgium's unwillingness to commit itself to joint preparations. Indeed, the neutrality of some of Hitler's victims, for example Denmark and Norway, gave his strategy of opportunist aggression a major advantage over that of his opponents. The key problem for

France was its lack of manpower, in the sense of men fit for active service, a lack that reflected the differentiation in population growth rates between France and Germany from the nineteenth century. This issue very much affected their strategies.[4] In 1938, there was also a shortage of shells to support a French offensive into Germany. The lack of men and means encouraged a French focus on the Maginot Line, as well as helping explain the value of any British contribution, however small. France, in addition, had to consider other threats. In order to be able to preserve its position from the Italian challenge in the Mediterranean as well as in response to the German naval build-up, much effort was put into building up a modern navy.

Britain also faced a range of challenges, and needed to adapt its strategic prospectus accordingly, a process complicated by drag factors. In a 'Note on the Development of the "Army Rearmament Programme"', drawn up in May 1939, General Sir Ronald Adam, the talented Deputy Chief of the Imperial General Staff, recorded that, under the plan approved in April 1938, the Field Force available for overseas commitment was:

> to be organised primarily with a view to reinforcing the Middle East . . . The crisis in September 1938 ['Munich'] emphasised the danger in the assumption that a Continental commitment was to be given a low order of priority. It also focused sharply the fact that, even when the programme was complete, our forces would be inadequate for a major Continental war.[5]

Another shock followed when, in order to facilitate action against Poland and offset Britain, Hitler concluded a Non-Aggression Pact with Stalin on 23–4 August 1939, a pact often named after the two foreign ministers, Ribbentrop and

Molotov, and celebrated by Stalin at the signing in Moscow with a toast to 'the health of this great man', the absent Hitler. The pact stipulated no war between the two powers for ten years, while secret clauses determined spheres of influence in Eastern Europe, spheres that both left no effective independence for local states and no role for other European powers, nor for international organisations. To his delight, Hitler was therefore freed from the prospect of a two-front war against major powers and, thereby, apparently from risking a repetition of the stalemate of the First World War.

The pact was also of great strategic importance, as Hitler was seeking to counter the effects of a possible British blockade with imports of grain, oil and other resources from the Soviet Union. That the Home Front could suffer, as it did in the First World War, might have been of greater concern to him, and thereby to German strategic planning, than the question of a two-front war. In combination, the pact made the war possible, certainly in the form it took in 1939; and thus the Soviet Union carried a major part of the responsibility for what happened, a responsibility it was subsequently largely to be able to evade. In turn, the pact finally ended Soviet fears of a Polish–Japanese alliance and the possibility that Germany might support such an alliance. Indeed, it brought to a close the acute anxiety that had come to the fore with the Japanese conquest of Manchuria in 1931–2.

In July 1919, a General Staff report in Britain had claimed that: 'Taking the long view, it is unquestionable that what the British Empire has most reason to fear in the future is a Russo-German combination',[6] a view that in part reflected Mackinder's geopolitical speculations, both then and before the First World War. This combination indeed offered much to both Germany and the Soviet Union. That had been seen in 1918 with the Treaty of Brest-Litovsk, which had enabled Germany to transfer troops to the Western Front; in 1922 with the Treaty of Rapallo, the prelude to mutual assistance in building up forces; and again in 1939 against Poland.

Such an agreement was not necessary in order to overcome Poland, which, in the face of a surprise German attack benefiting from air superiority and an offensive from a number of directions, lacked the necessary strategic defence-in-depth irrespective of Russia's deep enmity. However, the 1939 pact both helped speed Poland's defeat, and, for the same reason, was the key strategic element in the Fall of France in 1940. In the former case, Soviet policy over Poland demonstrated a habitual pattern, notably with Stalin, of allowing potential opponents to exhaust each other before deriving more direct benefit; an opportunistic, indeed in a way aggressive, practice that helps to explain what might otherwise be referred to simply as caution. The Soviet Union invaded eastern Poland after the Polish military had been defeated by the Germans. In the case of France, the pact enabled Germany to fight a one-front war, as it had done when successfully attacking France in 1870–1, and not the two-front war that had helped thwart success when it attacked in 1914.

The ideological rift between Germany and the Soviet Union had meant that the agreement between the two powers was not widely anticipated. Instead, it was Germany's allies under the Pact of Steel, Italy and Japan, that remained neutral in 1939. This was a key consequence of the Nazi–Soviet pact. By not informing his existing allies about his negotiations with Stalin, Hitler had offended them, especially Mussolini, who later on tried to 'counter' Hitler's solo runs with his invasion of Greece, launched on 28 October 1940. This unsuccessful invasion, at least in part, can be seen as the consequence of the mishandling of its allies by Germany. Japan was also offended.

In contrast to Hitler's existing allies, the Soviet Union not only failed to proceed to an anti-German policy in 1939, as Britain and France did, but, instead, moved to cooperate with Germany. This was political, economic and, in the destruction of Poland, military cooperation, in a way that totally contrasted with Britain and France in 1938. Abandoning the previous focus on opposition to fascism and the support, accordingly, for 'Popular Front' policies of alignment on the Left, notably cooperation with socialists, the Soviet Union instructed Communist parties in Britain and France to oppose the war, and also resumed its support for 'national liberation' movements in British and French colonies.

In turn, Anglo-French concern about Soviet policy as an ally of Germany was to lead, in the winter of 1939–40, to plans for military action, including the bombing of Soviet oilfields near Baku and assistance to Finland when it was attacked by the Soviet Union. Midway deployments accordingly were planned. Nevertheless, this offensive strategy, which offered scant advantage in practice, was not pursued; although its defensive counterpart was, notably, in the shape of consideration about how to respond to Soviet pressure on British India. In this case, and more generally, strategic planning had to cope with unexpected and rapidly changing contingencies. These included a military environment in which opposing capabilities, let alone intentions, were far from clear or fixed.

Britain and France, however, focused on the immediate threat – Germany. Indeed, the Soviet Union was able to invade eastern Poland (1939), attack Finland (1939–40), intimidate Romania (1940) and occupy the Baltic republics (1940); all without any significant concerns other than German attitudes about the respective territorial interests of the two powers. Whereas the British and French had acted to block Soviet expansionism in Eastern Europe in 1919–20, not least by deploying warships, this was no longer viable. Instead, the region was a 'happy hunting ground' for Soviet expansionism, one that was only really costly in Finland where there was initially successful opposition. Germany was appeased. Thus, there was to be no Soviet opposition to the German invasion of Yugoslavia and Greece in 1941 as an equivalent to the British guarantees to Poland and Romania in 1939. Indeed, in October 1940, a Soviet tanker delivered to Rhodes the aviation fuel the Italians, under the strain of the British naval blockade, needed to maintain their position in the Dodecanese until the fall of Greece in 1941 opened up supply routes to the eastern Aegean. The Soviet Union did propose selling modern weaponry to Yugoslavia in June 1940, and in April 1941 offered a security guarantee, but Stalin was not interested in substantiating any such step or, indeed, in the absence of a common frontier, able to do so.

That process throws a comparative light on Hitler's stance. Despite his *Reichstag* address on 6 October 1939, rejected by Britain on 12 October, Hitler failed to make any real effort to translate his initial victory over Poland in 1939 into a widely accepted peace. This can be seen as an aspect of Germany's more general failure of diplomacy, which is an important arm of strategy. However, adopting that position entails failing to appreciate the logic and drive of Nazi strategic geography. The idea of Hitler seeking a modest gain, and then accepting a new order based on Anglo-French consent, is seriously problematic, not least as it underrates his opportunism. Discussing such a concept in counterfactual terms does not aid the analysis, although it can recapture the uncertainty in which contemporaries operated. So does the argument that Hitler might not have attacked the Soviet Union in 1941.

Hitler's plan was *lebensraum* in Eastern Europe, an objective at once geopolitical and racist that affected every level of German war making in the east. This plan involved seizing the European part of the Soviet Union. Poland was a strategic obstacle, because it was between Germany and the Soviet Union and thus, unless in German hands, a challenge to German supply and communication lines when attacking the Soviets. This factor was also important in the case of Yugoslavia in 1941 as, in hostile hands, it challenged German action against Greece. So also with the need to bring Bulgaria into the Axis camp.

Moreover, although willing to cooperate with Poland, notably over Czechoslovakia in 1938, Hitler particularly hated Poles and had long planned the destruction of their country. In Hitler's mind, France had to be destroyed, one day or another. He did not care for any Anglo-French consent, either for the seizure of Russia or that of Poland as the preliminary step, but, had they been willing to back his plans, he would probably have spoken openly about his intentions, especially to Britain.

As in 1914, although in different circumstances, Britain and France were determined to fight on in order to prevent German hegemony. The British government was sceptical about Germany's capability to sustain a long war and was confident that, as in the First World War, the Allied forces in France would be able to resist attack, a confidence that was a necessary corollary of an alliance with France that required the dispatch there of a British army. Hoping to intimidate Hitler by a limited war, essentially with the damaging aspect pursued through blockade, British strategy relied on forcing him to negotiate, or on exerting pressure that led to his overthrow – although, as First Lord of the Admiralty, Winston Churchill sought a more aggressive strategy.[7]

The strategy of the slow burn, however, was undercut by Soviet supplies of raw materials, including grain and oil, to Germany, a process greatly facilitated by the common border that followed the joint conquest of Poland. In addition, British strategy was countered by the German strategy of the quick victory. Arguing that Germany enjoyed a window of opportunity, thanks to being more prepared for war than Britain or France, the view also taken by German leaders in 1914, Hitler feared that Britain would be able to build up its strength. This was indeed was the case from the late 1930s, and notably so as far as the air force and the navy were concerned. The establishment and build-up of RAF Fighter Command was important, as was the integrated RAF Command and Control system implemented by Air Marshal Sir Hugh Dowding, the first head of Fighter Command, from 1936 to 1940. Radar was an important tool. Hitler also remained concerned that Britain and France would launch air attacks on the Ruhr, Germany's leading industrial zone, which was very exposed to bombers based in France. In contrast, later British bombers had to fly from Britain in the face of the defence-in-depth provided by anti-aircraft guns and interceptor aircraft operating from, and over, the Netherlands and Belgium. They, however, were able to deliver far more serious blows and to impose higher defensive costs.

Victory over Poland and cooperation with the Soviet Union offered Germany the opportunity to fight on only one front. Moreover, this victory had demonstrated what could be achieved from a successful strategy of manoeuvre, and had enhanced Hitler's confidence in himself as a great strategist. In part, moreover, the German requirement – military, economic and political – for a quick victory drove out other strategic requirements. There was certainly an improvised quality to German strategy, one that reflected its opportunism in the face of war with Britain and France, two mighty empires, and in an unpredictable international situation.

This opportunism and unpredictability was seen with the German conquest of Norway in 1940, a conquest launched on

9 April, when, in addition, contiguous Denmark was rapidly and easily overrun. The risky nature of the invasion of Norway in the face of a stronger British navy was readily apparent. Indeed, far from a predetermined result, the Germans benefited from a comparative advantage that was not easy to plan. As a key advantage in strategy, that of responsiveness, there was less-flawed planning on the German side than by the Allied forces that intervened, let alone by the poorly prepared Scandinavians, and a greater ability by the Germans to respond, indeed improvise, under pressure.

Such improvisation was also shown by the Soviets in their war with Finland in 1939–40, the 'Winter War'. The initial Soviet strategy was poor, characterised by an inadequate coordination of advancing forces, a major underestimation of the fighting quality and mobility of the Finns, and Stalin's serious exaggeration of Soviet military capability and failure to commit adequate resources at the outset. In part, it was as if there was to be another version of the recent invasion of eastern Poland. Indeed, the Finns inflicted a series of serious and humiliating defeats.

However, in early 1940, the Soviets reorganised their forces to give effect to a different, more focused and deliberative strategy, which indeed delivered victory. This was not a victory of the German 'type' in 1939–41, as artillery played a far bigger role for the Soviets than armour, while the fixed fortifications of the Mannerheim Line were successfully assaulted. The Soviets were eventually victorious, even if not dramatically so; but this success, and the resilience it reflected, tended to be overlooked by those who preferred to focus on Soviet deficiencies.

THE FALL OF FRANCE

The German attack in the west on 10 May 1940 culminated in the strategic shock of the Fall of France, which accepted defeat and German terms on 22 June. This was a shock that was greater because it not only contrasted with failure in 1914, but also because, in 1870–1, France, though defeated, had fought alone and held out for longer. France's rapid collapse in 1940 was shared by the Netherlands and Belgium, which surrendered on 14 and 27 May respectively. Moreover, the forces of France's ally Britain were bundled out of the Continent with significant losses, notably in equipment, the scale of which impressed the Germans when they surveyed what they had captured.

The Germans had benefited from the role of politics in Allied strategy, namely the exigencies of alliance politics and the related strategic priorities. The Allies moved their mobile reserve into Belgium before they were aware of the main direction of the German attack. The Allies therefore were unable to respond to where the attack unexpectedly came from: through the Ardennes, which was not really tank country; across the mid-Meuse on 13 May, a high-risk approach; and to the English Channel, which was reached near Abbeville on 21 May. The ability of the German tank units to operate with open flanks in part reflected the disposition of Allied forces.

Nevertheless, rather than treating the Allied response simply as a strategic blunder, it is important to emphasise both the multiple contingencies of the 1940 campaign, notably in the Meuse crossing, and the degree to which the Allies abandoning Belgium would have been unacceptable politically, as well as risking the loss of part of the Allied order of battle, not least by also leaving the Dutch exposed. This point underlines the significance for the military of political factors, and the difficulties therefore of judging strategic choice. Indeed, in a different context, this was seen in the British intervention in Greece in April 1941, in an unsuccessful attempt to provide help against a German invasion. The operational failures of this intervention and of other aspects of Allied war making in the Battle of France (for example a lack of necessary preparation by the French army to counter the *Luftwaffe*) can also be discussed in terms of the strategic mistake of spreading effort and underrating German strength, both points made at the time.

Yet, there was also the strategic need not to abandon allies, the need that encouraged Anglo-French military intervention in favour of Norway, Belgium and the Netherlands in 1940, British in support of Greece in 1941, and British and Americans in support of the new Italian government in 1943. The reinforcement of exposed positions, for example Hong Kong prior to the Japanese attack in 1941, and Singapore in early 1942, was an aspect of the same situation. So also, to a degree, with the dispatch of American help, notably aircraft, to Australia in early 1942, although, as that both proved successful in itself and was followed by the triumph at Midway, the risks of the resulting dispersal of effort were underplayed. The reinforcement of threatened and attacked positions could be vindicated by success, as with the American response to the German Bulge offensive of 1944, or condemned by failure, as with the Axis reinforcement of Tunisia in 1943.

The Fall of France in 1940 represented the success of a risky strategy, that of Germany, over one, that of France, with serious deficiencies, both in planning and at the operational level. The French were outmanoeuvred in part because their attempt to take the initiative contributed to a disastrous position. Although Hitler's intervention over Dunkirk, stopping the advance of the German armour, was unwise, as well, possibly, as reflecting his misplaced confidence in the *Luftwaffe* as opposed to the army, the German army's greater intellectual flexibility proved decisive in responding to a fast-moving situation.

The French campaign demonstrated a key element of German strategy, in the shape of a strong cult about a decisive battle of annihilation, following Napoleonic patterns and, especially, the traditions of the Prussian victories of Dybbøl (1864), Sadowa/ Königgrätz (1866) and Sedan (1870) over Denmark, Austria and France respectively. This military tradition led to the seriously detrimental approach of viewing strategy considerations in operational or even tactical terms: planning campaigns with the ultimate target of forcing the enemy to a battle of annihilation, which would automatically lead to the end of the war, was the sum total of German strategy. The original plan for the attack on France was in effect a repetition of the 1914 plan, but there was no long-term strategic provision for what would happen after the initial clashes.

The replacement, 'sickle-cut' plan, was, in the event, an improvement, but still only an operational plan focused on cutting off and defeating Allied forces. The plan did not go further. In a clear case of the operationalisation of strategy, there was an expectation that victory would automatically lead to peace or the capitulation of France, which in the event it did not. Thus, operational success, at least in the short term, did not bring the desired strategic outcome. Instead, the French fought on, and reasonably well, inflicting more casualties on the Germans in June than in May, and the Germans had to improvise the later stages of the campaign. They did so effectively, which, however, ensured that German strategic mistakes were not analysed, either by the Germans or by others.

Although there were weaknesses, notably in the size of the French and British armies, and in the limited fuel-capacity of

French tanks, a more successful Anglo-French defence against German attack in 1940 might have repeated the 1914 situation. Major German offensives had been held in 1914, 1916 and 1918. Such a defensive success in 1940 would have enabled the Western allies to make more effective use of their superior economic resources and of their geopolitical position, specifically on the oceans and encompassing their empires, and their ability to thwart access to both oceans and empires by the Continental powers. In the First World War, French defensive strength was a crucial adjunct to British power, and vice versa.

The strategic consequences of the Fall of France were readily apparent. Aside from a strategic defeat for British naval dominance as a result of German campaigning on land and in the air,[8] any successful challenge to Germany would now have to overcome German dominance of Western Europe. That was an objective strategic consideration that Winston Churchill, the new British Prime Minister from 10 May 1940, understandably did not really address other than with the hope that something would turn up, a hope he was able to turn into confidence for the public with brilliantly phrased and delivered speeches that Hitler read in full.

The strategic means envisaged by the British governments – the use of blockade and air attack, and the support for resistance within German-occupied Europe – were unlikely to have the anticipated military consequences or have a direct strategic effect. So too Britain's successful attacks on the Italian overseas empire in 1940–1, attacks that were reminiscent, in strategic and operational terms, both of the Peninsular War of 1808–13 and of imperial warfare. These attacks were a form of indirect attack on Germany, but very indirect. A British strategic review of August 1941 argued:

Bombing on a vast scale is the weapon upon which we principally depend for the destruction of German economic life and morale. To achieve its object the bombing offensive must be on the heaviest possible scale and we aim at a force limited in size only by operational difficulties in the UK. After meeting the needs of our own security we give to the heavy bomber first priority in production.

Our policy at present is to concentrate upon targets which affect both the German transportation system and morale. As our forces increase we intend to pass to a planned attack on civilian morale with the intensity and continuity which are essential for success . . . we believe that by these methods applied on a vast scale the whole structure on which the German forces are based can be destroyed. As a result these forces will suffer such a decline in fighting power and mobility that direct action will once more become possible . . . Although these methods may themselves be enough to make Germany sue for peace we must be prepared to accelerate victory by landing on the continent . . . and striking into Germany itself.[9]

This review was not realistic, but reflected the poverty of options then available, as well as the need to maintain confidence, not only within Britain and its military, but also in the empire and, crucially, as far as the United States was concerned.

More broadly, the defeat of the imperial systems of France and Britain in their European heartland greatly increased German confidence and ensured that it would only be stopped as a super-power if the Soviet Union and, even more, the United States came into the war, while also making it more likely that Hitler would challenge both. This defeat also meant that a major American role would be necessary to defeat Japan if it went to war with Britain and the United States, as it did in December 1941.

Worried about German expansionism, both the American government and, increasingly, the Republican opposition, realised the need for preparation for war. This affected the options offered to the public in the 1940 election for president, as Wendell Willkie won the Republican nomination on the sixth ballot on 28 June 1940, instead of the initially better supported isolationists Robert Taft, Arthur Vandenberg and Thomas Dewey, the last of whom was to be the unsuccessful presidential candidate in 1944 and 1948. German success against France played an important part in affecting the mood among delegates, although the inability of Dewey, Taft and Vandenberg to agree on one of them as a candidate was crucial, as were other tactical factors.

In the subsequent election campaign, both sides agreed on peacetime conscription as well as the Destroyers for Bases Agreement with Britain. However, towards the end of the campaign, Willkie, who was critical of British imperialism, moved in a more isolationist direction, encouraged by signs of voter support for the view that the Battle of Britain indicated that Germany would not be able to invade Britain and that therefore the United States did not need to intervene. In response to Willkie's move, Roosevelt declared that the United States would not fight any foreign war. He won on 5 November with 54.8 per cent of the popular vote, but 84.5 per cent of the Electoral College.

The Fall of France also marked the end of limited war because the new British government under Churchill was not interested in a compromise peace dictated by a victorious Germany. This decision ensured that the war would continue until the actions of these other powers played a decisive role. It is too easy to say that the first period of the war had been fought by peacetime forces,[10] but they were certainly more limited than those that were to be deployed from 1941.

Churchill's role underlined the significance of individuals in the politics of the war; and that significance suggests a more unpredictable nature for strategy making than if the emphasis is on the state as a reified, and therefore somewhat homogenous, body. The concept of strategic culture can indeed lead to the latter emphasis but, in practice, the ideas bound up in the concept of strategic culture were interpreted by individuals, as well as in command structures that had an ad hoc character.

GERMAN COMMAND STRUCTURE

This was very much the case with Germany, the state where the General Staff system had been developed in the nineteenth century, presenting a model that was to be emulated elsewhere. However, there were serious deficiencies in the system itself, as was to be seen with the failure to achieve victory in 1914, a failure that was one of strategic planning and strategic practice.[11]

Hitler's distrust of the army leadership and his determination to wield total control came to a head in 1938 when the German War Minister and Commander in Chief of the *Wehrmacht*, Field Marshal Werner von Blomberg, and the Commander in Chief of the army, General Baron Werner von Fritsch, were dismissed on 27 January and 4 February respectively, and the ministry abolished. In its place, on 4 February, Hitler established the *Oberkommando der Wehrmacht* (OKW), the *Wehrmacht* High Command, with himself as Supreme Commander, and the ductile Lieutenant-General (from 1940, Field Marshal) Wilhelm Keitel, the Chief of Staff and, under him, his son-in-law, Alfred Jodl, as Chief of the Operations Staff.

In part, this restructuring in 1938 reflected a lack of support on the part of sections of the army for Hitler's risky bellicosity, one seen in the background to the annexation of Austria and confrontation with Czechoslovakia, with certain senior military figures conspiring and seeking to develop links with Britain aimed against Hitler. There was also an inherent clash between his position and that of the army: Hitler sought to wield far more power than that enjoyed by Emperor Wilhelm II in the First World War. Both men were seriously limited, but Hitler was able to grasp control, whereas Wilhelm lost most of his during the war.

In addition, there was the longstanding structural problem, one, moreover, seen with Japan, of a lack of cohesion between army and navy planning, which was amplified in the case of Germany by the addition of an ambitious air force. The OKW in theory oversaw all of the armed forces, but it had no real control over the air force or the navy, the commanders of which had direct links to Hitler, while that of the OKW over the *Oberkommando des Heeres* (OKH, Army High Command) was limited. The OKH was headed from 4 February 1938 by Field Marshal Walther von Brauchitsch, the Commander-in-Chief. His Chief of Staff, General Franz Halder, was the key figure in the planning of the 1939 Polish campaign, which OKH ran. Accused of defeatism because he was opposed to the invasion of France, believing it too difficult, Brauchitsch, who had borrowed heavily from Hitler, in part to afford his divorce, found himself ignored by Hitler in the planning and conduct of the campaign in the west in 1940.

On 19 December 1941, the failure of Operation Barbarossa led to Brauchitsch being dismissed by Hitler: the Führer liked to respond to failure by getting rid of people, which was in part a reflection of his lack of affinity with the military leadership.

OKW then came to direct all theatres other than the Eastern Front, which was left under the OKH. The dismissal of the pessimistic Halder followed on 9 September 1942, when the misconceived campaign of that year ran out of steam.[12] In turn, his successor, Kurt Zeitzler, who had increased his reputation with the successful defeat of the Allied attack on Dieppe, found himself ignored, including over whether the Sixth Army should be permitted to break out from Stalingrad in the winter of 1942–3. He resigned in June 1944, being replaced as an acting head by Adolf Heusinger, before Heinz Guderian replaced Heusinger, whom Hitler increasingly distrusted, in July. Although Guderian was an experienced figure, he found that he had scant influence on Hitler.

In addition to the heads of the OKW and OKH being weak, Hitler liked direct links with prominent generals, and he also rewarded them financially. That he had his headquarters to the east, notably at the mosquito-infested and heavily guarded *Wolfsschanze* (Wolf's Lair) near Rastenburg in East Prussia (modern Poland) for much of the period from June 1941 to November 1944, and for part of the period from July 1942 to 1943 at Vinnytsia in west Ukraine, made the direct links easy. So did a compactness in operations (compared to those of Britain and the United States), which made it readily possible to recall generals and to visit local headquarters, as on 2 December 1941, when he flew to Army Group South, on 3 July 1942, when he flew to the German forces advancing on Voronezh, and on 17 June 1944, when he flew to Soissons to meet his commanders in France. Despite the possibilities provided by long-distance aircraft, which were faster than warships, the situation for Britain, Japan and the United States was very different, although Churchill travelled to North Africa to meet commanders there.

The structure of German command, the assumptions that permeated it, the practices that it followed, its politicisation and Hitler's own role did not lead to cohesion, sensible intelligence assessment, notably economic intelligence, perceptive planning or the drawing of logical conclusions.[13] The situation was exacerbated by continual jockeying for position by figures in the Nazi regime, and by Hitler's lazy inability to provide any consistent leadership. Institutional politics was shot through with personalised leadership and ambitious policymaking. Uncertainty over Hitler's intentions encouraged this rivalry.

Moreover, this uncertainty means that historians need to be particularly careful in analysing and explaining his strategy. In practice, a range of views can be found in Hitler's remarks. In part, he was speaking for specific audiences, domestic and/or international, military and/or non-military, and sending messages accordingly. However, there was also a lack of consistency on the part of Hitler and, in particular, a paranoid reaction to what he saw as the threats made by others. The argument that he was more concerned about Britain and the United States than the Soviet Union rests on this issue.[14] In practice, the trend of his statements was one in which the latter was to the fore, with communism perceived as a threat to Germany that was both domestic and international. The opportunity for Germany was also at the expense of the Soviets. *Lebensraum* was to the east, not the west, and it was in the east that the slaughter of Jews was to be concentrated. There was no comparison in the case of gains from Britain, the United States and even France. Alsace-Lorraine was annexed to Germany but the population, seen now as German, was left in place.

The focus on a single figure who was not up to the task was also seen with Italy. The old and ailing king, Victor Emmanuel III, was head of state but Mussolini was minister for all the armed forces. Under Mussolini, the three services were in effect independent of each other, as Marshal Pietro Badoglio, the Chief of the General Staff, had no staff and scant power. The naval high command had a very different set of strategic parameters to that of the army. In 1938, Mussolini was made a marshal, and in 1940 persuaded Victor Emmanuel to let him exercise military command. There was no real coherence in command, however, and the situation in which the chiefs of staff of the individual services were the key figures, especially if, as with the navy and air force, they were also ministerial undersecretaries, was made more difficult by Mussolini's frequent interventions. His failure to base ambitions on a reasonable assessment of Italian capability was more serious, and was seen in his choice of opponents. At the same time, Italian options were affected by German success, and notably so in France and the Balkans.

In organisational terms, Italy, like Germany, suffered greatly from a failure to integrate intelligence into the understanding of the strategic situation and options. In addition, as in Germany where key figures, notably Admiral Canaris and General Oster, came to oppose Hitler, the Italian intelligence services were fractured and mutually antagonistic. In contrast, there was much greater unity in intelligence in the case of Britain, the United States and the Soviet Union.

Italy entered the war on the side of Germany on 10 June 1940. Aside from brief operations against France with limited advances against its effective Alpine defences, this entry created new zones of conflict centred on the Italian colonies in Albania, East Africa and Libya, and on neighbouring targets: Greece; the British colonies of Kenya, Sudan and British Somaliland; and Egypt respectively. Italian forces were initially successful in capturing British Somaliland, defeated the Yugoslav attack on Scutari in Albania in April 1941, and then swiftly occupied

Slovenia and Dalmatia. However, they totally failed in their invasions of Greece and Libya, and were completely defeated in East Africa. In June 1941, General Ugo Cavallero, Badoglio's replacement, created a larger Supreme Command and increased inter-service cooperation, but he found the navy and air force maintained their independent stance. Unfairly blamed for failure in North Africa, Cavallero was sacked in January 1943.

CONCLUSION

Strategic culture was a key element. Prussia, and then its successor, Germany, had been trying to keep their wars short since the days of Frederick, the Great Elector of Brandenburg (r. 1640–88), and Frederick the Great, Frederick II of Prussia (r. 1740–86), in part because they believed, rightly or wrongly, that a short war was the only kind that they could win due to respective resources. This tradition had been carried on into the nineteenth century, and Helmuth von Moltke the Elder, the Chief of Staff in the German Wars of Unification in 1864–71, proved the short-war commander par excellence. Nevertheless, the attempt to achieve a repeat in 1914 came to nought.

In 1939–41, there was a drive to return to this earlier tradition of strategy and operations. However improvised the campaign planning, the Germans had a doctrine that was designed to provide a war-winning strategy. This doctrine called for the strongest and most mobile force of the army, by 1940 clearly the armour, to be used where the enemy was weakest in order to encircle and destroy them, in a *kesselschlacht* (a 'cauldron battle' or encirclement). This was a modern version of Hannibal's devastating victory over a large Roman army at Cannae in 216 BCE, a victory that had long attracted the Germans as a model. The 1940 plan was based on this doctrine, as were most of the opening battles in the invasion of the Soviet Union in 1941.[15]

In practice, however, the presence of armour did not change the fundamental strategic situation, as long-range heavy bombers, able to devastate the productive centres of opposing economies, might just have done. Traditional German operational planning focused on a *Schwerpunkt* or point of main effort. In the First World War, the limited mobility of the combat arms, interacting with the scale and strength of defensive positions and firepower, had helped create a crisis for the initiative from the tactical to the strategic levels. The tank appeared to some to be an answer but, in fact, it was only a means and expedient. As with so many weapons, the tank did not offer a strategic solution. *Blitzkrieg* worked well against inferior armies but only in particular circumstances, notably relatively confined geographical areas. It was not a substitute for strategy. Indeed, Hannibal himself had ultimately failed completely and, totally defeated in battle at Zama by Scipio Africanus in 203 BCE and with Carthage having surrendered in 201 BCE, died in exile, possibly by committing suicide.

Repeatedly, both in 1914–18 and in 1941–5, German tactical skill and operational proficiency were not converted into strategic success. In part, this was due to the limited political grasp the Germans showed, and its serious impact on their strategy. Each war as a whole also demonstrated the degree to which attempts were made by participants to counter the capability advantages of opponents, and the Germans suffered accordingly in both struggles as their opponents caught on, not least by moving forward on their learning curve.

The basic flaw of German strategy was that it was operational planning with a focus on tactical events, this being mistaken for strategy. In contrast, the Allied approach had operational planning integrated into overall strategy. The lower level of military planning should always serve the higher one, so that operations should help achieve strategic goals, while battles should help fulfil operational plans. However, with Germany, there was a fatal twist in that operational planning was only focused on seeking and winning battle. Against France in 1940, this system helped to win a first stage in the campaign; but, in the Soviet Union in 1941, the approach totally failed. In large part this was because the improvised nature of German operational planning was not able to muddle through the second stage (as it had done in France) due to the strength and resolve of the enemy, and for geographical reasons. The inherent weakness of German strategic culture was to be greatly exacerbated by Hitler's strategic assumptions and priorities but, in practice, there was this more systemic weakness.

3

Germany and Japan
Plan New Worlds

Germany's repeated victories in the spring and early summer of 1940 provided opportunities for a reordering of strategy. The need for such a reordering was the key theme for Germany's opponents, but real opportunities for the refocusing of strategy largely lay with Germany and its allies, especially Italy and Japan. Discouraged by its serious and indicative defeat at Khalkin Gol at the hands of the Soviet Union in a short frontier war in August 1939, Japan was encouraged to revisit its goals and priorities by the new weakness of the European colonial empires. In addition, other powers needed to manoeuvre in the shadow of the German successes. In particular, neutrals had to take note of the new situation, several of them being forced to do so.

The common historical approach – the focus on the leading powers, and on how they sought to change the situation to their benefit – is an understandable one. At the same time, that approach both leads to insufficient attention to other powers, and is apt to drain them of autonomy. In practice, the situation was more complex. In starting here with Germany, and then moving to its allies, Italy and Japan, before considering other powers, I am not downplaying the role of the latter but, instead, noting their need to respond to the major states and their expansionism.

GERMAN WAR MAKING

Giving his ambitions a marked boost, the Fall of France certainly did not end Hitler's determination to create a new order. Nor did it settle how best to address the issue of prioritisation and sequencing, an urgent issue for all the powers. There was both an opportunistic, and thus inconsistent, pattern to Hitler's strategy, and a demanding ideological drive. The latter, however, took Germany in more than one direction. There was primarily a hostility to the Soviet Union, to its communism, its Slavism and the alleged (in practice greatly exaggerated) role of Jews in its politics; the last was an issue Hitler also misleadingly advanced in the cases of the United States and Britain. There was a hostility, moreover, to liberal democracies, notably Britain and France, but also the United States. These states were seen as inherently weak, and their tolerance was regarded as unimpressive and conducive to deracination due to the interbreeding of ethnic groups, which, Hitler argued, was particularly the case of the United States. Liberal capitalism was seen as sapping the liberal democracies through encouraging consumerism and hedonism. To Hitler, these characteristics affected military and civilian morale and cohesion, and therefore gave Germany an advantage and, similarly, were to help Japan.

Sequential war making played a major role in German thinking, but the prime objective was the Soviet Union. This was a matter of danger as well as opportunity. The latter was clearly present in terms of *lebensraum* and race war. The danger was in terms of Soviet expansionism in Eastern Europe. This was perceived as a threat in Berlin, but also more widely. The states threatened by the Soviets, for example Romania, looked to Germany and in some cases openly asked for German support, as with the three Baltic republics, especially Latvia, and Finland. Thus, for the Germans, prestige played a role in the issue in opposing Soviet expansionism. The Soviets were also an alternative patron, as with the Soviet–Yugoslav agreement signed on 5 April 1941 and intended as a military guarantee against Axis attack.

Linked to both factors was a spread of Soviet power, real or feared, direct or indirect, in Eastern Europe, that might facilitate a Soviet attack and/or make a German attack on the Soviet Union more difficult, both by expanding the Soviet buffer zone, which indeed was very much the case, and by compromising Hitler's ability to win allies, which was much less the case. As a consequence, Hitler in 1940 was planning to attack. The immediacy of developments in Eastern Europe encouraged an invasion. As a result, the apparent closeness of Britain to collapse was less consequential in the decision to attack the Soviet Union. Instead, it appeared necessary to attack and defeat the Soviet Union in 1941, seizing Moscow before the winter. After that, it seemed pertinent to mount an attack on Britain.

As a lesser issue, Britain, indeed, was very much still part of the equation. To conquer the Soviet Union, it would have been useful to have ended the war with Britain, which would have left Germany with a war on one front only. Conversely, defeating the Soviet Union would provide an opportunity to build up the air and naval forces necessary for war with Britain and even possibly to renew planning for an invasion of land forces. Equally, what became the intractable nature of the war with Britain led to a view that defeating the Soviet Union would become a way to bring Britain to a settlement by robbing it of options and, thereby, hope. As with Napoleon in 1812, Moscow was seen as a stage on the way to London, although for Hitler there was a strong ideological drive against the Soviet Union that was not the case with Napoleon.

In the case of Britain, German strategy was set by the failure to reach a settlement. Given that the defeat of France's army had led to its surrender, and that despite the continuing existence of the large French Empire and its strong navy, it was reasonable to assume that the British government would accept the same outcome. However, its failure to do so, much to Hitler's surprise and disappointment, apparently meant the need to reproduce the fate of France by invading Britain.

This goal confronted some of the grave limitations of German strategic planning, as mentioned in the previous chapter. In particular, there was a lack of the relevant tri-service (army/navy/air force) capability and cooperation. This lack reflected the institutional practices and strategic cultures of the individual services. The individual arms provided competing strategies, and there was no real attempt to reconcile them, either before the war or during its various stages. This failure was an aspect of the more generally dysfunctional nature of the Nazi regime, although this lack of coherence had longer roots, as the differences between the German army and navy in the First World War had fully indicated. The services were not focused on cooperation, and this was especially true of the army and the navy. The air force, the *Luftwaffe*, had experience of cooperating with the army in attack at the tactical and, to a degree, operational levels but not comparable experience with the navy, and there was scant cooperation with the latter. Britain greatly benefited from this situation in the struggle to protect trade from German attack.

These were far from being the sole aspects of German incoherence. The rivalries of the German intelligence systems also suggested a regime that found it difficult to focus key strands on its external enemies.[1] It was also instructive that appointment to the officer corps was only comprehensively Nazified after the traditional military leadership had been compromised by the role of some generals in the unsuccessful July 1944 bomb plot against Hitler. More generally, Hitler felt it necessary to bribe his generals with large amounts of tax-exempt money or seized Polish and German-Jewish property. Such bribery was in line with the frequently chaotic and kleptocratic (thieving) nature of German government under Nazi rule.

The bribery also revealed the extent to which there was a military autonomy in Germany that scarcely accorded with notions of totalitarianism, nor indeed with the practice of often vicious control, not least through political commissars, in the Soviet Union. There had been no purge of the German military comparable to the Soviet one that began in May 1937, and even the purge after the bomb plot of July 1944 was far more limited than the Soviet one, although, alongside a very different military culture, wartime conditions did not encourage a more comprehensive one: the Soviet purge had been in peacetime. At the same time, wartime failure by Soviet commanders was punished by executions, whereas the German equivalent was dismissal.

For the Germans, as for others, economic capability was linked to procurement and planning. Quantity as well as quality were at stake. Thus, Germany was seriously unprepared for amphibious operations. This factor did not preclude success in the case of Norway in 1940, but it greatly affected the situation as far as plans against Britain (1940) and the attack on Crete (May–June 1941) were concerned. In Norway and, even more, Crete, airborne assault was crucial to success. Germany lacked specialised amphibious capability. In contrast, the Allies were to develop many specialised designs for such operations, notably in landing craft and tanks. Moreover, the implausible and certainly risky 1940 plans to invade Britain revealed particular problems in Germany with devising and implementing a tri-service strategy. Whereas Soviet strategy did not rely on naval power, and Soviet air power was subordinated to the army and very much tactical in its use, the Western Allies were to prove far more effective than Germany in a tri-service strategy in 1944 when invading Normandy.

This issue of service cooperation was also to be a problem for Italy and Japan, Germany's principal allies. Indeed, that repeatedly provided a qualitative difference between the two sides in strategic conception and implementation. This point is part of the narrative, and also a key element of the conclusion. There was also for Germany, Italy and Japan the refusal to accept what others might consider objective strategic considerations, a refusal that might be traced to the nature of their regimes, as well as to their determination to overcome the constraints of domestic and international circumstances.

Nor in 1940 did the *Luftwaffe*, and notably its head, Hermann Göring, who was anyway hostile to Keitel and the OKW, have any real grasp of its serious limitations as a strategic tool. The *Luftwaffe* was determined to put itself centre stage in the attack on Britain in 1940, rather than acting as a preparatory adjunct to the role of the army and navy, as envisaged in Operation Sealion. The *Luftwaffe*'s focus on its own role was part of the usual service emphasis but, in addition, reflected a lack of German strategic understanding as to the relationship between air attack and invasion. There was also a serious pre-war failure to prepare for a strategic air offensive because the Germans, with their emphasis on tactical and operational imperatives, had not sufficiently anticipated its necessity. This was a matter of doctrine, but there was also a lack of an adequate aero-engine capability. In wartime, the German leadership came to see rockets as the means to leapfrog the situation but they lacked any effective guidance system and diverted resources that might have been used more effectively elsewhere.

The *Luftwaffe* was primarily intended to act in concert with German ground forces, in a combined arms role, something that was not possible in the aerial battle with Britain. There had been a serious failure to prepare for a strategic air offensive because its necessity had not been anticipated. There was a lack of bombers with the range and bomb capacity necessary to provide an effective strategic force, and a lack of the necessary long-range fighters.

The heavy bombing of London, from 7 September 1940, represented an attempt to dominate the strategic centre of British public opinion. However, this German strategy was based on a misreading of relative air capabilities, plus a consistent lack of grasp of the political context in Britain. Indeed, the hope that the British people would realise their plight, overthrow Churchill and make peace proved a serious misreading of British politics and public opinion; although also one that drew on pre-war discussion of air attacks, including those that took place in Britain, as well as on pre-war German views about the strength of pro-German sentiment.

As with the German aircraft raids launched on London in 1917, that strategy failed totally. The bombing led in Britain to a conviction of the need to keep going, as well as to increased hatred of Germany and Hitler. 'We can take it', the motto of, and for, civilians, proved a strategic response, one that was encouraged by government propaganda. It was a phlegmatic and fatalistic reaction, one captured by the BBC Listener Research Report in 1941. The 'Blitz', the bombing of British cities from September 1940, like the earlier plan for the invasion of Britain, was based on Germany's flawed assessment and provided a shared identification in Britain in the shape of fortitude, an element that became important to the post-war British understanding of the war.

Moreover, the inability to intensify the bombing, or even, in the face of British resistance, maintain its scale, was significant. In early 1941, much of the *Luftwaffe* was transferred for operations in the Mediterranean and against the Soviet Union. More generally in its air operations, Germany suffered greatly not only from failing to limit its goals, but also from not having any allies to offer capacity similar to that offered by the cooperation of Britain and the United States.

THE MEDITERRANEAN

The temptation in any discussion of the war as a whole is to rush on to the German attack on the Soviet Union in June 1941. Indeed, that attack was planned from the previous year, and was encouraged by growing Soviet–German differences over Eastern Europe, as well as by the lack of Soviet interest in cooperating with Germany to despoil the British Empire.

However, in the meanwhile, German rivalry with Britain – for example, concern that British bombers based in Greece might attack Romanian oilfields that were crucial to Germany – led to a strategic expansion by Germany to the south, specifically the Mediterranean. As with many instances of strategic choice, this can be seen as mistake or as opportunity, or as both; and that prefigures and, to a degree, matches the discussion over Britain's Mediterranean strategy, particularly in 1943.

In 1940–2, the British certainly felt vulnerable in the Mediterranean. On 25 June 1940, just after France's surrender, the talented General Archibald Wavell, Commander-in-Chief in the Middle East, observed: 'The internal security problem in

Egypt, in Palestine, and in Iraq, and elsewhere, occupy a very great deal of the attention and time of the Middle East Staff. An improvement in propaganda may help the situation, but only military successes or evidence of strength and determination will really do it.'[2]

The Royal Navy remained potent in the Mediterranean. After France surrendered, the British fleet had four battleships and one carrier at Alexandria whereas, as the British naval attaché in Rome reported in June 1940, the Italian navy had only two smaller and weaker, even if faster, modern battleships, in addition to older battleships. Two more modern battleships were ready by the end of 1940. Churchill pressed for a great decisive naval battle, and the action was fought off Calabria on 9 July 1940. The result was highly disappointing for the British, as indeed were other aspects of British naval operations later that year, with the exception of the Taranto raid on 11–12 November. The Italian supply routes to North Africa remained open, with most tonnage and personnel arriving. In contrast, the British commitment in the Mediterranean affected the availability of warships to oppose the Germans in the Atlantic, and the British were obliged to use the long Cape route to the Indian Ocean, which hit their shipping availability and the tonnage of goods moved.

The need to support an ally, Italy, was an important element for the Germans, but so also was the determination to weaken an opponent, hitting Britain where it could be readily attacked. Both played a role in Germany's intervention on land, at sea and in the air, first, in Italy's unsuccessful war with Britain in the Mediterranean and, then, with the decision in 1941 to act in the Balkans in order to help Mussolini and to thwart Britain. Due to the unexpected move of Yugoslavia into the British camp, plans for action against Greece broadened out to include the conquest of Yugoslavia, which was ordered on 27 March 1941. Both countries were attacked on 6 April, and were rapidly conquered.

The situation in North Africa was to be less happy for the Germans in the long term. In part, this contrast reflected the scale of operations there and the strategic depth enjoyed by the British on land, at sea and in the air; both very different to the position in the Balkans. There was also the issue of the integration of leading military figures in the strategic planning process. General Erwin Rommel, the commander of the *Afrika Korps*, the German force sent to North Africa in February 1941, certainly thought that he would receive more troops and materiel, and that Hitler had approved offensive plans beyond those of the official OKH orders to Rommel. Uninformed about the Barbarossa plans, Rommel mistakenly believed that he would receive more divisions as soon as the campaign against Greece was over. Rommel's offensive vigour and drive therefore appears justified from what he knew about the strategic situation. This point underlines the degree to which it could help for the commanders of major theatres to be involved in the strategic situation, in order for them to be able to shape their operational plans accordingly. Rommel was not, because the OKH thought that he had his orders. But from the incomplete knowledge of Germany's strategic plans, and possibly due to Hitler's encouragement, Rommel was convinced that he could deal Britain a serious, maybe fatal blow, by acting against his orders and attacking. His selfish personality also played a role. On the Allied side, commanders who acted contrary to their orders tended to be replaced, or were given the necessary reason to change their mind. In contrast, Rommel might be an extreme example, but he was an instance of the process by which Hitler, inherently an opportunist, allowed the war to expand unnecessarily.

At the same time, this strategic context did not lead to a different German expansion to the south. In 1940, Hitler was interested in the idea of a league of Germany, Italy, Spain and Vichy France (the post-defeat French state headed by a collaborative administration), although, characteristically, without giving sufficient attention to what that might entail. In 1939, the fascist victory under General Francisco Franco in the Spanish Civil War had been greatly aided by German and Italian military support and, thereafter, there was a determination to gain economic benefits from Spain. Franco, who had signed a Treaty of Friendship with Germany in 1939, was a keen supporter of Hitler's cause, a point greatly played down after the war. Francoists later pretended that Spanish neutrality was a result of Franco's brave and adept rejection of Hitler's pressure. In practice, Franco was a firm opponent of democracy and a sharer in Hitler's belief that Judaism, communism and cosmopolitanism were linked threats, and that Jews were responsible for the alliance against Germany. Franco did not want Spain to shelter Jews. A decree of 11 May 1939 prevented entry of 'those of a markedly Jewish character', and another of 23 October 1941 banned the passage of Jews to the New World on Spanish ships. Few Jews were given shelter.

To Franco, Hitler was bound to win. This likelihood apparently provided an opportunity to gain control of Gibraltar, French Morocco and even Portugal, a traditional ally of Britain, and thus to revive Spain, which had only lost its empire in 1898 at the hands of the United States. Neutral throughout the First World War, Spain had benefited economically but had gained none of the German overseas empire from the post-war settlement. Franco had served in Spanish Morocco from 1914 to 1917 and 1920 to 1928, as part of a major effort to expand and protect Spanish territory there. In Spain, there were calls for territorial gains, notably from the fascist Falange movement. Franco put his brother-in-law, Ramón Serrano Súñer, into control of the Falange in order to make it pliant. As Foreign Secretary from 1940 to 1942, Serrano Súñer was strongly anti-Allied. On 14 June 1940, Franco occupied the international zone of Tangier, which was annexed on 23 November.

Spain's entry into the Second World War could have led to an attack on the British base of Gibraltar. If successful, such an attack would have destroyed the British ability to operate in the western Mediterranean, which would anyway have been compromised if Germany had gained air bases in southern Spain. Furthermore, such an alliance would enable the Germans to gain submarine and air bases on Spain's Atlantic coast and in the Canary Islands. This would have made the Allied task of containing the German submarines in the Atlantic even more difficult.

The Battle of the Atlantic ultimately depended not only on ships there, but also on the control over coasts and islands. Alliance with Spain would also have influenced Portugal, a neutral that was more pro-British, both traditionally and in practice. Portugal had an important Atlantic presence in its coastline, Madeira and the Azores, as well as colonies that bordered the Atlantic and Indian oceans: the Cape Verde Islands, Portuguese Guinea, Angola, Mozambique and bases in India, notably Goa. In February 1942, the Portuguese colony of East Timor, which had been recently garrisoned in part by Australians, was seized by Japanese forces which held it for the rest of the war.

Hitler met Franco at Hendaye on 23 October 1940. Franco was keen to offer support, but Spain was kept out of the conflict. This reflected Hitler's views and, as he showed elsewhere, had he sought a different outcome, he had considerable success in pressurising neutrals. However, Franco's demands for armaments, food, raw materials, manufactured goods and territorial gains from French North Africa were seen as excessive by Hitler, and likely to weaken the Vichy regime in France, which was regarded by him as more important both politically and militarily. Vichy forces had already fought the British, and Hitler wanted to ensure that Vichy France did not move towards Britain.

This preference meant that, while talking about cooperation with Spain, Vichy France and Italy, Hitler lacked enthusiasm for alliance with Spain, which was by far the weakest of the three in naval strength. To Hitler, Spain was largely inconsequential, a source of minor advantages that were not worth major effort, not least due to the clear weakness of the Spanish economy. Due to the Allies' naval blockade, Spain was dependent on the Allies for fuel and food. Furthermore, Britain bribed members of the Spanish leadership, as well as planning to attack Spain, notably bombing its ports, if it backed Hitler.

A key factor was Hitler's wish to limit secondary commitments. To him, Italy was the ally that should deliver the Mediterranean, and that subsequently required protection, albeit with only limited forces compared to German interests in Eastern Europe. To offer protection to Spain, with its Atlantic coastline vulnerable to British attack (as the Italian coast was not to the same extent), was less welcome and a diversion of forces. Spain lacked Italy's large navy, its air force and its industrial capacity; a situation of weakness that was accentuated by the recent civil war. By this stage, moreover, preparations were beginning for war with the Soviet Union.

In contrast to Germany at this time, Italian strategic horizons were compromised by failure, and other powers were now willing to consider seizing Italian possessions. Greece and Britain had ambitions accordingly, and, prefiguring issues at the end of the war, the British held out the prospect of Trieste and Istria when seeking Yugoslav support in 1941. Entry into the war swiftly brought a surfeit of reality about Italian military weakness, in terms of its capabilities, effectiveness and will. The relationship with Hitler, always shot through on both sides with concern and doubt, became one of dependence by the Italians and contempt from the Germans.[3] As a result, although he sought to reassure Mussolini, Hitler, unlike his opponents, lacked the need to justify strategic choices in the face of strong criticisms from an ally who could not be overawed.

LACK OF GERMAN STRATEGIC CLARITY

This point underlines the different directions in which German strategy pulled, and the extent to which these directions had protagonists in the divided, uneasy and incoherent Nazi system; a system that was not held together by any clear structure, plan or even much of a narrative. Unwilling to be restricted largely to submarine warfare, the German naval staff, building on the attitudes and policies developed prior to the First World War, wanted Germany to become a power with a global reach provided by a strong surface navy. As Britain had become a more obvious opponent, so plans for the size of the German navy became far more ambitious, with schemes in 1938 and 1940 replacing the more limited one of 1934, which had been directed essentially against France.

The naval staff also sought Atlantic naval bases from which, helped by the geostrategic consequences of the return of naval ports to Ireland in 1938,[4] it would be possible to threaten the convoy routes that brought Britain crucial supplies, as well as to increase German influence in South America and to challenge American power. Hitler, who on 26 September 1940 declared his interest in the Canary Islands, certainly hankered after global domination, and wanted Germany to regain the African colonies it had lost to Britain, France and their allies in the First World War. Indeed, this was an aspect of his general desire to reverse the losses and humiliations of that conflict. However, regaining these colonies was very much tangential to his central concern of reversing the Versailles peace settlement as far as Europe was concerned and, moreover, with creating a new Europe. Separately, the naval staff was not central to his concerns. Its interest in the establishment of bases around the Atlantic and in the Indian Ocean were not credible.

It is possible to quote Hitler's remarks suggesting different priorities, for example his attempt on 13 November 1940 to get Vyacheslav Molotov, the Soviet foreign minister, and very much an ally of Stalin, to centre their alliance on the partition of the British Empire, but such remarks need to be qualified in terms of a scrutiny of the deployment of troops. In practice, as with Napoleon, Hitler's prioritisation of European goals was clear. He talked for example of bases in French North-west Africa in order to thwart American attack, but did nothing to establish them. Seeking, instead, to focus on addressing clashing interests in Eastern Europe, Molotov was not interested in Hitler's proposal of a partition of the British Empire, although a British approach to Turkey in January 1941 led to Molotov talking wildly to the Italian envoy of a possible Anglo-Turkish attack on Crimea.[5] Such an attack had been mounted during the Crimean War (1854–6), while, until the final Soviet triumph, Crimea had been held by British and French-backed anti-Communist forces in the Russian Civil War.

The German navy took its focus on the Battle of the Atlantic to the extent of some officers pressing in the summer of 1941 for a declaration of war on the United States and, by November, there was an undeclared naval war on both sides. However, Hitler was more cautious.

The range of strategic players in the incoherent Nazi regime was seen on 10 May 1941 when Rudolf Hess, Hitler's loyal deputy, flew to Britain on an unauthorised, uninvited and unsuccessful attempt to settle Anglo-German differences – this possibly reflected initiatives involving MI6, perhaps some British politicians keen to avert a German invasion of Britain, and even the Polish government in exile.[6] Hess thought there was a political group in Britain that would negotiate peace with Germany. This mission, indeed, was seen by Stalin as a possible means of negotiation designed to isolate the Soviet Union. This may have been Hess's intention, but was certainly not Churchill's response. Moreover, Hitler disavowed the mission. He was concerned that Italy and Japan would see the approach as an attempt by Germany to settle with Britain. Hess was imprisoned in Britain.

Hess's failure represented defeat for the geopolitical alignment advocated by Karl Haushofer and his son Albrecht, geopoliticians close to Rudolf Hess, that of good relationships with the Soviet Union and Britain, or, at least in May 1941, with Britain. This geopolitics would have required Germany to abstain from war, which would not have suited Hitler at all. The difference in strategies was readily apparent in this case, but there were also other less stark contrasts within the Nazi system. In 1941, prior to his mission, Hess sought the advice of Albrecht, who was to be executed by the Nazi regime in 1945.

With modest forces compared to those deployed by the Allies in 1944–5, although still with a large air force, Germany in 1939–41 had sustained an impression of indubitable success. This impression itself was important in influencing support, whether in occupied Europe or among allies, neutrals and opponents. Indeed, strategy was in part driven by the value of success. In Germany, the popularity of the regime, already high as a consequence of overcoming the Versailles terms and ending unemployment, was greatly enhanced by the defeat of France. This situation expanded the opportunities for German aggression, although there is scant sign that the domestic situation acted as a strategic constraint. Indeed, for Germany, even in 1945, there was to be no parallel to the collapse of domestic support seen in 1918, other than in the lack of continued resistance after surrender.

OPERATION BARBAROSSA

Attacked on 22 June 1941, the Soviet Union might appear simply to have been the next target on the conveyor belt of German success, but it represented a very different strategy in terms of goal, means and scale. Indeed, the German attack on the Soviet Union indicated that Hitler was very much adopting a strategy predicated on what he saw as an inevitable struggle for destiny, one that met ideological preconceptions while dealing with geopolitical and resource issues.[7] On 18 December 1940, Hitler gave the orders for Operation Barbarossa. Already, on 15 November, he had ordered the building of the necessary headquarters for himself, the Wolf's Lair, which was completed by June 1941 and where Hitler was in residence from that July.

At the same time, there were military factors underlying Hitler's choice for war with specific powers, and his choices of particular operational goals and sequences. In effect, the Germans, notably Hitler, mistakenly assumed that with the Soviet Union there would be a repetition of their success of 1940. This entailed transposing the deep penetration they had achieved in France in 1940 onto the enormous distances of the Soviet Union, and in a time sequence that would be hindered by the climate, weather, terrain and communication systems being far more challenging than in the earlier instance. The tactical and operational means of

1939–40, in the shape of a combined arms attack (or *blitzkrieg*) that had worked in a confined geographical space could not work over the far greater spaces of the Soviet Union. Scale was a key dimension of strategy and, not least through imposing different time parameters, an important variable in its implementation. In addition, the Germans had developed an operational level doctrine in an ad hoc fashion and improvised manner. Alongside a seriously misplaced self-confidence, this ad hoc character helped set them up for serious problems when they attacked the Soviet Union and faced opposition in depth.

A range of factors had played a role in German success, notably the nature of the response by other powers, both allies and opponents. In the case of Poland (1939), Yugoslavia (1941) and Greece (1941), Hitler had also benefited from being part of an alliance system that attacked his opponents from a number of directions or, at least, provided useful bases for such attacks, as with Bulgaria for the invasions of Yugoslavia and Greece. The Soviet Union was important in the case of Poland; Italy, Hungary and Bulgaria in that of Yugoslavia; and Italy and Bulgaria for Greece.

The situation was different with the attack on the Soviet Union. Alliance with Finland and Romania greatly extended the length of the attacking front, added to the attacking forces and, in the Finnish case, enhanced the vulnerability of Leningrad (St Petersburg), but that front was already long enough. Instead, Japan, which would have greatly altered the military situation by fixing Soviet forces in the Far East and Siberia, was not included in German planning and, in what became a clear variance, had negotiated a non-aggression pact with the Soviets earlier in 1941, a pact that held until the Soviets broke it in August 1945.

German strategy was geared to the future in a sequential fashion. The attack on the Soviet Union was designed as part of the establishment of a new geopolitical and racial order in Europe, and as a key stage in a wider geopolitics intended in part to lead to the replacement of the British Empire, with Japan left free to fight the United States, albeit with the help of the far larger German navy projected in the aftermath of the dominance of Eurasia. As such, the attack on the Soviet Union was an important episode both in the German drive to dominate Eastern Europe and in the much more long-lasting struggle over the succession to the British Empire, a struggle that was a key geopolitical theme during the twentieth century, and that linked the Second World War to the first half of the Cold War. In the case of Hitler, this succession was to entail a thousand-year German empire, one that both dominated Eurasia and was able to defeat the United States.

The resources necessary for this struggle were to be found in the east, even though Germany's economic experts sensibly warned that it would be difficult to deploy these resources: oil, for example, could not be as readily moved to the *Reich*, as some assumed, or indeed within the conquered zone. Bold plans for major new communication links did not match the scale of the problem. Moreover, there was concern about the availability of sufficient food in the Soviet Union for the invading force. In addition, land for settlement was a resource that posed issues, not least the provision of a docile workforce.

In the short term, having destroyed the Soviet state, Hitler intended to overrun North Africa and the Middle East, with the advance of Army Group South to the Caucasus, which was a formidable distance, preparing the way for the latter. Soviet defeat would lead, it was hoped, to British surrender as their empire was put under great strain, their forces defeated and their morale destroyed. Thus, victory on land would not only compensate for British strength at sea and in the air, but would also counteract the problems caused by the German lack of a unified command structure and joint staff. This was a grand strategy configured to the nature of the German military and to its planning system, and, more particularly, to the perspectives of the army. *Lebensraum*, thus, would become an immediate as well as a long-term strategic advantage.

Reflecting a characteristic concern with control over raw materials, the Soviets assumed that German strategy would be dominated by a different configuration to the nature of its military, in the shape of a grasp for resources for the German war machine, with any attack focusing on the grain and coal of Ukraine, and therefore mounted south of the Pripet Marshes, a large area in southern Belarus and north-west Ukraine. As a result, Soviet forces concentrated on the South-west Front, and these proved difficult to overcome in the initial attack. Germany's concern with Soviet resources had been made readily apparent in the economic treaty of 10 January 1941 between the two powers, a treaty that also reflected Stalin's willingness to go on supplying Germany.

By seeing struggle primarily as a means of national purification and race war, however, Hitler ensured that the largely successful (for the Germans) earlier stage of the Second World War was merely instrumental in moving towards what became a prolonged, indeed attritional, war in which the German military, war economy and policy-making, under the war plan of 11 March 1941, were all found wanting and repeatedly so. The nature of German strategic goals, including a new demographic order (which would involve the draining of the Pripet Marshes and handing them over to German colonists), meant that peace was not really an option. German military discussion, at the time, focused more on operational than on strategic questions. There was no real interest in a peace similar to that forced on

Lenin in 1918, the Treaty of Brest-Litovsk. Thus, the option for Stalin to claim that example was not offered by Hitler, even though it would have provided a means for Germany to deliver a low-cost victory and to retain the strategic initiative there and elsewhere.

In contrast, Italian and, to a degree, Japanese strategies were more limited in their goals and means. Territorial acquisition was the key point for Italy and Japan. However, the idea of Japanese strategies as limited can be overturned if the perspective is that of China, against which restricted goals had been progressively abandoned in 1937, rather than that of the war with the United States. Italy was not expecting war, and was not ready for it in 1939 when, indeed, it remained neutral. In June 1940, Mussolini thought that the war would be soon over, which encouraged him to attack.

As an instance of the degree to which the war, and the unpredictability it brought, led to a far-flung dissemination of fear, Brazil, a pre-war ally, greeted Italy's entry into the war that June with concern that Italy might attack South America with *Ilha do Sal* (Salt Island) in the Cape Verde Islands as a base area; an airport had been built there in 1938, as a stage in a new Italian air service from Rome to Rio de Janeiro via Lisbon, a service using civil versions of Italian bombers. There is no evidence of plans for such an attack.

German strategy was deficient at a number of levels. This was not a case of a good strategy that was poorly executed, which is one approach to the evaluation of strategy, an approach that leads to the focus on particular command decisions, such as the decision to turn troops southwards to overrun Ukraine. Instead, German strategy was a bad strategy, which is a very different conclusion. The Germans had failed to devise a time sequence of even limited plausibility, in part because it was assumed that the defeat of the Soviet forces near the frontier would lead to the Soviet collapse. Hitler indicated to senior commanders that he was determined to shatter the Soviet Union with one blow, another instance of the German commitment to the idea of a decisive battle.

Overconfident of the prospects for a swift offensive, reliant on poor intelligence and completely failing to appreciate Soviet strength, and notably their army size, tank developments and persistence, the Germans both failed to understand the contrast between winning frontier battles and the subsequent conflict in rear areas, and suffered from a lack of consistency. Their goals shifted over the emphasis between seizing territory and, in contrast, defeating Soviet forces, and also over the question of which axes of advance to concentrate on. As with the poorly coordinated pressure on Britain in 1940, Hitler revealed himself a seriously flawed strategist in attack.

The lack of consistency, one already more generally seen with German strategy earlier in 1941, led to a delay in the central thrust on Moscow, while forces, instead, were sent south from 14 July to overrun Ukraine (capturing its resources) and to destroy the numerous Soviet forces there, which had hitherto mounted an impressive resistance to Army Group South advancing from the west. Both these goals were accomplished in what most closely approximated to the *Blitzkrieg* operations of 1939–41.

However, the delay in the advance on Moscow hindered the Germans when they resumed it, and helped exhaust the resource of pre-winter time, a key aspect of the time continuum and one that had not been properly assessed, not least due to the tendency of armoured offensives to require periods of lull for resupply and maintenance. Conversely, the advance on this central axis had already faced major difficulties, a point that leads to an emphasis on Soviet resistance rather than simply German command decisions. Moreover, the opportunistic German move south provided them with a concentration of force that was otherwise dispersed between different army groups, and also an ability to encircle major Soviet forces on the southern flank of any German advance. These points underline the need to consider a range of factors when evaluating strategy and its relationship with operational planning.

A key element was provided by the failure of German intelligence and planning, in the shape of a stronger than anticipated Soviet resistance. Such resistance had also been the case with the Poles in 1939 but they had been beaten, not least due to lacking defence-in-depth and due to attack (eventually) from all directions. Neither proved the case with the Soviets, and their resistance affected German operations and accentuated the consequences of a prior failure to settle grand strategic choices. The strength and persistence of their resistance helped ensure that mid-August 1941 was a decisive moment on the Eastern Front, with German casualties mounting, planning thrown out and assumptions disoriented.

Part of the debate about Barbarossa focuses on whether, how and when the Germans could have captured Moscow. However, that alone, as Tsar Alexander I had shown against Napoleon in 1812, would not have ended the conflict. The Soviets intended to fight on, planning to hold the line of the River Volga east of Moscow, and this line would have forced the Germans to sustain the struggle at an even greater distance and with a more serious logistical strain. The Soviets were determined, at any cost, to persist.

Linked to this was the central aspect of Soviet strategy provided by the transformation in their military-industrial complex created by the ability of this highly authoritarian state to move large quantities of industrial plant and many millions of workers to the east; and thus far beyond the range of likely German advance or air attack. As a consequence of this determination and defence-in-depth, the issue of the stability of the Soviet regime was more significant than the usual Barbarossa counterfactuals, which focus on failings in German operations, notably the decision in July to turn forces towards Ukraine. Indeed, the scope and progress of Barbarossa highlighted the Third Reich's lack of strategic and operational options, and the many weaknesses inherent in the German reliance on improvisation, especially in logistics.

JAPAN

Like that of Germany, Japanese strategy was confused. There were parts that made sense. Taking control of French Indo-China in 1941 was of strategic importance as an axis of advance to the extensive 'southern resources area' of Malaya and the Dutch East Indies. The latter (modern Indonesia) posed a problem for Japan as, despite the German conquest of the Netherlands in May 1940, Dutch colonial officials rejected Japanese efforts to acquire oil and, instead, sought to align policy with Britain and the United States. Moreover, seizing Burma (Myanmar) would, the Japanese hoped, cut off a crucial source of supplies for China, as well as providing Japan with another source of oil. However implausible, there was concern that Germany's conquest of the Netherlands and France would lead to Germany establishing control of their colonies. That would be highly unwelcome to Japan.

More generally, Japan's strategy was one of action, and in part for its own sake. Seizing and keeping the initiative would enable Japan repeatedly to translate numerical inferiority into a more favourable position at the point of engagement. This was in line with the short-war, 'grab and hold on' strategy of the successful conflicts of 1894–5 and 1904–5: the Sino-Japanese and Russo-Japanese wars. Based on an assumption of air superiority, which indeed existed,[8] Japan could set operational goals that otherwise would look unrealistic. The mistake was to assume that these goals constituted a realistic strategy.

The headline sequence of Japanese success in 1941–2, notably the capture of Singapore on 15 February 1942, suggested a brilliant strategy or, at least, a brilliantly successful one but, in practice, Japan suffered from the lack of a viable one. This was most obviously because Japan's prime opponent was now the United States, but the situation had already been the case when China was in that position. Acting to retain and secure great-power status, Japan, in reality, took steps that jeopardised it. Against the United States, there was no prospect for Japan of a complete victory, and, unlike with China, there was the prospect of the opponent attacking Japan, and in strength. Moreover, the very character of the surprise Japanese attack at Pearl Harbor on 7 December 1941 meant that the basis for any compromise peace between the two powers was missing. There was a different basis for the similar situation between Germany and the Soviet Union, but also similarities – that such a peace was made far less plausible by the legacy of conflict – now added to very contrary ideologies.

Underlying the flaws in Japanese strategy, there was a systemic confusion in Japanese policymaking, with very serious differences both between military and civilian politicians, and between army and navy, interacting with rifts over strategy, and notably so over areas of prime geographical interest. The army's continental concern with China and the Soviet Union (and there were differing priorities within the army) was not matched by that of the navy, the concern of which was engagement with Britain and the United States. The structure was in theory given coherence by Emperor Hirohito being in total command and an interministerial imperial committee in charge of overseeing the war. However, as a reminder of the need not to be confused by formal structures, the latter became a forum for the rivalry of the army and navy, while the indecisive Hirohito refused to provide coherence. The Prime Minister from 17 October 1941, General Hideki Tōjō, found that he could not be an effective substitute, although Admiral Shigetarō Shimada, the Minister for the Navy from October 1941 to July 1944, proved reasonably pliant to him.

As with Hitler and his attitude to Britain, the Soviet Union and, eventually, the United States, a conviction of the weakness of the opposing system led to a failure by Japan to judge sensibly their resolve, as well as a refusal to make the necessary choice between competing policies. This led to the problem of accumulating policies (and failing to order priorities and develop synergies between them), a tendency that was avoided by the Soviet Union. Instead, there was an unwarranted response by both Japan and Germany to the problems of the war, namely that of extending it.

Japanese political strategy focused on an anti-Western pan-Asianism under the leadership of Japan. Indeed, Tōjō's predecessor, Prince Fumimaro Konoe, wanted Germany to mediate peace between China and Japan in 1940. On 21 January 1942, Tōjō, in a statement to the Japanese *Diet* (Parliament), referred to the benefits to be obtained from co-prosperity in a system in which Japan was the core helping other East Asian peoples find their proper place. This pointed the way towards the creation of the Greater East Asia ministry in November 1942, to the encouragement of pan-Asian thought and, as greater difficulties were encountered in the war, to the granting of titular independence to Burma and the Philippines in August 1943. That November, the Japanese-backed Provisional Government of Free India, which had been formed by the Indian nationalist Subhas Chandra Bose in October 1943, was given administrative control of the Andaman and Nicobar Islands in the Bay of Bengal, vulnerable British possessions which had been occupied by Japan in March 1942.

This policy, which matched Japan's attempt to create allied regimes in occupied China, as well as alliance with Thailand, offered stabilisation (also seen in the non-aggression pact with the Soviet Union) as well as winning recruits. On land, there was potential in this strategy, although it was greatly weakened by Japan's racialism and its harsh exploitation of its conquests. However, against the United States at sea and in the air, there was no comparable potential for Japan's strategy.

The Japanese were eventually to be forced, contrary to their mentality, to adopt a defensive strategy towards the Americans, but the scope of the defensive shield was unclear, and the concept itself allowed for a more aggressive stance. Thus, in 1942, initial successes, and the sequential nature of advances, did not suggest any stop to expansion. Indeed, success encouraged elements in the navy to press either for the invasion of northern Australia, using Port Moresby in New Guinea as an advance base, or for an advance into the South-west Pacific, notably to the Solomon Islands, New Caledonia, Fiji and Samoa. The latter was designed to cut off Australia and New Zealand from American support, and thus to lessen the prospects of attack on the Japanese-occupied zone, as well as to oblige the Americans to defend a different 'frontline'. In the event, the army, heavily committed elsewhere, including in China where there was a successful offensive that year, was opposed to any invasion of Australia.

The conquest of New Guinea was a different, more limited, matter, but that was thwarted when a fleet designed to cover an amphibious attack on Port Moresby was checked by the Americans in the Battle of the Coral Sea (7–8 May 1942), a carrier action. Subsequently, an overland advance on Port Moresby from the north coast of New Guinea was blocked by Australian forces that September in fighting in very difficult terrain as well as in the face of serious disease, notably malaria.

To the fleet commander, Admiral Isoroku Yamamoto, the South-west Pacific, and even more the Indian Ocean, had become clearly secondary to the determination to achieve a strategic breakthrough by staging an equivalent to Pearl Harbor. Identifying the American fleet as the strategic centre of gravity, a reasonable view, he wanted to destroy both its carriers and battleships. The significance of the former had been underlined on 18 April 1942 by the Doolittle raid, an American air attack on Tokyo, mounted from carriers, which was named after its commander, Lieutenant-Colonel James Doolittle.

Although essentially symbolic, a public relations event for the Home Front, this raid hit the crucial element of Japanese prestige and forced the relocation of fighter aircraft to home defence, further putting pressure on air resources. The raid had a strategic impact and recentred Japanese naval concerns away from the south-west towards the northern Pacific, where there was less of an extensive defence-in-depth for Japan and therefore apparently greater possibilities for an American advance. As a result, the Japanese decided both to seize the westernmost Aleutian Islands, lessening American options in the northern Pacific, and also to tackle the American Pacific fleet. To that end, and also so as to enhance the defensive perimeter, Yamamoto proposed to seize Midway and other islands that could serve as support bases for an invasion of Hawai'i, which he correctly assumed would lead to the battle he wanted. In this battle, he planned that Japanese battle-ships and submarines would destroy American carriers.

In part, the Japanese suffered, like Hitler's forces in the Soviet Union in 1941 and 1942, from the adoption of an offensive strategy that both contained too many goals and did not adequately address prioritisation, sequencing, the timetable and a response to opposing moves. Having operated into the Indian Ocean, the Japanese navy was expected first to obtain advantages and secure goals in the South-west Pacific, and then across the expanse of the North Pacific to seize Midway, destroy the American fleet, and capture Attu and Kiska in the Aleutian Islands.[9] This misconceived strategy was further weakened by poor execution, notably the loss of the Intelligence war, but also the events of the desired battle itself.

In the Battle of Midway, which began on 4 June 1942, American carrier aircraft sank four Japanese carriers. The battle demonstrated Yamamoto's insight into the significance of fleet action as opposed to seizing territory but, due to poor planning and execution, did so to the detriment of Japan. Although there was still the damaged *Shōkaku*, the *Zuikaku* and a number of smaller carriers, Japan after Midway no longer had a significant carrier fleet nor the linked air cover, and thus Japanese plans for further expansion in the Pacific lacked traction.

Even prior to Midway, the initial Japanese ability to mount successful attacks, to gain great swathes of territory, and to establish an apparent stranglehold on the Far East and the western Pacific, had not deterred the Americans from the long-term effort of driving back and destroying their opponents. The American government and public were not interested in the idea of a compromise peace with the power that had attacked Pearl Harbor. Even more than Germany towards the Soviet Union, Japan, the weaker power, had gone to war with the one power that could beat it, and in a way calculated to ensure that it did so. As a result, helped greatly by the superior command skill that made possible the effective use of resources at a stage when they were still in short supply, the Americans were able to exercise strategic leverage, and to take the strategic initiative successfully by the end of 1942.

GERMANY, DECEMBER 1941–2

Hitler followed up the Japanese attack on Pearl Harbor by declaring war on the United States on 11 December 1941; Mussolini had done so earlier in the day. Hitler argued that there was already in effect an undeclared war between Germany and the United States in the Atlantic, where American warships were indeed involved in active conflict with German submarines, albeit at a limited scale, and stated that the United States was, as he told Mussolini, part of a global Jewish conspiracy that he claimed to discern. To Hitler, declaring war showed that Germany was a great power and, linked to this, it was better than having war declared on Germany. Moreover, Japan provided in effect a navy that could be used against America, and thus Japanese entry into the war extended the window of opportunity for Germany.

The German declaration was the key event in making the war global, and one in which the power taking the initiative was to prove the eventual loser. As with the Germans bringing the Americans into the war in 1917 by switching to unrestricted submarine warfare, there was a failure to think through the possible consequences. Germany's allies were under pressure to follow suit and declare war on the United States, Hungary and Romania doing so on 12 December and Bulgaria on the next day, although Finland did not.

German submarines were sent into American coastal waters, inflicting much damage on unprotected or poorly protected coastal shipping, notably oil tankers, and thus affecting the overall Battle of the Atlantic and the crucial equation of losses as opposed to construction. However, the global perspective of German strategy was secondary in 1942 to the specifics of a renewed offensive against the Soviet Union. In June, having stopped initially successful Soviet attacks earlier in the year, the Germans launched a fresh offensive against Soviet forces. To Hitler, gaining Soviet resources, in particular oil, was the best preparation for conflict with the United States, specifically for opposing a so-called 'Second Front' in Western Europe (the 'First Front' was the Eastern Front). The initial plan in 1942 called for the destruction of Soviet forces west of the River Don, followed by an advance into the Caucasus Mountains, in order to capture the Soviet oilfields in the region, and then put pressure on Allied interests in the Near and Middle East. Cutting Allied supply links to the Soviet Union through Iran, links created when Britain and the Soviet Union jointly occupied the country in 1941, was seen as important.

There were also hopes of winning the support of neutral Turkey, a potentially pivotal power in the eastern Mediterranean and the Middle East, one with a very large army, although no significant air force or navy. Turkey borders Syria, Iraq, Iran and the Soviet Union, and, from Turkey, it would also be easy to threaten Cyprus, Palestine (Israel) and Egypt. In the event, resisting blandishments from both sides, Turkey remained neutral until joining the Allies in early 1945, although that delay helped ensure that the victorious Allies, over Turkish protests, in 1947 awarded the Dodecanese Islands to Greece, which retains them to this day.

The seizure of the Caucasus oilfields was regarded as a preparation for the lengthy struggle that American entry into the war appeared to make inevitable. Indeed, Hitler expanded the original objective in order to seize all the oilfields in the region, including the distant ones round Baku on the Caspian Sea. Resources were a key factor in strategic planning, and in terms of goals as well as means. In a classic instance of the repeated failure to consider lines of communications and logistics, the difficulties involved in moving any oil that could be obtained were dramatically underrated. Hitler understood the need to gain the Black Sea coast in order to be able to move the oil from the nearest oilfield close to Maykop, but not the problems that would subsequently occur in moving sufficient oil.

In 1942, as in 1941, German strategy on the Eastern Front was both misguided and poorly implemented. There was a misleading confidence that the Soviets would both fight where the Germans wanted – in the Don bend – and that they had been gravely (yes) and permanently (no) weakened by the war so far. Not envisaged in 1941, when the planning for the future had been perfunctory, the 1942 offensive was not, in conception or practice, an adequate stage two. The German plan, for the destruction of Soviet forces west of the Don followed by an exploitation notably to the Caucasus oilfields, with the flanks secured at Voronezh and Stalingrad (now Volgograd), was flawed from the outset because it was supported by insufficient logistical preparations, underestimated Soviet strength and offered a massive flank in the north open to Soviet attack. More generally, even if successful, the plan would not have countered the build-up of Soviet strength nor Soviet resilience. Nor would it have had an impact in northern and central Russia, other than indirectly.

As in 1941, the Soviets misjudged the likely direction of German attack. Stalin had anticipated the blow falling on Moscow, which was within the range of an attack by the German Army Group Centre, and had deployed his reserves accordingly. This enabled him to benefit from Moscow's central position in the Soviet rail network and to move troops to either flank as required.

Moreover, and producing a more specific problem, Hitler's growing conviction, as the campaign developed, that the city of Stalingrad on the River Volga had to be captured foolishly substituted a pointless symbolic goal for the necessary operational flexibility. This was a situation already seen with the Germans at Verdun in 1916, and one that captured the more general role of symbolical factors in strategic planning and implementation. Alongside regarding Stalingrad as a threat to north–south Soviet communications in the Volga valley and beyond, and thus a factor in future campaigning, Hitler, on the model of the unsuccessful plan for the Verdun offensive of Erich von Falkenhayn, the Chief of the German General Staff, hoped that Stalin would commit his forces to hold the city, which was within the grasp of his forces as other cities on the river, to north and south, were not. Thereby, in Hitler's view, the battle for the city would provide the strategic advantage of overcoming, both practically and conceptually, the distance of the Soviet Union by forcing a decisive clash; creating, as it were, a new battle of the frontiers.

In practice, Hitler's obsession with Stalingrad proved misguided at the strategic, operational and tactical levels. The obsession squandered German advantages in mobile warfare and the pursuit of the open flank, and, more specifically, the prospects offered by Soviet vulnerability in the Caucasus region, which was tangential to the major Soviet troop developments. In Stalingrad, the German force was fixed, the dynamism of strategy and operational warfare rapidly swallowed by the tactical dimension of capturing particular locations in an urban terrain broken up by German bombing and bombardment.

Even had the Germans succeeded at Stalingrad, the victory arguably would have been of limited value. The resource base (both German and captured Soviet) required for further conflict on the Eastern Front and, eventually, against the Western Allies, would have been attenuated (as it indeed was anyway), not strengthened, by the struggle. It is possible to suggest that an early German victory at Stalingrad would have enabled the Germans to sweep north on the eastern side of the Volga, cut Moscow off from the Ural factories, and draw off Soviet forces facing Army Groups North and Centre, thus enabling both Army Groups to achieve their goals. In this scenario, the Soviets are either beaten in an encirclement battle or driven to avoid this by withdrawing towards Siberia, Moscow is captured and the Soviet Union is defeated. However, aside from the commitment in the Caucasus, the Germans lacked the resources in manpower and, crucially, fuel for this scenario; and, to be ahistorical at best, they were in a situation more akin to that of Alexander the Great crossing the River Indus in 326 BCE, only to be obliged to turn back in the face of other large Indian armies, rather than being able to press forward to a major new conquest.

Having failed to sustain their advances in Stalingrad or the Caucasus, the Germans were subsequently defeated in Stalingrad with heavy losses by a Soviet counterattack, Operation Uranus, launched on 19 November 1942. This was, as it should not have been, a surprise. Strategy involves not only the fixing of sensible goals and the understanding of the relevant means, but also doing so with reference to a sound assessment of the likely ones of opponents. Germany totally failed to achieve this in the Stalingrad campaign. The German Sixth Army in Stalingrad was rapidly surrounded, and attempts to supply it by air and to relieve it by land both failed completely.

THE FAILURE OF AXIS ALLIANCE STRATEGY

The Axis, moreover, failed to provide a coherent strategy at the level of the alliance or, indeed, any basis for producing, let alone implementing, such a strategy. Hitler's inability to control his allies led to serious problems for him, most especially with their attacks on other powers, that of Italy on Britain and Greece in 1940, and of Japan on the United States in 1941. The total failure of Italy's attack on Greece – which had not been planned with German approval – partly affected Hitler's timetable for launching an attack on the Soviet Union in 1941: the attack was postponed to late June. However, the harsh weather in Poland and the Soviet Union that spring was also significant in this postponement, as was Hitler's decision to attack Yugoslavia alongside Greece. British intervention also increased the task posed by conquering Greece, and added the need to mount a separate attack to capture Crete.

As a result, the gap between Hitler's ability to impose his will on events and the pressures of reality became ever wider. This gap always exists in strategy, but it became too large in the German case. At the same time, this problem was made less serious in this specific case because the particularly wet spring in 1941 meant that the ground remained saturated until later in the year, and therefore highly unsuitable for tank advances.

Separately, with each power doing essentially only what they wanted, Germany and Japan were unable to create a military partnership, nor to provide mutual economic assistance that in any way matched that of the Allies. Hitler underestimated Japan's potential because he was focused on Europe and he was a racist, as his responses to Indian nationalism indicated. German plans for war with the Soviet Union, and later with the United States, made relatively little of the remote prospect of direct Japanese assistance, although Japan's entry into the war with Britain was seen as a way to harm it and to deter the United States. Instead, against the Americans, the Germans preferred to focus on their naval power alone and, to that end, on Atlantic naval staging bases, such as Spain's Canary Islands. Germany and Japan fought what were in essence two independent wars, and there was little in the way of coordination or cooperation between them or, as significant, any real attempt to work in tandem, or even to provide the context where it might be possible.

Still less was there any coordination between Italy and Japan. Unlike Germany, Italy had a colony on the Indian Ocean and a colonial presence on the route there. However, these colonies, Italian Somaliland and Eritrea, were conquered by the British in early 1941 before there was any prospect of coordination, their principal ports, Kismayo and Massawa, falling on 14 February and 8 April respectively; Mogadishu lacks a harbour. Based in German-occupied France, Italian submarines took part in the Battle of the Atlantic from 1941; while there was a presence in the Indian Ocean.[10] However, the large and modern Italian navy was essentially deployed in the Mediterranean, and only in the central Mediterranean at that. As a consequence, it was not in a position to cooperate with the German surface fleet in the Atlantic, other than in the important indirect sense of keeping British warships busy in the Mediterranean, which was the major reason why Hitler welcomed Italy's entry into the war.

The highpoint of the very limited German–Japanese coordination was Germany's decision on 11 December to declare war on the United States after the 7 December 1941 attack on Pearl Harbor. Concerned about the possible outcome of the negotiations between Japan and the United States in late 1941, Japan going to war with Britain and to a lesser extent the United States was a move that Hitler had sought to encourage. He did so by pressing forward his military operations against Moscow in Operation Typhoon, and thus made himself more attractive as an ally, and the Soviet Union less of a deterrent for Japan; although that was scarcely the sole, or indeed major, reason for his operations.

Furthermore, and this was also important for Mussolini, bringing Japan into the war offered another way to put pressure on Britain and on the cohesion and resources of its empire, including the ability to employ Australasian and Indian forces in the Middle East. Thus, an ability to think in broader terms of the interaction of strategic options was highly significant, Indeed, by entering the war, Japan certainly did apply this pressure, and notably so by making the defence of Australia and India major requirements for British imperial forces. Nevertheless, as part of his tendency to delusion and dream, Hitler exaggerated the extent to which his policies were of significance to Japanese strategy-making, other than the very important factor of keeping the Soviet Union busy.

The German declaration of war on the United States did not lead to any concerted attempt at grand strategy. This was not least because, despite German pressure early in the war with the Soviet Union, Japan had chosen not to attack the Soviet Union. Instead, it maintained the non-aggression agreement of 13 April 1941. Hitler hoped that the Japanese would change their mind after he declared war on the United States, but they did not. (Hitler, in turn, did not extend his support for Japan by declaring war on China, although Germany could not have done anything had he done so). The continuing pact lessened the problem for both Japan and the Soviet Union of being overextended on too many fronts, as well as raising the question of what might have occurred had Japan attacked.

In turn, the Soviet Union was not to allow the use of its territory for American air attacks on Japan, which would have effectively ended Soviet neutrality. This refusal lessened the strategic significance of the North Pacific, including the Aleutians, and left the Americans with the more difficult alternatives of bases in China and/or the western Pacific. The former were difficult to supply and protect; and the latter hard to conquer. Conversely, Japan did not attempt to block American supplies to the Soviet Far East as requested by Hitler, and the route was an important one, being enhanced by the building of the Alaska Highway, a proposal approved by the army on 6 February 1942 and Congress five days later. In practice, most supplies were sent by sea from west coast ports, including the large number of trucks that were to prove important to Soviet mobility in 1944.

The only sphere in which an attempt at Axis grand strategy might have been possible was the Indian Ocean region. In particular, there was the possibility of German pressure in the Middle East interacting with Japanese advances on India and in the Indian Ocean, to provide simultaneous pressure or, at least, sequential shocks. British policymakers were certainly concerned about this. They were worried about pressure on South Asia with, for example, the Germans possibly advancing through Turkey prior to the launching of Operation Barbarossa in June 1941, and subsequently through Turkey or the Caucasus.

These concerns, which echoed those in 1918 as the Germans advanced in Russia, were a second tranche of fears in 1940–1 about the Germans exploiting support and possibilities in Iraq and (Vichy) Syria. They had indeed sought to do so, with the Paris Protocols of May 1941 with Vichy France granting Germany access to military facilities in Syria, which was seen as a way for Germany to intervene in neighbouring Iraq. This threat led the British, in a successful forward-defence strategy, to invade both Syria and Iraq in 1941. The British underrated the extent to which nationalism, rather than support for the Axis, was the key element in Iraqi politics and policy, a pattern that was to be replicated during the Cold War. On the other hand, strategy frequently involved the subordination of the local realities of alignment to the directives of those exercising control at the level of grand strategy.

In 1941, a German advance into the Middle East did not materialise. Despite British concern, the German seizure of Crete (and the Italian presence in the Dodecanese, of which the leading island is Rhodes) was not followed by an Axis attempt to seize Cyprus, a British colony. This would have been vulnerable, as Crete had been, although not, due to factors of location, to the same extent nor, indeed, to that of Malta, which was not invaded. The Italians overestimated the size of British forces in Malta. Moreover, except in a few places, Malta was a difficult island to invade due to its steep and rocky coastline, and, at that time, it was known that the island was covered by an overlapping system of heavy artillery positions. Cyprus was further than Crete or Malta from ports and airfields that Germany or Italy could have used.

Nor was the conquest of Greece and alliance with Bulgaria followed up by an invasion of neighbouring Turkey. Had the Germans done so, a counterfactual that was later to be advocated by the military historian John Keegan, they would have found the Turkish army capable of mounting a formidable resistance. There was also no equivalent to the perimeter exposed to attack from a number of directions seen with Poland in 1939 and Yugoslavia in 1941, while, unlike Istanbul, Ankara was less vulnerable than the capital cities on which the Germans had advanced then and in 1940. An alternative, pressuring Turkey into granting transit rights, would have been a different question, but the situation would have had to be more dire for such pressure to succeed because, as a neighbour of the Soviet Union in the Caucasus, Turkey was exposed to its presence. Furthermore, any German move through Turkey on Syria or Iraq would have encountered very serious logistical and transport limitations and problems, even more so than advancing through Spain on Gibraltar, and the Germans were well aware of this. As a result, they gave very little thought to such operations.

In 1914, alliance with Turkey had given Germany strategic possibilities. In an offensive sense, these had not been realised, notably with the failure of the Turkish attack on the Suez Canal in 1915. However, thanks to the alliance, there had been a welcome diversion of British and Russian forces during the First World War. In 1941, there was such a diversion for the British as a result of confronting local powers in Iran, Iraq and Syria; but there was no Turkish attack on the Soviet Union nor on the British in the Middle East.

The risk of a German attack on the Middle East via the Soviet Union came to the fore as a result of the German conquest of Ukraine in late 1941. This suggested an axis of strategic interest and operational advance for Germany via the Caucasus; and that prospect appeared enhanced as a result of the German conquest of Crimea, finished in July 1942, which brought established air and naval bases into the equation. The Soviets, moreover, were not able to mount convincing opposition to the weak Axis naval forces in the Black Sea. In the event, in late 1941, the Germans were forced back from Rostov by a Soviet counter-offensive on Army Group South. Moreover, in late 1942, the planned German advance to the oilfields of the Caucasus region could not be brought to fruition due to Soviet resistance, a factor that it was too easy to overlook when considering axes of advance on a map, and as a result of Hitler's focus on the capture of Stalingrad.

By then, anyway, the British and Soviets, invading from 25 August 1941, had rapidly occupied Iran, overthrowing the ruler, Reza Shah Pahlavi, whom they suspected of Axis sympathies. As a consequence, and reflecting British attitudes towards Tsarist Russia in the nineteenth century, as well as the Anglo-Russian 1907 agreement over spheres of influence in Iran, British India was provided with defence-in-depth in the event of German success in the Caucasus and/or the Middle East. Iran was a larger target than Syria or Iraq, and Britain benefited from the support of the Soviet Union. At the same time, the suspicious government of British India in New Delhi would have preferred that the operation had been mounted without Soviet participation. It was overruled from London.

The occupation of Iran thus supplemented the earlier British conquest of Iraq, as well as providing control over strategic oilfields. A British strategic review of that month noted: 'Iranian oil and the Abadan refinery [in Iran] are essential to us. Our present positions afford a defence in depth to the shores of the Indian Ocean and Persian Gulf.'[11] The Abadan refinery, owned by the Anglo-Iranian Oil Company, produced 8 million tons of oil in 1940. With British and Soviet troops stationed in occupation zones, the new Shah agreed in January 1942 to provide non-military aid and, in September 1943, declared war on Germany. American and British aid to the Soviet Union was sent in part via Iran. Control of Iran and Iraq also left the Persian Gulf totally in British hands.

Japan was a more prominent part of the Axis equation because it also had a potent naval capability. With their conquest (as well as much elsewhere) of Malaya, Singapore, Sumatra and Burma (Myanmar) in early 1942, and notably of the naval bases of

Singapore (February) and Rangoon (March), the Japanese were well placed to advance into the Indian Ocean region, and far better so than the Germans or Italians. These advances had been made by land as well as sea, but the Japanese naval achievements – notably the attack on Pearl Harbor, the sinking, by land-based torpedo-bombers, of the modern British battleship *Prince of Wales* and the battle cruiser *Repulse* on 10 December 1941 off eastern Malaya, and the sweeping victory in the battles of the Java Sea from 27 February to 1 March 1942 over American, Australian, British and Dutch warships – showed how victory at sea could be the prelude to amphibious attacks and territorial gains. So also with later American naval successes in the western Pacific.

In April 1942, the Japanese made just such a move. Five carriers sailed into the Indian Ocean and inflicted serious losses on the British, including sinking a carrier and two heavy cruisers. The outmatched Eastern Fleet was obliged to retire while the Japanese launched devastating air attacks on India and Ceylon (Sri Lanka). This was a serious threat to the strategic resource and depth presented by British control of the Indian Ocean. Concern was readily apparent. General Sir Alan Brooke, the phlegmatic Chief of the Imperial General Staff, noted in his diary for 6 April 1942:

On reaching COS [Chiefs of Staff] I discovered that most of the Japanese fleet appeared to be in the Indian Ocean and our Eastern fleet retiring westwards. Up to present no signs of [invasion] transports. I don't like the situation much as we are very weak in the Indian Ocean. I have been trying to get First Sea Lord to fix up with the Americans some counter move towards Japan to cover this very predicament that we are in, but he has failed to do so up to the present.

There was no prospect of such American action. Brooke was even gloomier the next day: 'COS at which we looked into the unpleasant situation created by entrance of Japanese fleet into Indian Ocean . . . I suppose this Empire has never been in such a precarious position throughout its history.' On 10 April 1942, Brooke added, 'usual COS meeting, mainly concerned in trying to save India from the Japs. A gloomy prospect with loss of command of sea and air.'[12] In the event, the Japanese did not persist. Instead, their fleet speedily left the Indian Ocean. The advance therefore ended up as a raid, displaying capability. It was a raid that showed a degree of threat totally different to that posed by German warships entering the Atlantic, notably the *Bismarck* in 1941.

This Japanese carrier force was rapidly to be wrecked in a way that illustrated how Allied victories more successfully influenced the relationship between different spheres of activity. The Japanese fleet launched the Pacific operations that led, first, to the Battle of the Coral Sea (7–8 May) and, subsequently, to disaster at the hands of the Americans at Midway (4–5 June).

The loss of Japanese offensive capability at Midway, as a consequence of the sinking of four of their carriers, the destruction of many aircraft (much of their fleet strike force), and the loss of air crew and support staff, made thoughts of further Japanese advances in the Indian or Pacific oceans implausible, let alone ideas of joint action with the Germans. Thus, the events of a few minutes of Midway reset strategic parameters, both then and subsequently, and not only, as usually thought, for the war in the Pacific but also in the Indian Ocean and further afield. This was significant because the major role that Japan played in the Second World War was an important aspect of its novelty. As a consequence, Allied planners were obliged to confront challenges on a far greater scale than in the First World War. The trade-off with regard to Japan was not simply between the conflict in the Pacific and that in the Indian Ocean. China was also important, but it was not a factor at sea, not even as a diversion to Japanese naval strength.

Midway was made more significant by a more general emerging pattern of increasing American naval effectiveness and the attrition of the Japanese navy, alongside that of its American rival. Thanks to Midway and, more generally, the American–Japanese war in the Pacific, on which the Japanese navy overwhelmingly concentrated until the end of the war, the British needed only to deploy limited naval strength against Japan after April 1942. This situation did not change until the closing year of the war when, after covering D-Day on 6 June 1944, much of the British fleet was transferred so as to be able to play a major role in the war with Japan. Doing so provided Britain with a strategic capability in the Pacific lacking in the case of land forces and, in particular, a means to regain imperial prestige, to impress allies, notably the United States and Australia, and to be an influence in the re-creation of European colonial empires, particularly the British Empire.

Prior to that, the British had two carriers in May 1942 to cover the successful attack on Diego Suarez (Antsiranana), the main port in Vichy-held Madagascar, but from January 1943 there were no British carriers in the Indian Ocean until October, when an escort carrier arrived. No British warship was lost in the Indian Ocean in 1943; but no major attempt was made to launch another front against Japan on the land perimeter of its newly conquered empire south of Burma, and thus no effective British pressure was brought to bear to assist the United States and Australia.

The Vichy-governed, large French Indian Ocean island colony of Madagascar was very different. Indeed, its conquest, like that of Iran and Iraq, was part of the deep defence of the British imperial system. The German navy's 1940 plan for a *weltreich* (world empire) had included a base at Diego Suarez. In 1942, Britain feared that Madagascar might become a Japanese submarine base, thus greatly taking forward Japanese naval power and challenging Britain's ability to operate in the Indian Ocean and thereby its position in India (and ability from there to assist China), as well as the maritime route to Australia via Cape Town. In March 1942, intercepts of signals, which gave the British an important (albeit not continuous) strategic capability which the Germans generally lacked, indicated that Germany was urging Japan to occupy the island.

These fears were ended by the British conquest of the island between 5 May and 5 November 1942. Initially, it was only Diego Suarez, vulnerable to amphibious attack, that was seized, falling on 7 May after resistance that indicated anew the willingness of Vichy forces to fight, but that also displayed a marked increase in effectiveness since the unsuccessful British attack on Dakar in Vichy-held Senegal in September 1940. The cumulative nature of strategic ambitions led Britain, encouraged by South Africa, to take over the rest of the island with fresh landings from 10 to 29 September. These landings were the best way to capture the other ports. In part, the campaign was a reflection of South African concern in the First World War about German colonies in Africa. Although German and Italian submarines did link up in the Indian Ocean with the Japanese, and benefited from bases available to them at Singapore and Sabang, which is off the north coast of Indonesia, they did not mount any large-scale concerted operations.

Axis alliance politics might, indeed, have had most global geopolitical possibilities in the case of Germany and Japan. However, in practice, Axis alliance politics focused on bilateral relations between Germany and its European allies. Hitler sought to treat them as clients, with peremptory demands for troops and other resources, with the attempted imposition of anti-Semitic policies, and with assumptions that their territory both could be used for military operations and should be reallocated to suit German diplomatic goals. Thus, in 1940, Romania had to accept a German–Italian settlement of territorial differences, with northern Transylvania transferred to Hungary in August, and Southern Dobrudja to Bulgaria in September under the Treaty of Craiova, both reversing First World War gains from German allies. In accordance with the Nazi–Soviet Pact of 1939, Romania also had to transfer Bessarabia and Northern Bukovina to the Soviet Union in June 1940.

Such changes, nearly a third of Romania, caused serious tensions and, more generally, there was hostility or opposition to German requirements. On the other hand, Romanians could do nothing else and proved far more supportive to the Germans than they later cared to remember. Selective amnesia for the Romanian government as an ally of Germany was fostered by its help in regaining land from the Soviet Union lost in 1940, as well as land beyond the River Dniester, the latter against the wishes of politicians outside the regime.

This was more generally the case with Eastern Europe. More of the people in the region accepted or cooperated with German and/or Italian policy than they were subsequently to recall. In part, this process was encouraged by the extent to which Czechoslovakia, Romania, Poland and Yugoslavia had included ethnic minorities. In addition to Italy and Romania, Bulgaria and Hungary both gained land from conquered states.

Germany's allies were reluctant to agree with its priorities. General Ion Antonescu, Romania's Prime Minister and in effect military dictator, was pro-British as well as pro-German, and war between Britain and Romania was begun with reluctance on both sides and only because of Stalin's pressure. British pressure on Romania to stop military operations in the Soviet Union was of course unsuccessful, and Britain declared war on 7 December 1941. Seeking to remain neutral, Bulgaria did not declare war on Britain until 13 December and never declared war on the Soviet Union. Bulgaria, instead, sought to restrict its activity as an ally of Germany to Balkan expansion. No troops, even volunteers, were sent to fight the Soviets.

Tensions would have existed anyway, but were not eased by the character and content of German alliance politics. Instead, Germany's allies, many of limited military relevance due to poor equipment and limited training, were kept in the dark, there were no summits equivalent to those of the Allies, intelligence was not much shared, other than between Germany and Italy, and there was a general failure to sustain cooperation. This was a part of the more general character in Hitler's concept of Europe, namely his preference for a racial chimera over an acknowledgement of the legitimate political aspirations of others.

Irrespective of this, the Germans suffered from the lack of planning for collaboration and from the absence of any relevant organisation or staff. Instead, there was a very disparate practice, reflecting in particular the degree of formal independence remaining, as well as the nature of the German administration of occupied territory. There was also serious rivalry between German organisations that sought to profit from the control or influence over allies and occupied territories.

The problems in Germany's alliance system ranged widely. A lack of cooperation between allies was significant. This was particularly seen in former Yugoslavia, where the number of actors on the Axis side was made serious by their rivalry, the inability to control protégés and a willingness to take interests to the point of conflict. Alongside Germany, Italy, Bulgaria and Hungary as annexing powers came military occupation, self-government for the Germans in the Banat, and collaborationist regimes in Croatia and Serbia. The former, the Independent State of Croatia, had to accept the cession of territory to Italy, as well as German and Italian economic exploitation. This state quarrelled with that in Serbia, and its forces fought anti-Communist militias established by the Italians. Similarly, there was bitter opposition within the Resistance, notably between the Communists and the anti-Communist Četnici. Moreover, there were cross-alliances spanning the theoretical divide of Allies via Axis. The situation greatly affected chances of lessening opposition. Thus, alliance with the murderous *Ustaša* regime in Croatia made it harder for the Germans to win support in Yugoslavia and, notably, from anti-Communist Serbs. So also with the brutality of the Bulgarian occupiers of Macedonia.

Issues arose over independent initiatives by allies. This was particularly seen with Italy and Finland, although each posed different issues. More effective militarily against the Soviets than Germany's other European allies, in part because they only fought in areas they knew, the Finns refused a full-scale commitment against partly besieged Leningrad (St Petersburg), despite repeated requests to do so from the Germans. This was really important to the failure to conquer the city, as a further Finnish advance would have hit the supply links on which its defenders relied. From the autumn of 1941 to the spring of 1944, the Finns did little fighting.[13] The Finns were also reluctant to yield to German pressure to hand over Jews.

Constrained by inadequate resources and fighting on too many fronts, Italy proved a highly disappointing ally. Hitler at the outset thought that the two powers could act in parallel, and without melding their fronts and operations; while Mussolini did not want German dominance of the Axis. The defeat of Italian forces in 1940–1 and the degree to which they were forced to improvise responses, changed the situation, not least due to German successes in this period. However, even then, the degree to which Italian resources were mobilised was insufficient. Until 1941, there was no rationing, while, due to harvest work, many conscripts were released in late 1940. The economy, which was anyway weak in key industrial sectors, was not militarised. Italy thus became a drain on the German military. The Germans certainly undervalued their Italian allies militarily. This continued after the war, when German commentators used Italian failure to help explain the failure that was more truly German. The Germans did not provide Italy with much in the way of good or modern weaponry, nor indeed food. In September 1940, some Stukas (ground-attack aircraft) were provided, and, in the summer of 1943, some Messerschmitts, but no German-made tanks, little artillery and few lorries. Coal was delivered and a certain amount of oil, but these had to be paid for in goods or money. However, alongside limitations in German assistance, the Italian army failed to make a successful effort commensurate with Italy's industrial resources, while the more impressive navy and the small air force were squeezed, both as fighting forces and in terms of industrial capacity, as well as suffering the major handicap of limited fuel availability. Furthermore, repeatedly, there were also major problems in coordination between the Italians and Germans.[14] Both sides proved deficient in this respect.

More generally, Germany lacked the willingness or resources to provide appropriate military assistance to its allies, notably weaponry: for example, the anti-tank guns unsuccessfully sought by the Hungarians in early 1943 that might have helped their Second Army survive serious defeat and major losses at the hands of the Soviets near Voronezh. This defeat affected Germany, both in so far as that particular operation was concerned and because it was followed by Hungary adopting a less bellicose position against the Soviet Union. This inability to deliver aid was an aspect both of Germany's failure, in capacity and strategy, and of a broader limitation of the alliance system as a military process for diffusion, one also seen in the absence of any major success in transferring skills and experience through training and doctrine. The net effect was to leave large numbers of Axis forces with inadequate equipment and, therefore, unable to raise their game.

The provision of inadequate equipment was not simply a problem for Germany's allies. An indicative failure of the entire German system was the reliance in part on captured military equipment, notably tanks and artillery. This had consequences in terms of often difficult, if not incoherent, issues of ammunition supply and maintenance requirements.

Outside its alliance system, Germany was able to benefit from military success in 1939–41. It did so in obtaining the support of neutrals, as well as in conquered areas, by securing a measure of collaboration and, more widespread, passivity, and, further afield, by drawing on widespread opposition to imperial rule in the Western empires, for example in Egypt and Palestine, just as Japan was to seek to do, notably in Burma and India. However, Hitler's longstanding hostility to Indian nationalism, a hostility that drew on racism as well as to an inherent sympathy for imperial rule, was in evidence when he met the anti-British Indian nationalist Subhas Chandra Bose on 27 May 1942.

Supportive neutrals included Sweden for Germany, and Thailand for Japan. Sweden provided naval protection for crucial iron-ore exports to Germany (receiving coal in return) and, accordingly, fought Soviet submarines in the Baltic. This was a conflict that was subsequently to be greatly underplayed by the Swedes. So also with Swiss neutrality, while the Irish refusal to provide Britain with the use of naval bases helped Germany in the Battle of the Atlantic.

Spain was a self-declared non-belligerent, and Franco claimed that the country was exhausted. Yet, he actively collaborated, for example providing bases for German reconnaissance aircraft and Italian torpedo units, facilitating German espionage and propaganda, and refuelling U-boats. Franco also provided not only raw materials but the volunteer 'Blue Division' that fought on the Eastern Front against the Soviet Union in what was presented, in Spain and elsewhere, as a crusade against communism. About 47,000 Spaniards fought in the *División Española de Voluntarios*, which was known as the Blue Division because many of the early volunteers were fascist Falange militia who had that shirt colour. This was not a regular force, but it was justified as a response to Soviet intervention in the Spanish Civil War, although Franco did not declare war on the Soviet Union. There was a shortage of volunteers so that, by late 1942, even anti-fascists were being recruited. The division fought well and bravely. It was an instance of the large-scale military support that Germany was able to obtain or coerce in Europe. Forced labour was a variant on this, as much of this labour was delivered with the compliance of local authorities.

Although signing the Iberian Pact with Franco in March 1939, a pact expanded in July 1940 after the Fall of France, Portugal was more clearly neutral. This accorded with the view of its dictator, António Salazar, on the damaging impact of the First World War on the country. A traditional ally of Britain, including in that war, and with its empire greatly vulnerable to British naval action and to land attack by Britain and its dominion allies, Salazar, however, did not wish to offend the then victorious Germany in the early 1940s, nor to provide Spain, a militarily powerful neighbour, with an opportunity for conquest. Moreover, Portugal maintained its neutrality when Japan occupied its colony of East Timor in 1942. There was an important economic dimension to strategy and, as part of the process of making money by trading with both sides, Portugal sold tungsten (wolfram) to both.

There was also, as in the First World War, an attempt to recruit support from opponents of the imperial systems of Britain and its allies. Arab anticolonial nationalists that looked to Germany included Syria's Social Nationalists and the Young Egypt movement. With other Tunisian anticolonial leaders, Habib Bourguiba was freed from a Vichy prison in late 1942 by the Italians and sent to Tunis where, however, he remained prudently in a political no man's land in 1943. Italy supported the rebellious Faqir of Ipi, Mirzali Khan, on the North-West Frontier of British India in 1940–1, and the British were concerned about Italian intrigues in Aden. Then, in 1943, there was an unsuccessful attempt by German agents parachuted into Iran to bribe the Qashqai tribe to block supplies en route for the Soviet Union. In 1944, the Germans parachuted arms into Palestine to help Arab nationalists who, pre-war, had looked to Italy.[15] The Germans also supported the IRA, just as they had backed Irish nationalism during the First World War, and there were feelers towards Welsh nationalism. In practice, Germany derived few benefits from this process.

In occupied, allied, neutral and opposed Europe, the Germans sought to draw, as well as on anti-Semitism, on widespread anti-Communist and anti-Soviet sympathies, and notably so after the Soviet Union was invaded in 1941. However, the Germans failed to exploit these opportunities, particularly, but not only, in Ukraine, Poland and Lithuania, in part due to the flow of the conflict and in part due to the brutality of the German military, and the racism of its policies. This was a major strategic flaw.

It was part, indeed, of a wider failure of both conception and implementation. It proved impossible, and unsurprisingly so given Hitler's attitudes and policies, to ground the new German empire in popular support from the conquered peoples, and to win much effective backing from them for Germany's wars; or, alternatively, to persuade Britain to end resistance and/or to define the basis for a settlement with the Soviet Union. Moreover, even partial success proved only limited and transitory for Germany, and that also was a serious flaw. Soviet troops essentially fought on in order to survive.[16]

Reflecting the more general divisions and tensions within the Nazi system, there were significant cross-currents in German policy, in conquered territory as well as towards allies. In the former case, there was brutality as well as attempts to win over hearts and minds. Among army officers were fanatics who would draw no distinction between partisans and the rest of the population, as well as moderates and self-styled pragmatists.[17] There were similar cross-currents in the Japanese system, but a harsh exploitation repeatedly came to the fore.[18]

The failure to win support was more important than the tactical and operational successes, best summarised as *blitzkrieg*, because this failure helped to ensure an underlying weakness in the German position, and also that of Japan. This was a weakness that was exploited from 1942 by the superior resources and, eventually, much improved fighting effectiveness of their opponents.

THE HOLOCAUST

By the summer of 1942, Germany and Japan had made greater conquests than either power had ever done before. These conquests were ruled as part of the same strategic culture, one predicated on violence, as seen for example with the large-scale massacre of Chinese in Singapore after the 1942 conquest, part of a murderous strategy of terror by Japan as well as Germany. There was scant sign of any attempt at accommodation, in war making, diplomacy or the rule of conquered territories. Indeed, that situation can be seen as most significant in the ideology of these conflicts. This ideology, in turn, drew on the practice of power in the conquered areas.

The most dramatic aspect of this was the Holocaust. That understandably characterises much of the current discussion of German policy and should, indeed, be seen as an aspect of Nazi strategy. Doing so captures the importance of genocide to the Nazi regime, as well as the role of the German military in cooperating in its implementation. A significant part played in the Holocaust was also played by many of Germany's allies, notably Romania, but also Vichy France, Croatia and Slovakia.

At the same time, literature on the Holocaust throws up an instructive parallel to the general discussion of German strategy in the shape of its ad hoc character. Alongside the broad generalities of genocidal intention towards Jews, and notably so on the part of Hitler, there was a more complex and confused pattern of implementation, one that frequently lacked coherence both pre-war and during the conflict. To a degree, this contrast can be viewed as a difference between policy and strategy, but that offers a distinction that was frequently absent. There were similar inconsistencies in the treatment of client states and allies, and by both Germany and Japan, but also an underlying continuity in intention, attitude and brutality. Yet, to turn in greater detail to the background to the Holocaust and to its planning indicates a range of factors affecting and comprising German strategy. That range can be pushed even further by assessing the situation for Germany's European allies in addition.

From the outset of the war in Europe, the Germans killed Jews in atrocities. In Poland, this was a matter of the *Wehrmacht* as well as the SS, although the role of the former was later consistently underplayed. Soviet conquests and acquisitions in 1939–40 from Poland, Romania and in the Baltic republics brought many more Jews under Soviet control. The German military's schemes and contingency plans for a war intended to keep the Soviet Union in its place were co-opted by Hitler into a broader conflict designed to fulfil his hopes for the destruction of Jewish Bolshevism, and to create a new territorial order able to fulfil what he saw as Germany's destiny to lead Europe and to rescue culture. Conquest brought forward the possibility for utopian Nazi thoughts and plans, while enhancing their violence through the possibilities, pressures, practicalities and ideology of repression. In this conflation, military operations and occupation policy were to be linked. Conquest also brought greater power and centrality to the SS, and with far fewer institutional and practical restraints than were the case in Germany. War brought under Hitler's control areas where most of Europe's Jews had settled, and took forward the millenarian strain in Nazism, encouraging Hitler to give deadly and urgent effect to his aspirations and fears, the two being linked for him and for many Germans.

To Hitler, identity was a key element in strategy, both the means and the goal in an attitude that was at once existential in its scope and sequential in its understanding. Only through securing German racial and cultural identity in his eyes could superiority be guaranteed, and this goal could only be achieved by the prompt, total and irrevocable removal of Jews from a German-dominated Europe. Linked to this, the war against the Soviet Union was conceived from the outset as a genocidal war, one that would permit a complete ethnic and geopolitical recasting of the Soviet Union, and ensure food for the invading army and territory for German settlers. The latter would include German-Americans whom Hitler hoped would be attracted to their 'Fatherland', thus providing vital manpower, especially for the war with the Soviet Union.

As with Poland, but far more so, massacres of Jews were carried out from the start of operations and before the offensive into the Soviet Union encountered difficulties. Falsely attributing opposition to 'Jewish Bolshevism' encouraged a brutal response, which was seen as appropriate and necessary by the participants. The army was fully complicit in the slaughter, which was largely carried out by *Einsatzgruppen*, SS task forces, advancing close behind the troops. Thus, operational success provided the opportunity for the pursuit of this strategy, on the usual pattern of operational–strategic interaction.

Advancing into the Soviet Union in 1941 was not the sole issue for the Germans. The increasingly brutal anti-Semitic ideology encouraged and legitimated by Hitler's rhetoric and instructions was given a different focus that September when Hitler decided to deport the German, Austria and Czech Jews to Poland. Establishing this policy put even more Jews into position for mass slaughter. Opportunity was also a problem in that the scale of any such slaughter would also have to be stepped up were there to be new Jews brought under control. That indeed followed as plans were drawn up to make all of Europe *judenfrei*. Mass killing prepared the way for the extermination camps, while the exigencies of the German war economy combined with a brutal racism led to the use of Jews as goods: for murderously harsh labour or for products such as hair and gold teeth.

PROPAGANDA

Confidence was a key strategic resource and was understood as such at the time. In 1940, the views of both victors and defeated had combined to endow the German military with extraordinary strength and proficiency, not least overwhelming mechanised forces, when the reality was of a weaker mechanised sector than believed and of the bulk of the army as slow-moving infantry. A conviction of Axis effectiveness was an important element in the contest over morale. This contest was seen as important in a strategic sense; both with reference to the maintenance of war economies via popular support on Home Fronts, and also as operationally significant, specifically for countries that were invaded. Yet, the extent to which Germany in 1940 had been helped by a lack of French determination and a willingness to surrender has been controversial since.

Morale as a strategic enabler was not only an issue in the case of France. In April 1941, Lieutenant-General Sir Henry Wilson, the commander of the British force in Greece, which was then under successful attack by the Germans, wrote of: 'the question how to raise the morale of the people as well as that of the Greek forces who are showing signs of disintegration.'[19]

This focus ensured that the combatants made major efforts to try to influence domestic and foreign opinion. The emphasis on public opinion back at home in some instructions to commanders is notable, and this emphasis reflects the numerous factors involved in strategy and that those involved were willing to avow. In June 1941, Robert Menzies, the Australian Prime

Minister, wrote to General Sir Thomas Blamey, then command-
ing the Australian forces in the Middle East, about the direct
impact at home of the war in which Australian units were
involved: 'A disaster at Tobruk [in Libya] coming on top of those
in Greece and Crete might have far reaching effects on public
opinion in Australia, and a reverse in Egypt itself would, I think,
produce incalculable difficulties in Australia.'[20] So also with the
determination in Britain to maintain morale in the face of popular concerns in 1940–42. Allied strategic responses in part were
an aspect of this battle for opinion on the Home Front.

For all combatants, there were major concerns about morale
and resilience; and these concerns encouraged attempts to gather
intelligence and to influence opinion. This situation was certainly
true of democracies, and reflected a broader process of democratisation there. In 1937, John Buchan, the Governor-General of
Canada who had played an important role in the successful First
World War British propaganda effort, declared in a speech to the
Canadian Institute of International Affairs:

> The day has gone when foreign policy can be the preserve
> of a group of officials at the Foreign Office, or a small
> social class, or a narrow clique of statesmen from whom
> the rest of the nation obediently takes its cue. The foreign
> policy of a democracy must be the cumulative views of
> individual citizens, and if these views are to be sound they
> must in turn be the consequence of a widely diffused
> knowledge.

Yet, totalitarian societies, including Germany and the Soviet
Union, also had to be concerned about public opinion, and had
to get their mechanisms of authority and power to work to that
effect, which, given their paranoia, was a difficult task. The

German reading of the First World War, and in particular of failure in 1918 as a result of the army being 'stabbed in the back' by domestic disaffection and alleged Jewish conspiracy – a view very much held by Hitler who was convinced of the malign impact then of British propaganda – led to a great emphasis being placed by the Nazi regime on propaganda in Germany. It was argued that civilian society was more vulnerable than the military to war-weariness, and that the Home Front was the most fragile. Obedience was insufficient; there had to be positive mobilisation for the war effort.

Hitler also argued that propaganda should be aimed at the feelings and, if at an intellectual level, should be geared to those of limited intelligence. In practice, intimidation of the public in a propaganda of threat and menace became more pronounced in Germany as the war went badly and rumour flourished. The Gestapo responded with great anxiety to the public mood after the devastating British firebombing of Hamburg in 1943, a fire-bombing that proved without doubt on the part of the public that the *Luftwaffe* could not protect German civilians. This episode challenged Gestapo confidence to a degree greater than the subsequent Allied bombing of German cities in 1944, when the damage was more familiar.

PROPAGANDA MAPS

As part of an increasingly visual age, maps had a major role to play in propaganda. They were used in a variety of mediums including film, which reflected the range offered by that medium. *Why We Fight*, a series of seven motivational films made from 1942 to 1945, commissioned by the American government and directed by Frank Capra, included *Prelude to War* (1942). This depicted a hemisphere of light and another of dark dictatorship, with the New World being surrounded and then conquered, while the maps of Germany, Italy and Japan were transformed into menacing symbols.

Propaganda maps in films could be animated and thus more readily grasp the imagination of the public. In the German film *Sieg im Westen* (Victory in the West, 1941), animated maps served to create an impression of inevitable military success, with the Germans being those who had the initiative. Over thirty such maps displayed German's rapid success on the Western Front in 1940. This film in turn became an inspiration to other work. It was cited in developing literature on the subject, which included the German refugee sociologist Hans Speier's 'Magic Geography' in *Social Research* (1941) and Louis Quam's 'The Use of Maps in Propaganda' in the *Journal of Geography* (1943).

Maps were primarily produced for nationals of the state in question. Families at home were able to know where their fathers, husbands and sons were. Maps repeatedly encouraged the public to feel that success was both news and prospect, and exaggerated the contribution made by the forces of the state producing the map. For example, the German map of the invasion of Poland in September 1939 published in the book *Die Soldaten des Führers im Felde* (1940) ignored Polish resistance and, unsurprisingly, made German advances far more prominent than those of their Soviet counterparts. Italian maps in 1940–2 showed the expansion of Axis control. British newspapers produced in 1940–5 maps of British successes, although not only those. For example, at a time in which American and Australian forces were driving back the Japanese, the *Daily Express*, a major British newspaper, on 16 July 1943 showed them rolling back the rays of Japan's key image, the Rising Sun, the narrative located on a map of the Pacific. More definitively, the issue of 2 April 1945 had Allied soldiers from both east and west roll up the map of Europe, with the defeated Hitler looking on.

Nationals of the state in question, however, were not the sole audience. There were also maps designed to influence opinion among allies, neutrals and in conquered areas. In the struggle for American opinion in 1939–41, the German Library of Information in New York published propaganda maps. A prominent and dramatic instance of the attempt to influence opinion in conquered areas was those produced for a French audience by the German propaganda department based in Paris in 1940–4. One depicted Churchill as an octopus reaching out to attack the French Empire, as at Dakar (1940) and Syria (1941), with the attacks being bloodily repelled. From the beginning of Operation Barbarossa in June 1941, a key theme of German propaganda in occupied and allied Europe was provided by the idea of a crusade against communism. This was intended to suggest a united Europe under German leadership. The Germans did not make a comparable effort to win over public opinion in Eastern Europe: the emphasis there, instead, was on direction and more overt exploitation.

Reportage and propaganda very much overlapped in the case of maps for the military. Army newspapers contained maps; for example *Yank*, an American weekly with a circulation of over 3 million, contained National Geographical Society maps. They were also used by the Americans for the *Newsmap* series employed for instructional purposes. In addition, morale-shredding maps were published and distributed. Sometimes they were dropped from aircraft. Such propaganda was intended for civilians or for opposing troops.

The many problems of alliance politics and strategy were a subject kept well from the eyes of contemporaries. Instead, these politics were especially prone to propaganda designed to make alliances appear natural and strong. This was especially so of Anglo-American propaganda about the Soviet Union during 1941–5, and of German propaganda in 1940–3 about the value of the alliance with Italy.

CONCLUSION

From the outset, the Germans were successful, but there was also a gap between Hitler's determination to impose his will on events and the multiple pressures of reality, both military and diplomatic. This element came to the fore when Britain refused to be coerced into a settlement in 1940; but the potential seriousness of that for Germany was lessened by continued American neutrality, however much there were policy initiatives that helped Britain. Moreover, the limited ability of Britain to affect the situation on the Continent was demonstrated in April–May 1941 by its costly failure to save mainland Greece, or even Crete, an island far from German bases.

The German decision to attack the Soviet Union was crucial to the transformation of this situation. It led for Germany to an unsuccessful struggle, one that also did not have the desired intimidatory effect on Britain. Indeed, by early 1942, Hitler was worried about the possibility of an invasion of Norway, a worry focused by British commando raids there from March 1941, and he deployed troops accordingly. He was also having to plan for armaments production against Britain, the United States and the Soviet Union. As Hitler knew, he could not match their capability. At the same time, as Hitler pointed out in a speech of 8 November 1942, Germany was in a better position than Frederick the Great, Frederick II of Prussia, during the Seven Years War (1756–63), not least as it now held territory far from its frontier.

In responding to opportunities and challenges, there were opportunity costs. Thus, the extent of *Luftwaffe* operations in the Soviet Union limited the availability of aircraft and aviation fuel for the Battle of the Atlantic and for control of the Mediterranean. Linked to this, the *Luftwaffe* remained better at support for the army than for the navy, and at the strategic, operational and tactical levels. This contrast reflected issues of personality among the leaders, but also, more centrally, the role of the army in German society, the Continental dominance of German strategy, and the extent to which support for army attacks fulfilled the *Luftwaffe*'s image of activity.

The Battle of the Atlantic was different to that of the western Pacific, as Germany did not deploy shore-based aircraft in significant numbers in support of fleet action and lacked any carriers. The *Bismarck* was sent out in May 1941 with the heavy cruiser *Prinz Eugen*, but without other heavy warship support. Geographical factors made a concentration of German warship effort difficult. Nevertheless, until February 1942, when they sailed back to Germany via the English Channel, the two battle-cruisers at Brest, the *Scharnhorst* and the *Gneisenau*, with the *Prinz Eugen*, could have sortied into the Atlantic, as they had done in early 1941 attacking British trade. On the other hand, the Germans only had two proper battleships, the *Bismarck* and the *Tirpitz*, and the former was sunk by the British in May 1941. The loss of the *Graf Spee* in December 1939 had confirmed the weakness of the German pocket battleships, which were really heavy cruisers.

The problem with war is ultimately that of forcing opponents to accept your will. That is the outcome sought. Output, the 'boys and toys' of killing and conquest, is very important to the process, but generally only if linked to a political strategy that will deliver the outcome. That strategy involves maximising international advantages, as the Germans did in 1939 and continued to do in 1940 with Italy's entry into the war; and also dominating the political agenda of your opponent's society. Propaganda was designed both to sustain domestic support for the war and to affect opinion abroad. Germany and Japan both failed to do the latter and were obliged, as Hitler indeed wanted, to rely on continued struggle. That, however, they could not win.

4

Allied Responses, 1940–2

The Australian government regards the Pacific struggle as primarily one in which the United States and Australia must have the fullest say in the direction of the Democracies' fighting plan. Without any inhibitions of any kind, I must make it quite clear that Australia looks to America, free of any pangs as to our traditional links with the United Kingdom.

John Curtin, Australian Prime Minister,
Melbourne Herald, 27 December 1941

Allied strategy has to be approached both in terms of cooperation between the Allied powers and with regard to the strategies of individual states. The tensions of cooperation are better understood in terms of the strategies of individual states, and we shall therefore begin with them. At the same time, alongside individual strategic cultures, the likely responses of other states were a determinant of these individual strategies.

It is the major change in the position of the powers in question that comes to the fore. In 1939–40, cooperation between Britain and France, and between Britain and the leading members of the British Empire, notably Australia and Canada, were the key elements. In June 1940, with the surrender of France, it became the latter. In turn, the situation changed from June 1941 as, first, the Soviet Union and, then, the United States perforce as a result of attack, entered what in effect was an anti-Axis alliance and, with that, transformed it, albeit in different ways.

The marked broadening out of the war when Italy came in on Germany's side in June 1940 was also important to the accentuation of the imperial dimension, as British imperial forces, notably from India, Africa and Australasia, but also for example from South Africa, played the key role in the campaigning against the Italians in North and East Africa. They were also important to the conquest of Iraq and of the Vichy territories of Lebanon, Syria and Madagascar.

There were many issues and differences in imperial relations, including over how best to prepare against Japanese manoeuvres and concerning the destination of Canadian forces which that government was unwilling to send to North Africa and the Middle East. The dispatch of some to Hong Kong, where they arrived in November 1941, was to prove controversial when it fell to Japanese attack the following month. Such issues were handled more easily than was subsequently to be the case, notably for Australia and New Zealand, after Japan entered the war. It was seen as significant that visiting Commonwealth prime ministers were treated as *ex officio* members of the War Cabinet in London.

There was an understandable reactive character to British and Allied strategy as a result of German successes. This reactive character also owed much to the force structure of the British military, and to the character of Britain's alliance with France. There was no equivalent alliance that was so important for Germany.

Successes both greatly enhanced German capability, notably with the acquisition of total control over the Norwegian and French coastlines, and accentuated concerns about what other powers might do in response to this German capability. The Atlantic was at the forefront of British attention, as was the naval dimension. Thus, British fears about German oceanic intentions led to the occupation of the Danish colony of Iceland in May 1940 once the Germans conquered Denmark. There was less anxiety about Greenland, which backed the Free Denmark movement. British concern also resulted in planning, in early 1941, for landings in the Azores and the Canary Islands to pre-empt possible German moves; but in the event they were not carried out.

Vichy France was essentially a Mediterranean empire, with Vichy controlling southern France (while the rest of the country was occupied by German forces) as well as French North Africa (Morocco, Algeria, Tunisia), Lebanon and Syria. Further afield, Vichy also controlled French colonies in West Africa, South-east Asia and Madagascar. Moreover, Vichy had a powerful fleet. Anxiety about Vichy's intentions, and the possibility that the Germans would be able to take over the French fleet, led to the still-contentious British attack on the Vichy fleet at Mers el Kébir near Oran in Algeria on 3 July 1940, as well as to a subsequent unsuccessful British attack on 23–5 September on Dakar in Senegal, the main Vichy position in West Africa as well as a naval base. This attack, which was not repeated, made it easier for Vichy to cooperate with Germany and compromised support for its opponent, Charles de Gaulle, the leader of the Free French.

For Britain, Vichy was not an attacking opponent, by land, sea or air, but Italy was. That led to a very different reactive pattern to that against Germany, one that provided more opportunities for action and for cooperation within Britain's imperial system. Italy's attacks led to British counterattacks.

For Britain, the difficulty of moving from striking blows against Vichy and Italy to doing the same against Germany helped ensure growing emphasis on an air offensive against the latter. This emphasis drew on a number of factors, which underlines the mistaken nature of monocausal explanations in strategy. There was an important psychological dimension in terms of responding to the damaging German air offensive and, in turn, demonstrating German vulnerability. This was a currency that had meaning in terms of British public opinion and the government. In addition, pre-war doctrine about air power contributed greatly to the strategy. It was believed that serious damage could be inflicted on the German war economy, and that this would affect German resilience.

Moreover, this was a strategy that made sense of Britain's power and position. There was an existing bomber force, and the country was within bombing distance of major German and German-occupied industrial sites, notably the Ruhr, and ports, including those, such as Brest in occupied France, from which vital British trade routes were under threat and/or being attacked.

The many factors that were drawn together in leading to support for a bombing strategy are more generally significant for the nature of strategy: it is often fitted to the existing force structure and to the military interests involved, and is frequently accretional. Moreover, the strategy was pursued despite many problems, including the limited accuracy of bombing, the deficiencies of the bombers initially available, not least in bombload, the lack of long-range fighter escorts, and the extent to which this use of aircraft and crew for bombing ensured that fewer of both were available for anti-submarine patrols and for ground support for the army. These problems were all eventually under-stood, although their consequences were up for discussion.

Alongside that of Britain, there were the strategies of its allies who had become governments in exile. The first, setting the pattern but also being most complex in its international implica-tions, was that of Poland. Its strategy, in what to a degree was a repeat of the response to the three partitions of 1772–95 by Austria, Prussia and Russia, was to coordinate the fight both at home and abroad against the fourth partition, that of 1939. The Polish government provided the legitimate authority for Polish forces in the West, so coordination with the British was vital. Moreover, Britain had to be kept in the fight and kept to the promise of restoring an independent Poland.

The international situation became very different in late 1941 as Britain's alliance system became 'the Allies', with the latter crucially including the United States, as well as the more vulner-able Soviet Union. The Moscow Conference, held on 29 September–1 October 1941, saw Britain and the United States agree the principle of aid to the Soviets. For the Soviet Union and the Western Allies (Britain and the United States), the fundamental contrast was that the former was only fighting Germany, while the other two, from December 1941, had to decide how best to prioritise between Germany and Japan. Hitler's declaration of war on the United States on 11 December 1941 undercut any American idea of a 'Japan First' strategy, although it did not automatically end it. Instead, the declara-tion, combined with the policies of President Franklin Delano Roosevelt (r. 1933–45), helped lead to a 'Germany First' strat-egy on the part of the United States, the priority already settled, in very different and much more urgent circumstances, by Britain. Under this strategy, the bulk of American land and air assets were allocated to preparing for an invasion of Europe, and that commitment underlined the significance of securing the safety of Atlantic shipping lanes.

The 'Germany First' strategy, which was in line with the US Army's War College exercises from 1935, had already been outlined in a memorandum drawn up in November 1940 by Admiral Harold Rainsford Stark, the Chief of Naval Operations from 1939 to 1942,[1] known as Plan Dog. It was also already present in pre-war plans by the American and British military staffs, in the Rainbow 5 war plan, which, once revised by November 1941, became the actual war plan, and in the Anglo-American-Canadian ABC-1 Plan talks of 29 January–27 March 1941. These had envisaged a defensive strategy in the Pacific in the event of war with the three Axis powers.[2] In a clear instance of prioritisation, and of its centrality to strategic planning, Roosevelt had supported this because of concern that Britain might collapse.

However, this preference was controversial to some Americans at the time, notably those involved in the Pacific War, especially General Douglas MacArthur and some naval circles, and has remained so, as every conversation with Americans about wartime strategy appears to bear out. This is linked to a tendency, as a result of the focus on Pearl Harbor, to forget that Germany declared war or to treat that declaration as not amounting to a real threat. In reality, in early 1942, more German submarines were in American coastal waters mounting attacks than Japanese ones.

The logic was clear: Germany, the stronger adversary and the power with the more globally ambitious ideology, had a greater potential than Japan to overthrow its opponents, as well as to intervene in South America. In contrast, Japan, faced by the far greater distances of the Pacific and not able to draw on an economy comparable to that of the German-run sphere, was best placed only to defeat its direct opponents, with the exception of China and, possibly, Australia. The Japanese navy and amphibious forces could only achieve so much. This was very much geopolitics as a guide to grand strategy. Although colonies might be conquered, as they were in 1941–2, Britain was far less vulnerable to Japanese power. In practice, however, the pressures of the war in the Pacific were to encourage the allocation of more resources there than might have been anticipated under 'Germany First'.

It was argued that only a land attack, which would require American participation, could defeat Germany.[3] Prior to the Japanese attack, Roosevelt also offered to extend Lend-Lease (the supply of food, oil and military hardware) to the Soviet Union, although Harry Truman, then a relatively obscure senator, remarked that, if it appeared that the Soviet Union was winning, the United States should aid Germany and vice versa. The 'Germany First' strategy led the American army manoeuvres in the summer of 1941 to focus on preparing for European theatre conflict, notably with the training of armour, and, once the war had widened, was confirmed by the Washington Conference that began on 22 December 1941. The conference resulted in the creation of an Anglo-American planning mechanism based on the Combined Chiefs of Staff, as well as the establishment of the Anglo-American Combined Raw Materials Board. This was both a significant indication of joint planning, and one followed by other such planning. It was also agreed both that American forces should be moved to Northern Ireland to prepare for operations in Europe (and provide an additional guarantee of British security), and that the Americans should plan an invasion of Vichy-held Morocco.

This invasion would deny Germany the possibility of taking over another part of the Atlantic coastline, lessen the chance of

Germany establishing bases in the Canary Islands and the Azores, and provide a western anchor for operations in the Mediterranean. Moreover, although at a great range, Atlantic Morocco was vulnerable to American amphibious attack, and this attack could to a considerable degree be sealed from Axis naval interdiction as, indeed, was to be the case in November 1942. The preparation for the fightback had begun, and North Africa provided a peripheral operational theatre whereby American troops could gain necessary combat experience in preparation for the invasion of Continental Europe. There was no potential in late 1942 for a comparable operation against the Japanese system, although the long Guadalcanal campaign (7 August 1942–7 February 1943) did provide valuable experience, and notably so for the navy as well as for land forces.

'Germany First' had consequences throughout the war. An American emphasis on fighting Germany, rather than Japan, greatly helped the Soviet Union by diverting German resources to resist American attacks, and the impact of the Anglo-American invasion of Sicily helped to end the Kursk offensive in 1943. In contrast, an American focus on Japan would definitely not have weakened the pressure on the Soviet Union, as Japan and the Soviet Union had agreed a neutrality pact on 13 April 1941. The Soviets were assured of Japanese priorities by their effective spy in Tokyo, Richard Sorge, the press attaché of the German embassy and a committed communist.

Conversely, however, an emphasis on the United States fighting Japan might have assisted China, with consequences for the results of the post-war Chinese Civil War (1946–9), and might have also ensured that the Japanese were not able to mount offensives there, as they did in 1942 and, more seriously, 1944–5, and against India in 1944. This point was increasingly to be made after the war, when the claim that the United States had 'lost' China to communism in the Chinese Civil War by an inappropriate strategy gathered traction and political weight as part of a broader attack by Republicans on the Democratic legacy.

Yet, as is often forgotten, military assets are not readily transferable and usable in the simple fashion that such remarks about choices might suggest. There were major problems, particularly, but not solely, logistical, associated with the allocation and sustaining of units and resources. Linked to this, the capacity of the very extensive Pacific theatre to take more American troops in 1942 and 1943, and to employ them effectively, was limited. The infrastructure of effort took longer to assemble, although by late 1943 and even more by 1944 it was in place so as to support plans involving large-scale moves, notably the successful invasion of the Philippines in late 1944. It is an appreciation of such points that is so important to a scholarly appraisal of the war, and one that ensures the need to handle counterfactual (what if?) speculations with particular care.

The American 'Germany First' or 'Japan First' question had an echo in Australia, although differently so. There, concern about the allocation of military resources was intertwined with increasing anger about British assumptions that, as part of the worldwide distribution of the empire's resources in response to multiple challenges, the Australasian forces should help to protect the Middle East against Italian and German attack. There was already anger prior to Japan's entry into the war. Australian concern, indeed bitterness, about what was seen as a British unwillingness to heed and respond appropriately to the Japanese challenge was greatly accentuated by Japan's attack on the British Empire, and then by the humiliating surrender of Singapore on 15 February 1942 and, with it, of a large army. Under the threat of apparently imminent Japanese invasion, the minutes of the Australian War Cabinet make clear anxieties about British priorities in goals and force allocation, notably of British reluctance to release Australian forces from the Middle East, and, once released, a British attempt to have them used to defend India against Japanese attack. These anxieties were shared by the New Zealand government. In July 1942, the Australian War Cabinet cabled Churchill, 'superior sea power and airpower are vital to wrest the initiative from Japan and are essential to assure the defensive position in the Southwest Pacific Area'. Britain was not in a position to provide either.

America, in contrast, both could and would provide air and sea power in the Pacific theatre, as the events of 1942 made abundantly clear. After the devastating Japanese carrier-borne air attacks on Darwin on 19 February, designed to cover the successful invasions of Java and Timor, American aircraft helped protect northern Australia as part of what became a significant deployment of American forces. In April, MacArthur established his South-West Pacific Area headquarters in Brisbane. Two of the three Australian divisions in the Middle East were recalled, but the 9th Division remained and played a major role in the Battle of El Alamein in Egypt that autumn.

Roosevelt's strategic choices in part looked back to the navalism of A. T. Mahan, and drew heavily on the naval power projection of President Theodore Roosevelt (r. 1901–9), his own experience as Assistant Secretary of the Navy from 1913 to 1920 and his interest in geopolitics. Roosevelt was very committed to the invasion of Vichy North Africa in 1942. Many of his civilian advisors were also influential in strategic planning.

COMMAND STRUCTURES

Both the Soviet Union and the United States had to adapt their command structures in order to cope with the unprecedented demands of the war. For the Soviets, there was the requirement to meet Stalin's desire for control and the need to cope with the problems posed by failure in the opening months of the war. In response, there was the establishment and revitalisation of institutions. The State Committee for Defence (*Gosudarstvennyj komitet oborony*, GKO), of which Stalin was the chairman, provided a cohesion lacking in Germany and Japan. Under it came *Stavka*, the general headquarters, over which Stalin came to preside as Chairman and Defence Commissar (minister) from 9 August 1941. The General Staff answered to *Stavka*, as it was the planning and executive agency. When he wanted, however, Stalin was able to ignore the General Staff, as in the spring of 1942 when he decided to try to break through near Kharkov and drive towards Kiev, against the advice that he revert to defence. Always overly keen on attacks, a characteristic he shared with Hitler and with Japanese leaders, but also with Churchill and Roosevelt, Stalin failed in this instance to heed intelligence reports and military advice. Typically, he chose to put much of the blame for a costly failure on the lack of a Second Front in Western Europe.[4]

Although similarly reliant on terror, which was applied at an intense rate during the war, and keen on absolute, personal control, Stalin directed a more organised, bureaucratic and hierarchical system than Hitler. However, this system was also made uneasy by his practice of interventions in command decisions, by his playing off of his fearful commanders against each other, and by the roles of the secret police and the Communist Party organisation. These characteristics made failure very dangerous, not least for those who could be held responsible. The initiative of commanders was sapped throughout the command chain. Until Hitler's retribution after the 20 July Bomb Plot of 1944, German army commanders were less fearful of him than their Soviet counterparts were of Stalin.

Mistakes by Stalin, of course, were ignored. He totally failed to heed warnings of the German attack in 1941 and proved ill-prepared for the crisis it caused. Stalin's subsequent instructions, notably for broad-front attacks in early 1942, were maladroit and reflected a mistaken belief that the Germans could readily be defeated, thus blocking the danger of a renewed offensive. Instead, the Germans, having initially been pushed back, checked the Soviet attacks and did so again near Kharkov in May 1942. This led Stalin to draw back in late 1942 and, instead, to provide Aleksandr Vasilevsky, the Chief of the General Staff, and Georgi Zhukov, the talented Deputy Supreme Commander, both members of *Stavka*, with the opportunity to plan operations, a situation that continued into 1943. They improved the competence of Soviet operational planning, although there were still to be major failures in particular operations. Moreover, Stalin kept major issues of strategy under close control and did not take generals into his confidence.

The United States, in contrast, had not only to expand its existing national structures – a process very much seen with the scale of the Pentagon, the headquarters building of the Department of Defense, built in 1941–3 and the world's largest office building – but also to develop Anglo-American structures. The latter focused on the Combined Chiefs of Staff, a coordinating body based in Washington that essentially responded to the decisions made by Churchill and Roosevelt at their meetings. The Combined Chiefs then separately directed, through their national bodies, the national military structures while also overseeing high commands in particular theatres of operation. This was most significant when, as in the Mediterranean and Europe, there were large numbers of both American and British forces. That was not the case in the Pacific nor in South-east Asia.

In February 1942, the Americans established the Joint Chiefs of Staff Committee, which was subordinate to Roosevelt as the President was Commander-in-Chief. The Americans benefited from a number of excellent senior commanders, notably General George Marshall, the Army Chief of Staff from 1939 to 1945, who had been head of the War Plans Division. Marshall proved an effective peacetime commander able to make necessary preparations for war; and, in war, helped provide cohesion for the American military and was an adroit member of the Combined Chiefs of Staff Committee. His naval counterpart, the cantankerous Ernest King, was also highly effective, although he did not have Marshall's capacity for emollience. King benefited from a determined Secretary of the Navy, Franklin Knox, a Republican in a Democratic president's administration. Germany, Italy, Japan and the Soviet Union would never have looked so widely for talent.

STRATEGY AND SITUATIONAL AWARENESS

Situational awareness was a major element in strategic planning, and in moulding and responding to circumstances. Notwithstanding the serious failure in 1941–2 to comprehend Japanese power and motivations, the Allies eventually proved better than the Axis at understanding the areas in which they campaigned, and in planning accordingly. For example, an appreciation of the role of climate, notably for air operations and amphibious attacks, led to considerable efforts in accumulating and understanding meteorological information. Weather stations in Greenland and Iceland played a key role in providing data that helped determine the date of D-Day, the 1944 invasion of Normandy. The improvisation seen with the Axis was not present to the same extent with the Allies, and certainly not in strategic planning.

The Americans sought not only to develop their command structures, but also to strengthen their strategic capability, notably with the establishment of the Office of Strategic Services (OSS) on 13 June 1942 under William 'Wild Bill' Donovan. Building on the role of Co-ordinator of Information created in July 1941, this provided a central agency for intelligence, which had hitherto been lacking. The OSS was instructed to collect and analyse 'strategic information' as well as carrying out special services, in effect espionage. The Research and Analysis Branch produced high-grade analytical reports. The OSS also developed an international system of outposts, a key element in the strategic infrastructure of intelligence capability.

MAPS

Like Churchill, Roosevelt was very interested in maps; indeed, he created a map room in the White House. For Christmas 1942, he was given a huge 50-inch, 750-pound globe designed to rotate freely without an axis, thus increasing an understanding of strategic options. It was manufactured by the Weber Costello Company under the supervision of the Map Division of the Office of Strategic Services and the War Department, and presented to him by the Army Chief of Staff, George Marshall. This photographed occasion was intended to show Roosevelt's interest in maps and, through that, global strategy.

Strategic intelligence was highly significant to planning. This involved an understanding of spatial factors, but in a context in which the available information was limited in both range and content. An important element of the strategic nature of mapmaking was provided by Anglo-American cooperation. Under the Loper–Hotine Agreement of May 1942, the American Army Map Service was given full responsibility for mapping the Americas, Australasia, the Pacific, Japan, the West Indies and the North Atlantic; and the British for the rest. This allocation accorded with the systems the British had already in place for overseas production, most significantly centres in Egypt and India. As part of a broader pattern of cooperation, the Geographical Section of the British General Staff and the US Army Map Service exchanged map and geodetic material. The Western Allies initiated the World Aeronautical Chart 1:1 million-scale map series.

Mapmaking initiatives were of particular importance for air-power strategy and operations, while air power was a key driver of requirements for mapping. The acquisition and protection of air bases reflected strategies carefully plotted in spatial terms, with reference to maps and with particular interest in the range of aircraft; and the bases helped determine strategic options and operational means. The range of war led to the movement of air, sea and land units into areas with which they were unfamiliar, for example the Germans into Egypt in 1941, and to demands for the (improved) mapping of these areas and for a degree of consistency in mapping.[5]

TIMING

Strategy is about timing as well as prioritisation and space. Major, and apparently inexorable, Japanese successes in early 1942, combined with those of the Germans against the Soviets that summer, led to American pressure for swifter action than the British envisaged and were prepared for, in the shape of an invasion of France that year. The mid-term Congressional elections due in November were a factor because, unlike Britain, where, because of the wartime shelving of that due in 1940, there was no general election between 1935 and that in 1945 held after the end of the war with Germany, the United States continued with its usual electoral practices, which entailed elections in 1942 and 1944. In turn, these practices imposed a timetable of expectations and, therefore, were part of the strategic equation, and not only for the United States.

Pressure for action also arose from Stalin's totally misplaced anxiety that Churchill wanted a separate peace with Germany. This misplaced anxiety reflected not only Stalin's paranoia, but also the nature of his strategy. The Soviets were influenced by Harry Hopkins's deliberately indiscreet and out-of-character remarks to Molotov that the Americans could mount a so-called 'Second Front', to be initiated by the invasion of France, in 1942. In the event, there was no Second Front to join the 'First', Eastern Front that year. In the Washington Conference of 20–5 June 1942, the United States and Britain agreed on the North Africa landing, Operation Torch.

There was another factor affecting the American timetable. The need for speed had been pressed in the Victory Plan, the statement of American strategy drawn up in late 1941 by the War Plans Division of the War Department General Staff that defined the resource requirements to fight a war against the Axis powers simultaneously:

time is of the essence and the longer we delay effective offensive operations against the Axis, the more difficult will become the attainment of victory . . . we will be confronted in the not distant future by a Germany strongly entrenched economically, supported by newly acquired sources of vital supplies and industries, with her military forces operating on interior lines, and in a position of hegemony in Europe which will be comparatively easy to defend and maintain.[6]

The rapid success of Operation Torch, the largely American invasion of Morocco and Algeria on 8 November 1942, was helped by the careful prior cultivation of the French military leaders in North Africa. As a result, resistance by the far more numerous Vichy forces was rapidly overcome, although some units, especially of the navy, resisted firmly.

Torch's success could not conceal the risks of an invasion of France that year, not least in terms of Atlantic and Channel weather, lack of the necessary shipping, experience and training, and significant German opposition, including U-boats in the Atlantic. Furthermore, concern about the threat from German and Italian air and naval power in the central Mediterranean helped mean that there was no simultaneous amphibious invasion of Tunisia. German and Italian land forces were not available to resist Torch, and there were no armoured divisions to move up to support resistance. Torch therefore did not provide good guidance to any Second Front attack on France.

There was still a need to win the Battle of the Atlantic against German U-boats and to gain air dominance, as well as to plan operations and train, equip and move forces. The need for training had been made readily apparent by the deficiencies revealed in operations earlier in the war. The British were concerned about the risks of a premature invasion of France, in large part because they were aware that resources alone could not counteract German fighting quality. This was a sound assessment.

Training, crucially, was necessary, and 1943 was to be the great year of training for American and British forces.

Nevertheless, in April 1942, prior to the result of the peak campaign season of that year, it was accepted by the United States and Britain that France would be invaded in 1943, and the pace of the movement of American forces to Britain was stepped up so as to prepare for that invasion. This movement was dependent on success in the Battle of the Atlantic, but the presence of increasingly large American land and sea forces greatly magnified the strategic challenge to Germany from Britain, by giving Britain an offensive capability as far as Atlantic Europe was concerned.

In this and other cases, the location of forces was a key element in the implementation of strategy, although, in turn, it could influence the formulation of the latter. Location was also a response to the perception of threat. Thus, the build-up of the garrison of Ceylon (Sri Lanka) to a strength of two divisions by the close of March 1942 was a response to concerns about the Indian Ocean. The troops deployed in Ceylon were not sent to protect against a Japanese advance from Burma into India, as the Commander-in-Chief in India, Field-Marshal Sir Archibald Wavell, wished. Instead, their location reflected the determination of the London-based Chiefs of Staff to maintain oceanic links.

RESOURCES

The greater significance of aircraft, tanks, lorries and oil-powered warships increased the prominence of oil supplies in strategic planning. Moreover, seizing oil-producing areas, it was argued, would deprive opponents of such supplies. This factor was seen in strategy, notably in so far as the war in the Soviet Union[7] and the Middle East was concerned, and was also of growing significance to the Allied air offensives on the German and Japanese empires.

Other resources also attracted attention, including coal, copper, iron and nickel. Hitler was well aware of the significance of particular areas as a result, and deployed troops accordingly, for example to protect the Finnish nickel mines of Petsamo (which were significant for the manufacture of armour plate), Hungarian and Romanian oilfields, and the coal of the Donbass in eastern Ukraine. Resources were translated into strength through transport links and productive capacity. This explained the significance of a bombing directed not to the goal of wrecking morale, but at particular industries and transport sites. So also with the importance of providing resources to the assistance to allies. The Soviet war effort depended heavily on help from the United States and Britain, not least with lorries and tanks. After the war, this factor was greatly underplayed by the Soviets.

GAINING THE STRATEGIC INITIATIVE

The year 1942 saw a reversal in the direction of strategic initiative. In part, this was a matter of defeating Axis offensives and then using counterattacking as the basis for Allied successes and advances. At the same time, that reflected a range of capabilities that included the deployment of resources, the utilisation of relevant intelligence information and fighting effectiveness, the last closing the gap the German and Japanese had enjoyed in initial offensives. All of these factors played a role, and they did so in part by multiplying the impact of the others. When going over to the offensive, finding an appropriate choice of the place and time for attack was highly significant; but only if this choice could bring these advantages to bear, and only if they could be sustained in the face of the Axis response, notably counter-attacks. This outcome was achieved in late 1942 by the Americans at Guadalcanal, the British at El Alamein and the Soviets in the Stalingrad counterattack, achievements variously brought to fruition in early 1943. In each case, success over Axis counter-attacks was, subsequently, enhanced by the failure of the Axis powers to limit, at least for a while, the subsequent Allied advance. Thus, retreating from El Alamein, Rommel ignored Italian advice to hold a defensive position at the Halfaya Pass or in Libya, which might have delayed the British advance on Tunis. Cumulative pressure was also important. Total German losses for 1942 were over 1.9 million men.

The idea of a decisive battle has to be handled with care. There are many attractions to thinking of a sequence of such battles in 1942, including Midway, as changing the course of the war. At the same time, and not necessarily as an alternative, it is possible to qualify and contextualise the significance of these battles. The decisive turning points on the Eastern Front can be dated earlier, to 1941, indeed to August 1941. In North Africa, Rommel's chances can be regarded as limited, not least for logistical reasons. Moreover, the naval battles in the Pacific in 1942 can be seen as wearing down the Americans as much as the Japanese, with the Solomon/Santa Cruz Islands naval battles from August to November 1942 presented in part as Japanese victories, notably Santa Cruz on 25–7 October. By late November, the Americans had lost many ships and pilots, and were down to one damaged carrier, the *Enterprise*. Despite the tactical and or operation skill of Admirals Fletcher, Mischer, Spruance and Halsey, the American navy was in a very difficult situation by the end of November. Yet, the Japanese had also lost many ships. On Guadalcanal itself, the Japanese forces lost far more heavily from malaria and other diseases than from American action, but the latter was important in denying them success, fixing them and inflicting serious blows. A variety of factors led to the Japanese decision to evacuate Guadalcanal and it was not a defeat on the scale of the British one at Singapore in February 1942, but it was significant.

CONCLUSION

The challenges of a global war were in part conceptual and organisational. It was necessary to determine how best to understand and organise war at a distance, a strategic necessity to which mapping and other forms of information and intelligence were crucial. Once regional commands were established by the Anglo-American alliance, it was important to determine their relationship to each other, to the overall war effort and to existing service structures. Moreover, the pattern of advance and retreat posed additional tensions. Regional commands also acquired distinctive strategic agendas, and these challenged centrally directed priorities. For the Americans and British, there were the additional problems posed by the need to adapt to the requirements of allies. The Soviet Union proved less willing to do so.

5

Axis Responses, 1943–5

On 18 February 1943, Josef Goebbels, Hitler's propaganda chief, delivered in Berlin's large *Sportpalast* a statement of total war, one broadcast by radio across Germany. The statement came soon after German resistance had collapsed at Stalingrad without providing the heroic fight-to-the-last desired (for others) by Hitler. In practice, Goebbels's statement was a call to action, rather than a description of already-existing means and results. Nevertheless, by 1943, the war had taken on an attritional character for Germany and Japan, as well as for their opponents.

At the same time, this attritional character did not preclude the dynamic of operational campaigning, with all the characteristics and skills involved, including generalship. The high tempo of campaigning used up troops and materiel. Nevertheless, the availability of massive resources enabled the Allies to attack on a number of fronts at once, and to return to the attack despite high casualty levels, particularly on the Eastern Front, and serious wear and tear. Moreover, the greatly superior nature of Allied air and naval power was of strategic significance in terms of ground operations and tactics. The Allies adopted a strategy of forcing unconditional surrender on their opponents, a decision announced by Roosevelt at the press conference after the Casablanca Conference of January 1943.

GERMANY, 1943–4

This approach proclaimed by Goebbels underlined the flawed strategic insight of the German military leadership. Their willingness to accept Hitler not only morally corrupted them, as the military came to collaborate in Hitler's genocidal policies, but also led them into a conflict in which, from 1941, limited war and political compromise ceased to be options. Thus, conflict was linked to a war in which victory and total defeat were the sole options. That strategic choice lessened the value of operational success.

Just such a compromise was urged on Hitler by his Axis allies. Allied successes and potential led Italy, Japan and Germany's Foreign Minister, Ribbentrop, to press Hitler to settle with Stalin. Thus, in December 1942 and April 1943, Mussolini urged Hitler to make a separate peace with the Soviet Union, which was not really the problem for Italy and Japan. They wanted Germany, instead, to focus on the Western Allies, which, it was correctly anticipated, would greatly lessen the pressure on them.

Wishing to retain his Soviet conquests and their resources and possibilities, and concerned about his prestige and mission, Hitler did not make such a peace, a choice that undercuts the argument that Britain and the United States were his major rivals; or, at least, certainly so at this stage, for the war very much proceeded through contrasting stages, as with German–Soviet relations. In reality, Hitler made such varied comments that it is difficult to find consistency in his arguments.

Geopolitically and militarily, the Germans could not translate their central position into lasting success because peace was not an option at that time. As a consequence, the operational ability of the German military was linked to a task that risked and, in the end, caused not only their own defeat but also their dissolution, along with the total conquest of Germany. In narrower terms, the Germans, throughout, had not planned for the lengthy conflict into which, despite all Hitler's rhetoric, they had blundered. Neither the military-industrial complex nor the armed forces were prepared for the lengthy conflict that resulted. Strategy, resources, capabilities and doctrine were all inadequate; and this was true on land, at sea and in the air.

So also for Italy, where support within the regime for the continuation of the war, which had ebbed from July 1942 after the sudden collapse of Mussolini unleashed a struggle for the succession among the Fascist and army chiefs, dramatically fell from January 1943 as a result of developments in North Africa and on the Eastern Front. A British bombing campaign launched against northern Italy in October 1942, after over eighteen months' absence from those skies, did not cause a breakdown in the stamina of the people and was not militarily crucial; but it scarcely increased Italian confidence in the situation. The Fascist leaders fell out. Mussolini on 31 January–5 February 1943 sought a strategy of resolve, dismissing Marshal Ugo Cavallero, Chief of the Italian High Command, as well as all members of the government except one. However, the situation, international and domestic, military and political, was totally outside Mussolini's control. Italy's desperate improvisation had arisen from serious pressure on the excessive number of fronts on which it had become committed.[1] In effect, Hitler was having to prop up Mussolini, not yet by the direct military intervention seen later in 1943, but by providing the aura of victory and its deterrent to peace feelers to the Allies.

Discussion here of German strategy in 1943 focuses on the Eastern Front, notably the Kursk offensive. In practice, there were also other strategic choices made by Hitler as he faced the continual need to decide how best to deploy units. American and British advances in North Africa made the situation there hazardous for Axis forces and their wider prospects in the Mediterranean, and the speedy Axis occupation of Tunisia left unclear what should be done. Understandable in light of the risk of Axis air attack, the refusal of American commanders to include eastern Algeria and Tunisia among the landing zones for Torch was followed by the German–Italian occupation of Tunisia by troops moved from Italy by air and sea. Due to the acquiescence of Admiral Jean-Pierre Estéva, the Vichy Resident-General of Tunisia, there was no opposition.

In contrast, 250,000 tonnes of warships, most of the Vichy navy, an impressive fleet, were scuttled by the French when German forces attacked the great dockyard at Toulon. Having fought their way in, the Germans reached the quaysides as the explosives in the ships were detonated. Beaten to Marseille and Toulon by the Germans, the Italians took control of Corsica, Nice and Savoy, all of which had belonged to Italian states before being ceded in 1768, 1860 and 1860 respectively. Mussolini wanted to incorporate them into Italy.

The German position in Tunisia was more hazardous because of the British ability to use Malta as a base to damage Axis supply routes in the central Mediterranean. Ignoring Rommel's advice, delivered in person in November 1942, to withdraw from Tunisia, the German forces there were heavily reinforced by Hitler, who feared the impact on Mussolini's position of such a withdrawal. Tunisia, therefore, became the forward defence for Italy, as indeed it was in terms of preventing the Allies from having threatening air and naval bases able to support an invasion. Hitler, who had not angered Vichy by sending troops to French North Africa in 1940–2, felt obliged, in contrast, to send forces to protect Tunisia. Including the troops retreating from Egypt, this amounted to a larger force than that sent on the different task of conquering Egypt the previous year. Yet, the German troops dispatched to Tunisia were in part found by scraping the barrel. They included a penal brigade and *Luftwaffe* troops. The Tiger tanks and other weapons sent had been intended for a new offensive scheduled at El Alamein for December 1942. These forces made the Allied task of conquering Tunisia more difficult, but also eventually ensured a larger German (and Italian) defeat.

Indeed, capturing on a smaller scale the strategic dilemma facing Germany in a two-front war, an impact of Operation Torch further west was to handicap Rommel's resistance to the British advance via Libya, and vice versa. By 13 May 1943, all the German and Italian troops in Tunisia, possibly 180,000 (100,000 German, 80,000 Italian) in total, had become prisoners. A figure of 250,000 was given, but that was based on the inclusion of the Italian male civilian population in Tunisia who were seized by the French in May 1943. They also deposed the *Bey* (nominal ruler) of Tunis, Muhammad VII al-Munsif, replacing him with a cousin.

Two months earlier, helped by the problems the Soviets encountered in their advance, not least climate, logistics, losses and serious deficiencies in planning, the Germans had been able to consolidate their position on the Eastern Front. Field Marshal Erich von Manstein, the commander of the reconstituted Army Group South, counteracted successfully, recapturing Kharkov on 12–14 March 1943, this providing the last German offensive victory on the Eastern Front. However, a point that can be overlooked due to the general focus on campaigning, this was an operational-level victory and not the strategic triumph that the Germans required, and that they had sought in 1942. While reversing some of the Soviet advance and destroying Soviet units were successes, they were compensatory ones at most and, for the Germans, it was not good enough in strategic terms to return to the position they had occupied at the beginning of the 1942 counteroffensive. Indeed, in early 1943, Hitler felt it necessary to abandon earlier hopes to resume the offensive in the Caucasus and gain more of its oilfields.

Meanwhile, the Soviets at Stalingrad had destroyed the largest German field army on the Eastern Front, while the build-up of American forces threatened to open a Second Front in Western Europe as well as strengthening the air assault on Germany. As a result, Germany had to provide more resources to protect positions in the Mediterranean, Western Europe and Germany itself, which lessened their capability and affected their options on the Eastern Front. This was particularly so in aircraft, but was also seen in other capabilities, such as the fortifications constructed on the Atlantic coast.

On 5 July 1943, the Germans launched their last major offensive of the war on a principal theatre of the Eastern Front. This was an attempt to break through the flanks of the Soviet Kursk salient and to achieve an encirclement triumph to match the Soviet success at Stalingrad the previous winter. Still engaging in strategic wishful thinking, or rather in wishful thinking as strategy, Hitler saw this offensive as a battle of annihilation in which superior will would prevail and ensure the destruction of Soviet offensive forces. More mundanely, the elimination of this salient would rob the Soviets of a position from which they could attack two neighbouring German salients. Had Operation Citadel succeeded, the Germans were considering a further advance both to the north-east, thus avoiding the direct approach eastward from Army Group Centre against strong Soviet defences on the route to Moscow, and more generally. In practice, however, they were not ready for such an advance, no more than they would have been to exploit success at Stalingrad in 1942.

Hitler was not temperamentally prepared to accept the idea of staying on the defensive and conserving resources, while trying, through defensive operations, to make success cost his attacking opponents dear and lessen their will. Such a strategy, anyway, appeared politically unacceptable as it would test the morale of the German population, already under growing pressure from heavy Anglo-American bombing, undermine the cohesion of the Axis coalition, and, at best, produce defensive successes and buy time rather than bringing victory. Instead, Hitler hoped that victory in the Kursk offensive would undermine the Allied coalition by lessening Western confidence in the likelihood of Soviet victory and, correspondingly, increasing Soviet demands for a speedy Second Front in France. Matters of temperament on the part of the ruler are often crucial to strategy. The offensive would also demonstrate that Germany retained the initiative, and that Hitler therefore remained consequential, and did so on the world scale.

The decision to change the naval leadership and to move from the surface navy to a total emphasis on submarines, under the new commander, Karl von Dönitz, was an aspect of the same equation: the apparent need to take the initiative. Initial German submarine success in March 1943, in what Dönitz termed 'tonnage warfare', nevertheless was followed in May by a failure, in the face of effective Allied anti-submarine capability and tactics, that led to the temporary withdrawal of U-boats from the Atlantic.

As was generally the case, however, Hitler was scarcely alone in the decision-making of Kursk, a point greatly underplayed later by German generals. Although there was opposition, including from OKH staff and Heinz Guderian, Manstein was the principal architect of the Kursk plan, and his general agreed with Hitler that Germany could not afford to relinquish the initiative, an approach to strategy that, in itself, was not without point.

In the event, when they attacked from 5 July 1943 the Germans, although doing well on the southern side of the Kursk salient, were defeated by a strong Soviet defence-in-depth. Although the reasons for the outcome have been a matter of controversy, they were more than simply a matter of Soviet tactical strength and operational capacity. In addition, the fate of the campaign reflected wider German commitments as, on 10 July, Anglo-American forces invaded Sicily in Operation Husky. Hitler, by then disillusioned by the Kursk offensive, wished to move troops in order to protect Mussolini. However, no transfer was ordered before 26 July, when it followed an inaccurate intelligence assessment that the Soviets would not persist in attacking that autumn. In part, Hitler abandoned Operation Citadel as a result of the invasion, which, at least in part, suggests that Churchill's instincts were correct about the wider strategic value of an attack on Italy. Moreover, this response on Hitler's part to a degree reflected the damage done earlier in the year by heavy German and Italian troop losses in Tunisia, as well as the losses earlier in the year in the Soviet Union. Again, this point reflected the wider significance of the campaigning in the Mediterranean or, at least – and the distinction is important – that in early 1943. The accretional nature of the campaigning was apparent, although that was not the same as an attritional character.

Just as the campaigning in North Africa and Italy had shown the Germans to be beatable by the British and Americans, both on the offensive and the defensive, and led to major territorial shifts, so the 1943 campaigning on the Eastern Front demonstrated that the Germans were beatable, both on the offensive and on the defensive, and led to major Soviet territorial gains, as well as the prospect of more gains. Under great strain, Hitler's health itself was hit hard, with particular difficulties on 18 July. Moreover, as they were mostly heavily exposed to the situation on the Eastern Front, the confidence of Germany's allies fell rapidly.

The strategic advantage had passed to the Red Army, as its strength, confidence and operational capability all increased, which underlined the value to Germany had it regained the initiative earlier in 1943. There were failures for the Red Army, notably the attempt to conquer Belarus that began in October 1943 and suffered from harsh winter weather,[2] unlike that made the following summer. Nevertheless, the general shift to the Soviet advantage was important to the dynamics of the Allied coalition. The Soviet Union was now clearly going to play a major role in the future of, at least, Eastern Europe. Linked to this, the Soviet demands at the Moscow Conference of October 1943 proved a shock to the British and the Americans. Soviet confidence, a key strategic resource, improved and this was important for alliance relationships.

Furthermore, the Germans now were less able to spare troops for the Italian campaign, while the mobile armoured German reserve necessary to oppose successfully a Second Front in France was being destroyed in the Soviet Union. German tank and other losses on the Eastern Front in late 1943 and early 1944 were heavy. As a result, although these campaigns after Kursk (as opposed to Operation Bagration, a major Soviet success, from June 1944) commonly receive relatively little attention in general histories of the war, they were important in the degradation of the German army, and even more so because the bulk of the German army was deployed on the Eastern Front, as was consistently the case from 1941. On 1 June, 228 divisions were on that front compared to 58 on the Western Front. Moreover, the latter included units that were recuperating.

As in other instances, Hitler proved a poor strategist on the defence, with his general attitude taking precedence over operational considerations. This was especially so with his unwillingness to yield territory, and his consequent preference for static, over mobile, defence. In large part, this attitude was a reflection of Hitler's obsessions with willpower and, as a related point, with battle as a test of ideological and racial purity, as well as his ingrained suspicion about the determination of subordinates, a suspicion that reflected his longstanding distance from the ethos of the German officer corps, one that could lead him to rage against them, as in late 1939. In some respects, however, his focus on battle, rather than on a more complex understanding of war, was a repetition of German First World War practice, and one that captured a more general German inability to set sensible military and political goals.

Hitler himself had increasingly poor health, and this was linked to his inability to control his temper. Strategy with tantrums is not a good way to receive or understand measured advice. Yet, more was at stake. His consistent attitudes, notably a reluctance to yield territory, were linked to strategic assumptions, particularly his view that such territory might then be used as the base for bombing important targets. Thus, Crete in 1941 and Crimea in 1941 and 1943 took on significance as areas from which the Romanian oilfields at Ploeşti, the most important in Europe west of the northern Caucasus, could be bombed. Hitler was also determined to retain control of areas deemed economically significant, notably Ukraine with its grain and coal.

After the war, Manstein criticised Hitler for his preference for holding positions rather than turning to mobile defence, but the latter posed serious logistical challenges, especially for the limited fuel supplies. Moreover, both approaches underrated Soviet resilience in the attack. At any rate, in 1944, defensive 'hedge-hogs' were less significant than in 1942 in resisting Soviet broad-front attacks, especially when the defenders could not rely on armoured counteroffensives.

In defence of Western Europe against invasion, Hitler placed his emphasis on fortified positions supported by mobile units, as the French had done in their defence against invasion in 1940. For Germany, a lack of fuel and other resources was part of the equation, but so was the German strategy for victory. Hitler hoped that defeating Anglo-American forces when they landed would weaken Churchill while causing Roosevelt to lose the November 1944 presidential election, after which Hitler planned to turn against Stalin.

However, aside from Hitler's exaggeration of the scale and effectiveness of the Atlantic Wall defences, this strategy still left the initiative to the Allies, which meant that German forces were allocated with reference to threat assessments that were at best problematic. This had been the case from early 1942, as the United States' entry into the war and Germany's loss of the stra-tegic initiative in the winter of 1941–2, more particularly on the Eastern Front, meant that defensive considerations became more pronounced. This was even more the case in the winter of 1942–3. The result was a large German effort expended on the defence, indeed a larger portion of military effort than in the case of Japan. That focus lessened the resources available for attacks, and notably so because U-boats after May 1943 did not serve as a potential strategic enabler. The defensive focus also left unclear where the Allied attack was likely to come, as had been seen in 1943 with German concerns about Sardinia and Greece lessen-ing the forces available for the defence of Sicily and mainland

Italy. Moreover, this German focus did not necessarily greatly guide Allied plans as part of a defensive German strategy able to impose a reaction on that of the Allies. Thus, the large German force in Norway did not lead to the Allied choice for Normandy. Instead, this force lessened the number of German troops available elsewhere.

The location of defensive support was a key issue, one shot through with concerns about prestige and resources, both of which affected prioritisation. There was also the question of how to act when the attack came. The German preference, as shown in response to the Salerno and Anzio landings in Italy in 1943 and 1944 respectively, was to fight the Allies at the waterline. This reflected concerns about the ability of the Allies to manoeuvre once they had broken forward from a beachhead, and an awareness of the vulnerability of German forces to Allied air attack. However, a forward position also lessened the flexibility and mobility of the defending forces.

This factor was seen with the planning for D-Day, a subject that has attracted particular attention but that also offers an example that is valid for other episodes. In the Pacific, American planners assumed that the first seventy-two hours would determine whether they could hold a beachhead, and for Normandy, Allied planners were greatly concerned that the German *panzer* divisions would drive in the beachheads before they could become established and, in particular, supported by sufficient anti-tank guns and tanks. Alongside providing firepower against German defences, this factor helped explain the Allied wish to land tanks, as on Omaha Beach. In contrast, the German commanders were divided both about where the Allied attack was likely to fall and about how best to respond. There was particular disagreement over whether to move their *panzer* divisions close to the coast, so that the Allies could be attacked before they could consolidate their position, or massed as a strategic reserve, the latter the advice of General Leo Geyr von Schweppenburg, the commander of Panzer Group West, who had the armour concentrated near Paris. Rommel, Commander of Army Group B, in contrast, wanted to defeat the Allied invasion at the waterline. Field Marshal Gerd von Rundstedt, Commander-in-Chief in the West, agreed with the plan to hold back forces away from the beachheads.

The eventual decision, made by Hitler, was for the *panzer* divisions to remain inland, which exposed them to air attack when they moved forward. The issue reflected the tensions and uncertainties of the German command structure, which accentuated major failings in intelligence and which by 1944 were linked to differences over army loyalty to Hitler. There was opposition to him among some of the officers in France, although several were very probably not active conspirators, including Rommel and Field Marshal Günther von Kluge, Rundstedt's replacement, both of whom committed suicide in 1944 after the failure of the 20 July Bomb Plot.

The course of campaigning in 1944 would have been less serious for Germany had the political situation been different, a situation repeating that in 1943. The strategic context was clear: the failure to obtain peace with any one of their opponents (as had happened for Germany and Austria-Hungary with Russia in early 1918) put the Germans in a difficult position to secure victory or, at least, avoid defeat on any of their fronts. The German strategic quandary was exacerbated as it was increasingly likely that an intractable conflict on the Eastern Front would be joined by fresh commitments in France in the shape of the Second Front. This quandary helped explain the Allies' adoption of the policy of unconditional surrender and the strategy of relentless pressure from multiple fronts leading to annihilation.

The failure to knock the Soviet Union out of the war led to growing unease among Germany's allies. It had begun with the Soviet counteroffensive in the winter of 1941–2 and resumed as the 1942 campaign ran out of steam, becoming far more serious with that second Soviet counteroffensive. This was seen with growing disagreement in Romania, as Marshal Ion Antonescu, the military dictator who was *Conducător* (leader) and Prime Minister, faced pressure from Constantin Brătianu and Iuliu Maniu, the leaders of opposition parties with whom Antonescu maintained links. They urged him to withdraw from the Soviet Union, which Romania was scarcely in a position to do given the prospect of German intervention if it did. In early 1943, however, Romanian interest in a change grew, with an approach to Italy for a joint proposal to the Allies for neutrality. Mussolini rejected this and, instead, the Romanian government approached the Allies via the Papacy and Portugal, both of which were neutral. However, Antonescu's suspicion of the Soviet Union and unwillingness to abandon Hitler, combined with the Allied stress on unconditional surrender, handicapped armistice negotiations.

For Germany, meanwhile, effective cooperation with its allies had collapsed after Italy signed an armistice with the Allies announced on 8 September 1943, being at once attacked by the Germans. The fast-moving Germans took over much of Italy, as well as the Italian occupation zones in Mediterranean Europe, producing a new geography of occupation. When Italy was an ally, this had included Italian occupation zones in former Greece, Yugoslavia and France, for example the Ionian Islands, much of Dalmatia and Slovenia, and Montenegro. German control was violently imposed in 1943, with many Italian troops killed (as on Cephalonia) or imprisoned before being deported to work in Germany.

In Italy, a more radical Fascist regime was established at Salò in northern Italy under Mussolini, who had been rescued by the Germans. There was in effect a civil war in northern Italy, with the Resistance fighting both Salò and its German backers. Anglo-American forces had conquered Sicily and much of southern Italy in 1943, but the Germans were not driven from central Italy until the summer of 1944, and from northern Italy until the closing weeks of the war.

After Italy changed sides, effective cooperation with Germany's remaining allies continued to be non-existent but, given the pace of the Allied advance in 1944, the options for such cooperation collapsed. In August–September, Bulgaria, Finland and Romania abandoned Germany and switched sides, with Romania in particular providing the Soviets with plentiful forces. Antonescu had refused to abandon Germany, and an armistice only followed after he was arrested on 23 August in a coup instigated by King Michael. The following day, Romania entered the war on the side of the Allies, against Germany and Hungary. It was to regain Transylvania from the latter. Antonescu was handed over to the Soviet occupation forces who sent him back in 1946, after which he was tried and shot.

By 1943, the Hungarian government under Miklós Kállay was seriously considering how best to switch to the Allies, but without leading to German occupation. After January 1943, Hungary did less fighting on the Eastern Front, and negotiated with Britain and America. This encouraged Churchill's interest in an advance into South-east Europe. In the event, thanks to effective German intervention on 19 March 1944, Hungary's position in the Axis camp was strengthened, with the Hungarian army taking a more active stance against the Soviets, while large numbers of Hungarian Jews were seized and sent to be slaughtered at Auschwitz. In turn, Soviet success and, crucially, the defection of Romania led the Hungarian head of state, Admiral Miklós Horthy, a conservative but not a fascist, to change the government on 29 August and to agree an armistice with the Soviets on 11 October. In response, the Germans helped ensure a successful coup. Thanks to the installation of the puppet Ferenc Szálasi government on 16 October, the Hungarians were unable to switch side, but their morale fell and, in the defence of Budapest against Soviet attack in 1944–5, the morale of the German defenders proved higher.

The support from Germany's allies largely evaporated when the war went badly. Assistance then would have proved most valuable. However, prior to 1944, the Germans had already found this support generally conditional and transactional.

Neutrals also moved away from the Axis. The Allied conquest of Vichy Morocco and Algeria in November 1942, and the impressive transatlantic amphibious capability it reflected, made Spain appear vulnerable, even though the Axis occupation of Vichy France that month increased the German presence on Spain's northern border. After Sicily was invaded and Mussolini overthrown in July 1943, the Franco regime became more accommodating to the Allies; while Portugal also moved towards them, allowing the United States and Britain to establish in the Azores air bases which were important to the Battle of the Atlantic. As the war continued to look less good for the Axis powers, the Franco regime tried to make itself look less fascist: Franco, an anti-Semite, became more sympathetic to Jewish refugees, while the Spanish forces fighting the Soviets were largely withdrawn in 1943, the remainder, nevertheless, staying as late as February 1945. Under threat from the United States, Franco, in May 1944, agreed to hand over all interned Italian ships, to expel all German agents and largely to cut off the supply of tungsten to Germany. The same month, he expelled all

German diplomats from the international zone of Tangier. In October 1944, Spain recognised the government of Charles de Gaulle in France. Diplomatic relations with Germany, however, were not cut until 1945, intelligence aid to Germany was provided until the close of the war and, due to its wartime conduct as well as fascism, Spain was not invited to the United Nations founding conference in 1945.

Spain's changing stance was mirrored in Asia. In July 1944, the month in which the Japanese government had to resign, the pro-Japanese Thai government of Field Marshal Pibul Songgram (also known as Luang Phibunsongkhram) fell as a result of its association with an increasingly risky policy, and Thailand progressively abandoned Japan.

More broadly, as the war went badly, the German attempt to win support from anti-imperial and anti-Soviet forces across the world became less credible, as did the Japanese counterpart with anti-Western movements. The raising of non-German recruits for the SS was stepped up, for example among Muslims in Kosovo, but there were fewer areas than before in which to recruit. Whereas, in 1943, the course of the conflict had led to Hitler's loss of his Italian alliance, in 1944 his entire alliance structure in Europe collapsed and only marginal forces, instead of national armies, continued to fight alongside the Germans.

In addition, as Germany and Japan began to lose, so they increased their pressure for support on conquered areas, but also no longer appeared a viable long-term prospect. Their attitudes and brutality had already encouraged Resistance activity, and this now became stronger. Resistance activity against both Germany and Japan benefited from Allied support and became more effective, not least as air superiority was gained.

Never strong, Hitler's diminished grasp on reality, seen for example in his determination to move much of the industrial capacity underground so as to protect against bombing, exacerbated the difficulties of German command. It was also matched within much of the military, for example the *Luftwaffe*.[3] Having survived the 20 July Bomb Plot in 1944 and, in response, further radicalised the German state and military, Hitler was able to continue with his fantasy that willpower would prevail and that his opponents could be divided.

This offers a valuable strategic contrast with the First World War. For Hitler, war with the Soviet Union, which he saw as a land of Slavs and Jews, was an end not a means; and, indeed, a metahistorical and existential struggle without finish, one that would strengthen, even purify, the German people. The situation would have been different without him. The First World War also indicated that the German military leadership, at least then, was unprepared to end an apparently intractable struggle by negotiations in which they paid serious heed to their opponents' views. Hitler's racial paranoia and prospectus gave German policy in the Second World War a distinctive character. Aside from the Allied focus on German unconditional surrender, Hitler's views helped ensure that Germany could not negotiate an end to the war after defeat in 1944, as it had done in 1918 when, due to Russia's effective defeat, the circumstances were less serious. Thus, in ending the prospect for independent action by the military, the 20 July Bomb Plot was an important strategic moment in the Second World War. Yet, already well prior to the Bomb Plot, German army occupation policies had become even more brutal, in part in response to the strength of partisan activity.[4]

Yet, even though they had lost all realistic hope of winning, the German position in September 1944 was still better than that of Britain in June 1940 or the Soviet Union in November 1941; and both had continued to fight and with eventual success.

As with Napoleon in early 1814, facing his opponents' advance into France, Hitler's lack of realism was the key factor in Germany fighting on; but, in addition, much of the German military leadership did not see a viable way out. Germany also remained in occupation of much of Europe. Furthermore, continuing the war provided the opportunity to bring the Holocaust to completion, which was very important to Hitler.

Germany benefited from its central position and, related to that, shorter lines of communication and logistics, notably in moving units in late 1944 in preparation for the Battle of the Bulge, using the excellent and still tightly controlled German railway system. In addition, after the Bulge offensive, the Sixth Panzer Army was successfully moved to the Hungarian Front in order to launch an attack on the Soviets. Nevertheless, the pressure on this mobility was accentuated, both by the need, notably from late 1943, to disperse armour on the Eastern Front in order to counter Soviet attacks, an operational goal; and by a strategic factor: the extent to which, in the summer of 1944, the war in Europe had become a multi-front one with the Germans, unlike the Japanese, on the defensive on all the fronts. The latter had a multi-front war but, in 1944, were on the offensive in China and on the Burma–India frontier.

At the same time, although its leaders clashed over the allocation of resources and over command arrangements, the German army did not collapse. Fighting for Germany helped motivate the troops, not least due to the unattractive offer of unconditional surrender combined with fear of the Red Army, although Nazi commitment, defiance, German nationalism and military values were all, variously, significant factors in encouraging Germans to fight on.[5] Determination included not only fighting on, but also the ability to keep parts of the war economy going even under increasingly destructive Anglo-American bombing.

Hitler's strategic beliefs lay directly behind the German surprise offensive, launched on 16 December 1944, that led to the Battle of the Bulge. The strategy then was that of weakening the Anglo-American forces so as to lead them to abandon the struggle, which was a total misreading of the situation, both militarily and politically; indeed, it was an attempt to repeat the strategy of 1940, but in a completely different context. The self-serving assumption that the Americans and Britain could be forced to abandon the war was fundamentally misplaced. There was also no opportunity for the rapid manoeuvrability that the Germans had earlier used so well. Facing tough American resistance and short of fuel, the Bulge offensive, though initially successful, failed. Had it been more successful militarily, it would still not have worked politically, which is a comment on some of the counterfactuals that are offered. Willpower, after all, was not the sole factor, resource and remedy.

There was also, on the part of Germany, more particularly Hitler, an interest in new weaponry as a strategic enabler rather than solely one of tactical or even operational enhancement. This lay behind significant investment in rocketry, jet aircraft and new-type submarines. In December 1943, large-scale production of the ME 262 jet aircraft and the Type XXI submarine was authorised. The V-2 rocket was seen as a way to reassure the German public that there were reprisals for the Allied bombing campaign. In part, this reliance was an aspect of the process already seen with the use of more powerful tanks and tank destroyers from 1943, and with interest in still more powerful tanks, which further strained the rather limited materiel available. Yet, there was a major difference, in that, unlike the tanks, the submarines, rockets and jet aircraft were intended to have strategic effect: in destroying Britain's resolve and capacity to act as a staging area for an invasion of Western Europe. Hitler insisted that the jets should be used as bombers, and not as fighters for the defence of Germany against Allied bombers.

Alongside the development of advanced weaponry, the Germans considered the prospect of further unrealistic advances, notably with long-range bombers, multi-stage rockets, space bombers and submarine-launched missiles. These schemes included plans for rocket attacks on New York City and Washington, DC.[6] These were intended as a strategic magic bullet, in effect similar to atomic weaponry, but drawing on a totally flawed assessment of what was practical at this stage. Although German expertise proved important for both the Americans and the Soviets, the rocket technology necessary for a trans-oceanic attack was not to be developed until the 1950s. Moreover, the difference was that the Americans could develop and deliver what became their capability. German innovations generally proved less workable and practicable. Those that were workable were not employed with success (V-rockets, jet aircraft), in part due to mistakes in conception; involved the use of resources that might have been more effective employed differently; or were ready too late (Type XXI submarines). The Germans overengineered and produced too many prototypes, inhibiting their ability to focus on one or two models. The development of the submarines affected strategy, as Hitler, in response to requests from Dönitz, the head of the navy, sought to maintain security for the Baltic testing grounds, retaining, largely to that end, over 200,000 troops to control marginal Courland in western Latvia, rather than concentrating units on the Eastern Front to oppose the main Soviet axis of advance on Berlin.

Hitler, for whom a stalemate peace was unacceptable, realised that final victory was out of reach. Nevertheless, he was determined to fight on in order to destroy Europe's Jews, as well as to achieve what he regarded as a moral victory for his concept of the German people. As a consequence, a notion of heroic self-destruction, for himself, the military, the regime and the nation, which may always have been present, became a decisive part of the regime's ideology and therefore of its strategy. Never clear, the distinction between them had collapsed.

Always a struggle of the will in Hitler's eyes, the war was increasingly organised in those terms, notably in the extent to which political commitment was crucial to military appointment and subsequent promotion. The *Volkssturm* (People's Storm), a Nazi-run, compulsory, local defence militia for men between sixteen and sixty, was established in July 1944. It was designed to inflict casualties on the advancing Allies such that their morale could not tolerate, and also to indoctrinate the German civilian population for a total struggle. The *Volkssturm* therefore served a political as well as a military function. This strategy encouraged the appointment as officers of those who were politically committed.[7] The strategy was similar to that of the Japanese. Thus, the politics of the war became a matter of will as, in Hitler's view, it had been throughout.

This, however, was not a dimension forced on an unwilling army and public. Instead, the degree of Nazi commitment on the part of the officer corps, both young and old, recent and longer-established, was considerable. At dinner during the Tehran Conference, Stalin suggested the need to kill tens of thousands of German officers as a consequence of victory, only to find that Churchill recoiled with shock.

At the same time, the term strategy has in this context to take note of the sheer destructiveness of the German and Japanese forces towards those unable to protect themselves, including German and Japanese civilians, forced labourers and, more specifically, Germans who were suspected of defeatism and therefore hanged, or the inhabitants of Japanese-occupied

Manila who fell victim to the brutality of the Japanese, who notably burned much of the housing as part of their defence. Sadism combined with death-wish destruction on the part of all-too-many German and Japanese commanders and soldiers in what was increasingly an anti-societal determination to fight to the finish in a form of perverted heroism. That was not a strategy for victory, but it was one for death and destruction. Japanese *kamikaze* tactics were emblematic of a broader strategic culture that became a strategy for Japan and, in part, for Germany.

JAPAN

Thanks to Japan's major commitment to China and Chinese resilience, Japan, which anyway had a more limited economy than Germany, had fewer resources to deploy against the Western Allies or the Soviet Union. In what had become an intractable struggle, a key Japanese goal – to have a number of client regimes in a divided China – had been advanced without any real sense of how the goal was to be achieved, maintained and made effective to the benefit of Japan. There was a mismatch, there and elsewhere, between goal and process, as well as between ends and means. At the same time, the relatively limited amount of non-Chinese scholarship devoted to the fighting in China, and the heavily politicised nature of Chinese scholarship, mean that questions about potential and achievement there can be difficult to assess.

More generally, despite talk of a 'Co-Prosperity Sphere' in Asia (by which swathes of the continent would supposedly prosper economically and culturally under the leadership of Japan rather than Western colonialists), Japan, like the Germans, did nothing that would consolidate support in captured territory.

Nor did it even make the most of the raw materials that could be extracted. In part, this was due to military factors, in the shape of effective Allied and especially American submarine attacks, notably on shipping from Singapore to Japan, the key maritime route in the Japanese Empire. In greatly disrupting the articulation of the Japanese system, these attacks had an impact comparable to that of the Allied air assault on Germany but, irrespective of these attacks, there were also very serious weaknesses in the Japanese war economy.

These weaknesses, however, did not prevent a major rebuilding in 1943 of the Japanese fleet and of the related air arm, although numbers, rather than skill, now characterised the latter. This force was to be destroyed in the Pacific in 1944 by an American navy that had been far more significantly expanded in 1943, but, in the meantime, it gave Japan potential. For the navy, this rebuilding was the principal strategy in 1943, and while it was being undertaken, it appeared important to hold on to as much of the area conquered in the Pacific as possible, even if the perimeter of conquest was breached. This was done, and Prime Minister Tōjō's willingness in September 1943 to abandon the major anchorage and heavily protected airbase of Rabaul on the island of New Britain in modern Papua New Guinea was blocked.

However, the defence-in-depth such bases apparently allowed was, to a great degree, compromised by the American adoption of a leapfrogging strategy, as with Rabaul, which was extensively and successfully bombed in November 1943. The 70,000-strong Japanese force that surrendered there in August 1945 had achieved nothing significant. So also with Truk in the Caroline Islands, a Japanese base that was bypassed after destructive American air attacks in February and April 1944. By greatly lessening the number of islands that had to be conquered, the Allied strategy directed even greater attention to the struggle for air and sea dominance.

What might appear to be a rational assessment of strategic possibilities was impacted within a strategic culture that was anything but rational. With Japan in 1944, as with the Germans, there was a conviction that a decisive victory could be obtained on one front that would overcome the more general role and consequences of Allied resources. There was a certainty that victory would sap the inherently weaker will of opponents, and thus give the Axis the success to which they were entitled. The Japanese were encouraged in this by the shock in the United States over the casualties suffered in capturing the island of Tarawa on 20–3 November 1943: 1696 killed and 2101 wounded, the losses brought home to the American public by vivid photography, notably in *Life*. There was subsequent controversy over the value of the attack, with General Holland Smith, Commander of the V Amphibious Corps, arguing that the island was not worth it.

The Japanese military structure was reorganised in February 1944 when Tōjō persuaded the Emperor to replace the Navy Chief of Staff, Osami Nagano, with the Naval Minister, Shigetarō Shimada, who also kept that post. Tōjō, in turn, dismissed Hajime Sugiyama, the Army Chief of Staff, and added that position to his own of Prime Minister and Army Minister.

In practice, success for Japan, or indeed for its ally Germany, would only have delayed eventual defeat. Aside from following a questionable military strategy, the accompanying political one was deeply problematic as it was based on a total failure to appreciate American resolve. So also with Japan's flawed belief that Asian public opinion could be won over, as with the granting of titular independence to Burma and the Philippines in August 1943, the anti-Western war aims declared as part of a revival of the Co-Prosperity Sphere by Tōjō at the Greater East Asia Conference in Tokyo on 5–6 November 1943, and the treaty of 9 January 1944 with the collaborationist Nanjing-based government of Wang Ching-wei through which Japan surrendered extraterritorial rights in China. The previous June, that government had been allowed to take over the administration of the International Settlement at Shanghai where the Japanese were powerful as the Germans were not at Tangier. In reality, the harshness of Japanese control won scant support, both in China and elsewhere, for example Java where many lives were lost to famine as rice was shipped away.[8] This was a famine that was deliberate unlike that in Bengal.

The Japanese planned a series of major victories in 1944. An offensive from Burma (Myanmar) was designed to forestall a British invasion by the Fourteenth Army, the prime objective, by overrunning the Imphal base area and destroying the British 4th Corps. More ambitiously, it was also hoped that the offensive would knock India out of the war by causing a rising there. This was a strategy similar to that attempted by the Germans, via the Turks, in the Islamic world in the First World War. Partly for this reason, anti-British Indian nationalist forces played a major role in the Japanese advance. This operation was also designed to force China out of the war by cutting its supply lines from India. It failed in all its objectives. The support in India for the 'Quit India' campaign was separate to the nationalists aligned with Japan.

In contrast, Operation Ichi-Go, a large-scale Japanese offensive in China launched in April 1944, made significant territorial gains, notably in southern China, and overran important American air bases from which Japan could be bombed, an objective that had been only partly fulfilled in a more limited offensive in 1942. The Japanese, however, failed in 1944, as in earlier offensives, to knock China out of the war, which would have released significant forces for use elsewhere. Chongqing, the Chinese Nationalist capital, was not taken.

Nevertheless, extending their control of the railway network crucial to their army's operations, the Japanese occupied, for the first time, a continuous ground route from Manchuria to Vietnam. This gave Japan a land axis that was independent of American maritime intervention and provided Japan with valuable strategic depth. The loss of Chinese air bases obliged the Americans to focus on seizing Pacific islands that could provide air bases, such as Saipan and Tinian. The Japanese campaign also gravely weakened the idea of a China-based American invasion of Japan, which itself was deeply problematic in logistical terms, in light of the strong Japanese position in China, and as a result of Japanese control of likely staging areas, notably Korea and Formosa (Taiwan).

In the Pacific, on a longstanding model, the Japanese aimed to destroy the spearhead of the advancing American fleet by concentrating their air power against it. The Japanese plan was for the American fleet to be lured into the range of Japanese island air bases, while the naval air force was to be concentrated in order further to minimise the American lead in carriers. There was the hope that the total success of the Japanese fleet over a Russian one that had sailed from the Baltic, at the Battle of Tsushima on one day in 1905, could be repeated. This reflected a more general conviction, also seen in the Midway operation in 1942, and with the Germans at Kursk (1943) and the Battle of the Bulge (1944), that a decisive victory could be obtained on one front, which could overcome the more general role and impact of Allied resources. As seen from the outset of the attack on the United States in 1941 (as indeed also that on China in 1937), Japanese assumptions arose from the sway of historical examples that supposedly represented national greatness and destiny and, even more, from the role of factors of will in Axis thinking. There was a conviction that victory would sap the inherently weaker will of opponents, and thus give the Axis the success to which they were entitled, a conviction reinforced by the political investment in its repetition.

Aside from the lack of political understanding underlying Japan's policy, it was anachronistic militarily. Defeat in 1944 on one front, notably that of the Leyte invasion force, would have delayed the Americans, but nothing more. Despite heavy casualties, American resolve would have been maintained. Moreover, by concentrating a target for the Americans, Japanese strategy made it more likely that the American attack would succeed in causing heavy casualties. Thus, operational and strategic factors were closely aligned.

The Americans had a better and more mobile fleet, a far greater ability to replace losses and far more capable leadership than the Japanese. In the event, the Japanese failed totally in 1944, in the battles of the Philippine Sea (19–20 June) and of Leyte Gulf (23–6 October). In the former, the Japanese carrier air force was destroyed; in the latter the surface fleet.[9] An inexorable sense of success increasingly characterised the American effort and affected planning.

By the end of 1944, there was a breakdown of strategic thought on the part of the Japanese, indeed an inability, in the face of Allied power, to think through any option once the decisive naval battle, Leyte Gulf, had been lost. With the angry Emperor keen for change, the Tōjō government had already had to resign on 18 July after the loss of Saipan to the Americans that summer. From the Mariana Islands, all of Japan's major cities could be bombed, whereas, from China, only those on the southern island of Kyushu could be reached by B-29 'Superfortress' heavy bombers. Attacks from the Marianas on

Japan were mounted from 24 November 1944. From Tinian in the Marianas, the B-29s were to set off to drop the atom bombs.

Japanese successes in China could not be translated into a broader strategic achievement or even into knocking China out of the war. Indeed, having more territory to control proved a strategic burden and, faced with mounting casualties, the Japanese ran out of impetus in early 1945.

The destruction of naval assets, moreover, made it difficult to consider any further large-scale action. Instead, the state of the navy and air force reduced the Japanese to a defensive-offensive position predicated on tenacious defence coupled with destructive suicide missions, both of which were designed to sap their opponents' will. Neither did so. Aware that the military leadership was against surrender, the weak government had no real strategy left other than for the military to die heroically in *kamikaze* attacks. The government felt unable to explain to the public that all had gone wrong and, like the previous Tōjō administration, was worried by domestic opposition, from both left and right.

The last major Japanese attack failed. The *Yamato*, Japan's remaining major battleship, was sunk by American aircraft on 7 April 1945 in the Battle of the East China Sea. This was in effect a suicide mission, designed to show that the navy was doing its bit to defeat the American force successfully invading the island of Okinawa. On land, in China, the Japanese had a better prospect with the Battle of West Hunan launched on 6 April, in an attempt to force the American bombers out of the air base at Zhijiang and take over regional rail links, and eventually, if successful, to invade Sichuan and advance on the Chinese capital, Chongqing. Initially successful, the attack was held, and the Chinese then launched a successful counterattack, benefiting from supplies brought via northern Burma.

GERMANY, 1945

In 1944 and early 1945, for example in Courland, the German army fought a skilful rearguard action against the Soviets, several times forcing them to a halt. Nevertheless, the direction of success was clear. As with Japan, Hitler was reduced to vain hopes. His sense of his own destiny interacted with his ideological drives and his determination that there should be no repetition of the surrender in 1918. Indeed, the Germans fought on, their effort including killing those suspected of defeatism or whose political views were unwelcome. Moreover, atrocities against prisoners and the slaughter of the Jews continued until the end of the war. This determination indicated the difficult task facing the Allies.

Indeed, Hitler hoped that the alliance against him would dissolve because of Germany's resolve and its own inherent divisions. Goebbels was told by Hitler on 11 March 1945 that, due to what he saw as Churchill's determination to exterminate Germany and refusal to ally against the Soviets, and what Hitler claimed was Roosevelt's wish that the Europeans destroy themselves through war, it was necessary for Germany to fight sufficiently well to lead Stalin to seek a separate peace. Hitler's views were unfounded. As Prime Minister again in 1951–5, Churchill came to see a reconstituted German army as important to the defence of Western interests against the Soviet Union.

More specifically, Hitler relied on the death of Roosevelt on 12 April 1945, which he saw as proof of a providential salvation that would lead to a change comparable to the death of Tsarina Elizabeth of Russia in 1762. That had unravelled the alliance against Frederick the Great of Prussia during the Seven Years War (1756–63). Another instance of resolute defence finally successful was echoed in the German film epic *Kolberg*, released in January 1945, which dealt with heroic resistance in 1807 against a French siege. The success against larger invading Russian forces at Tannenberg in East Prussia in 1914 was another possible example.

The focus on the life or death of the opposing leader was a very traditional way to look at strategy. It did not work for Hitler. Nor did the emphasis on new weapons. The Soviets launched their final offensive on 16 April 1945 and, with his victorious opponents having fought their way into the centre of Berlin, Hitler committed suicide on 30 April. He had not fled to an Alpine redoubt, as was thought possible by the Allies, in part because he thought his Eagle's Nest retreat in Berchtesgaden in the Bavarian Alps was vulnerable to American air attack, as indeed it was. Moreover, flight did not match Hitler's monomaniacal vision of his destiny and legacy.

Based at Flensburg, Hitler's designated successor as Chancellor, head of the armed forces and Nazi Party leader Admiral Karl Dönitz, wanted to maintain resistance to the Soviets while negotiating surrender terms with the Americans and British. Dönitz hoped that this strategy would enable more Germans to escape Soviet occupation. However, the Western Allies insisted on unconditional surrender to all the Allies, and Dönitz complied on 7 May.

6

Strategies for Allied Victory, 1943–5

QUESTIONS OF EMPHASIS

Agreed at the Casablanca Conference of 14–24 January 1943, unconditional surrender was designed to fix the alliance and thus the pressure on Germany, as well as to avoid the problem of settling on terms both for the Allies and for the different Axis powers. Thus, the policy objective fulfilled both military and diplomatic goals, kept the two in synergy, and provided the context for a multi-front offensive geared to total victory. This was also an instance of a more general context for strategy, that of easing the tensions in coalition warfare: the coalitions being both between and, as it is all-too-easy to forget, within states, coalitions that were both military and political.

At the same time, this situation still left questions of emphasis for the Allies. Making gains at the peripheries of their opponents' position was important, but did not establish how best to operate, other than through an incrementalism based on success in particular areas. Far more was required, in theory and practice, from strategic planning. Indeed, at the end of 1943, both Germany and Japan continued to benefit from controlling large territories far from their home country, a point Hitler made.

Moreover, they benefited in defending their empires from interior lines. However, as the campaigning of 1943 had shown, Germany and Japan were unable to retain their peripheries and, in part related to this, faced serious resource issues, notably over the availability and movement of oil. Furthermore, the dwindling of Japan's maritime capacity in the face of Allied, especially American, submarine attacks reduced the value of Japan's conquests and made it harder to articulate the empire. In very different circumstances, and reflecting the greater vulnerability of maritime systems, this was so even more than Allied air attacks on Germany, its allies and conquests.

At the same time, the pressure of Allied attacks left Germany far less able to undertake offensives, although it was to mount significant counterattacks until the winter of 1944–5. In contrast, Japan was able to do so in China and on the Burma–India frontier in 1944, the first largely successfully but the second completely unsuccessful. Yet, the situation was very different for Japan in the Pacific, which indicates the difficulty of readily transferring resources and military assets under wartime circumstances.

In the case of Japan, the Americans were able to combine both their Pacific options: the southern drive on the Philippines, largely favoured by the army, and the Central Pacific drive that was backed by the navy and the marines. That is a simplistic juxtaposition, not least due to the naval dimension in the former, but it is still a largely valid one. As with Japan, this juxtaposition also captures a tension between the services. The emphasis in discussion on states therefore provides a degree of abstraction that is misleading. In particular, there was tension between the individual armed services, as well as within them. At the same time, such tension did not preclude effective planning. Indeed, superior American interwar leadership development, based at the war colleges and focused on the solving of complex higher operational and strategic problems, contributed to wartime successes. In particular, the American 'twin drives' in the Pacific were a great military operational feat; one, closely related to this achievement, that was logistically unprecedented. There was not the concentration on a decisive battle seen with Germany and Japan.

The situation proved very different in the assessment of strategy towards Germany, in part because, having to defend a smaller area and without any dependence on maritime routes, it was better placed than Japan to move forces to respond to attacks. In particular, there were major disagreements between the United States and Britain over the timing of an invasion of France, and concerning the extent to which there should be an Allied offensive strategy in the Mediterranean and, if so, what it should concentrate on and with what resources.

The Americans did not fully understand Hitler's paranoia about the south, including the Balkan approaches to the Romanian oilfields and refining facilities at Ploeşti, and, closely related to that, the Italian airbases from which they could be bombed. Oil supplies and movements were elements of the contrasting strategic depth and operational vulnerability of the two alliance systems. The Romanian oil was indeed significant, and fuel supplies played a role in subsequent campaigning, notably in the reasons for the vigorous German defence of Hungary, its second most important source of oil following Romania.

The interdependence of land and air warfare was also shown by Hitler's concern to retain control of as much of Italy as possible, in order to keep Allied bombers as far as possible from German targets, such as Munich. Such bombing was a brutal demonstration of complete failure to the German public, and an economic threat as well. Exposure to Allied aircraft from Italy was to place yet more of a burden on German air defences that were already under great pressure from Allied bombers based in eastern England. This interdependence of land and air warfare had been seen at a tactical level during the First World War, but now it was relevant at an operational and strategic level, and in a way that Germany could not also impose on its opponents.

The Americans were reluctant to support an invasion of Sicily and, even more, mainland Italy because they feared that it would distract resources from both the invasion of France and the war with Japan, and also be a strategic irrelevance. Such operations also posed far more of a logistical strain than cross-Channel ones, and notably so in the case of shipping. Opportunities lost were a key element in the assessment of strategic options.

More generally, American strategists, who were as much subject to groupthink as those of any other state, and as much unwilling to accept the point, were opposed to what they saw as the Mediterranean obsession of British policy and its determination to preserve the empire,[1] a situation that has remained the case with subsequent American commentary. The American army did not really understand the partly maritime environment of the Mediterranean theatre. Moreover, an emphasis on focusing on key targets reflected persistent concerns, notably on the part of George Marshall, the Army Chief of Staff, about limits to the American people's support for the war, in the shape of anxiety about how long the public would be prepared to have patience for a protracted struggle.[2] These concerns did not have to wait for the Cold War, when they were seen during the Vietnam War. Marshall was strongly opposed to the Mediterranean campaign.

What, in practice, was a commitment to the Mediterranean and not an obsession, however did reflect British strategic concerns in the region. These were the product in part of longstanding imperial geopolitical interests, interests the Americans did not view with sympathy, but also of the legacy of conflict in the Mediterranean with the Axis since June 1940. There was war there with Italy, as well as, from early 1941, Germany – war on land, at sea, and in the air – and resources had been, and were, allocated accordingly by Britain. Moreover, there was a support infrastructure for them.

The British preference for an indirect approach, weakening the Axis by incremental steps as the preparation for an invasion of France, was also important. As a reminder of the varied causes of strategic choice, this preference was a longstanding aspect of British strategic culture, one seen from the seventeenth century, and notably with the Peninsular War of 1808–13 waged against French forces in Portugal and Spain, and linked to the emphasis on maritime power and themes. The heavy casualties of the First World War had led in the 1920s and 1930s to a revived and very conscious interest in the idea of an indirect approach. This pref-erence was also a response to the specific military circumstances of 1942–3, and a reasonable one at that.[3]

Both strategic culture and the impact of specific circum-stances, or, to employ a distinctive term, reactive strategy, have to be considered together. Each provided a context, and it is mistaken to see one as necessarily more significant. At the same time, the legacy of experience was an aspect of the 'effective stra-tegic decision-making and direction'[4] discerned in the British case.

The British were concerned that a direct attack across the English Channel on France would expose untested forces to the battle-hardened Germans and where the latter were close to reserves. The British experience in 1940–2, notably in France and Norway in 1940, in Greece in 1941 and in North Africa in 1941–2, had made them wary of such a step until the Germans had been more generally defeated. This lesson was underlined by the total and costly failure of the cross-Channel raid on Dieppe on 19 August 1942, a raid designed to show the Soviets, the Americans and the British public that action was being taken. This failure also demonstrated the problems of focusing on a defended port. Instead, in the summer of 1944, beaches away from ports were the Allied targets, and both in Normandy (6 June) and in Provence (15 August), as they had earlier been in Sicily and mainland Italy. The force used for the Dieppe attack was largely Canadian, which reflected the Canadian government's determination to be seen to act combined with its refusal to send troops to the Middle East and North Africa.

In contrast to the British stance, the Americans repeatedly argued that Italy was a strategic irrelevance that would dissipate Allied military strength; although there is also the claim that Roosevelt had wooed the Italian-American community for electoral reasons, and that this concern influenced American strategy.[5] Instead, the Americans sought a direct approach: a landing in northern France, an engagement with the major German forces in Western Europe, their destruction and an advance into Germany. This was a variant on the German quest for a decisive battle. German weaknesses in 1943 suggest that this might have been an option that year. Many key German units were allocated to the Kursk offensive, the Germans lacked the build-up in munitions production that 1943 was to bring, and their defensive positions in France were still incomplete.

Moreover, the Soviets mentioned their suspicion of their allies' failure to open a Second Front to the Germans when probing the possibility of a separate peace with Germany in September 1943. Hitler, however, was not interested in pursuing this option. Nevertheless, the possibility of such a development indicated the potential impact of strategic decisions on geopolitical alignments. The paranoid Stalin, who throughout the war, as well as subsequently, misunderstood and played down the Anglo-American war effort, did not appreciate the 'Germany First' policy, let alone the war against Japan as a whole. Instead, he was suspicious about the failure to launch a Second Front. In particular, drawing on his experience of earlier rivalry, notably during the Russian Civil War, Stalin exaggerated British commitment to the cause of hostility to communism. On 17 January 1944, *Pravda* inaccurately reported Anglo-German talks, and Churchill's reasonable complaint about this report was rejected by Stalin.[6] The latter also questioned Churchill that year about Hess's mission in 1941. The Soviets, furthermore, mounted a major intelligence offensive against Britain and the United States, one that laid the basis for the acquisition of American nuclear secrets, and that was greater in scale and far more hostile than equivalent British and American activities against the Soviet Union.

Yet, as part of a strategy of providing a misleadingly good face to the world, Stalin assisted by abolishing the Comintern (the Communist International) on 8 June 1943. This decision was explained in terms of the need for Communist parties to serve within anti-fascist coalitions, which was what the Soviet Union was doing at the international level. From the summer of 1941, the Soviet Union ceased to focus on support for 'national liberation' movements in British and French colonies, telling Indian Communists, for example, to delay demands for independence. Moreover, the Communist Party of the United States eased its tone.

With far more conviction and integrity, Churchill declared in an address to a Joint Session of Congress in Washington on 19 May 1943, 'We must do everything in our power that is sensible and practicable to take more of the weight off Russia in 1943.'

He sought to demonstrate this with the Combined Bomber Offensive and, indeed, Stalin was sent by Churchill film depicting the results of the heavy British bombing of Essen, the site of the major Krupp armament works in the Ruhr industrial belt.[7]

Nevertheless, rather than supporting an invasion of Normandy in 1943, the British were correct to draw attention to serious deficiencies in Allied preparedness. As yet, there was only limited experience in (and equipment for) amphibious operations. There was a shortage of landing craft and there was not yet the capability for the undersea pipeline that was to be used to move oil to the invading forces in Normandy in 1944. Moreover, it was unclear, at the beginning of 1943, how far it would be possible to vanquish the U-boat threat, while American aircraft production (and the supply of aircraft to Britain) took a while to reach full capacity.[8] So also with tanks.

Aside from the need to build up forces for an invasion, there was also the requirement of assured and sustained, rather than simply transient or partial, air and sea superiority, a situation that would have threatened any German invasion of Britain in 1940. The most important Anglo-American decision in 1943, one made in January, was to focus on winning the Battle of the Atlantic. The Allies had already reached the point where they were not going to lose it, and certainly had done so by mid-1942. However, only once the U-boat threat had been contained as a serious operational challenge (and thus eliminated as a real strategic threat) could Britain and the United States begin to plan properly, because major maritime invasions are not practical unless most (in this case, nearly all) shipping is getting through. From that, everything else flowed for Britain and the United States. Indeed, naval and cargo shipbuilding, particularly by the latter, was crucial to Allied strategic capability.[9] Winning the Battle of the Atlantic required this shipbuilding, as well as the successful strategy won by the achievements of British, American and Canadian warships against the U-boats. The latter was not assured until the late spring of 1943.

This was the background to the Second Front sought by the Allies, and it underlined the strategic quandary faced by the Germans, with an intractable conflict on the Eastern Front likely to be joined by fresh commitments in France, if not in 1943, in 1944. Despite the hopes placed by their advocates, the U-boats were proven to have had only an operational capability. This repeated the situation in the First World War, and notably so after the German declaration of unrestricted submarine warfare in 1917. Moreover, in 1943, this operational capability shrunk to a tactical one. Large-scale and rapid American shipbuilding helped ensure this outcome and made the equations of effectiveness very much move against the U-boat.

Destroying the *Luftwaffe* was also a very sensible strategic decision, as it made Allied strategic bombing less costly – and thus easier to sustain and more effective – and eased land operations on all the fronts. It would have been premature to invade Normandy without total air cover and the possibility of interdicting the battlefield or, at least, of limiting the movement forward of German reinforcements. The task of isolating a zone was very necessary. This was because with an invasion, the key issue was not so much the initial success, which (despite the example of Dieppe) should be assured by the local superiority provided by surprise, but, rather, the consolidation of the beach-head and the subsequent breakout. Indeed, there was an echo of the significant difference between break-in and breakout in the trench warfare on the Western Front in the First World War.

In the Battle of Normandy in June–August 1944, the Allied breakout in what was a crowded battlespace was to prove very difficult and to require a formidable effort against a determined opponent as well as large-scale air support. Moreover, even the operations on D-Day itself could have gone badly wrong, not least if Allied deception schemes had failed and the German reserves, especially of armour, had been deployed further forward.

Since, by early 1943, the Japanese threat had been much reduced, notably in the Pacific (although, as 1944 was to show, certainly not yet in Burma or China), the decision to continue to focus Anglo-American, more particularly American, strategy on defeating Germany remained valid. Thus, the invasion of southern Italy in 1943 was not a bad idea at the time it was launched. Moreover, amphibious operations in the Mediterranean in 1942 (Torch), 1943 (Sicily, and, separately, mainland Italy) and 1944 (Anzio) provided valuable experience in planning and execution for the eventual invasions of France, those in Normandy and Provence. They also, notably at Salerno in September 1943 and still very much with the Anzio landing in January 1944, offered dramatic warnings about the grave difficulties posed by the exploitation of such operations by the Allies and, as a related matter, by the rapid German response, which was a serious threat to the entire beachhead in each case. In this respect, the situation had not fundamentally changed since the Gallipoli expedition of 1915, although the outcome was different in the cases of Salerno and Anzio.

In 1943, that would have been a more serious problem in France than it was to be in practice in Normandy in 1944, as the Allies did not yet have sufficient air dominance to seek to isolate the area in conflict and, at least, to impose a cost and risk on movement, which was to be the situation in 1944. Moreover, in the event of failure at Normandy, there was not really the manpower available for a comparable repeat attack. This element can tend to be overlooked, but there were serious manpower issues for both Britain and the United States, and also for Canada. Partly as a result, there was almost an over-provision of air and sea support on 6 June 1944; although, looked at differently, this did not prevent comparable support for the landing in Provence that August, and it would not have been prudent or necessary to move the warships earlier to operate against Japan.

Thanks to the cumulative nature of military proficiency or training in action, operations in North Africa and Italy in 1943 were also important in improving military effectiveness on land. Both the American and the British armies benefited greatly from this experience, just as the British were more effective in 1943 thanks to their experience in fighting the Germans in 1941 and, more particularly, 1942. Experience was significant in closing the capability gap enjoyed by the Germans and Japanese as a result of their early preparedness, a gap that had been very important to Axis success.

Moreover, as another vindication of the Mediterranean strategy, heavy German losses in Tunisia, 'Tunisgrad', in 1943 meant fewer troops available elsewhere in Western Europe or for the Eastern Front. It is a significant element of post-war coverage that the Soviet victory at Stalingrad received, and continues to receive, far more attention. German combat losses on the Eastern Front were certainly greater than those in North Africa, but German and Italian troop and materiel losses and, even more, commitments, in the Mediterranean were very important to the war on the Eastern Front, and greatly helped the Soviet Union.

Prior to the opening of the Second Front, the invasion of Italy, alongside the Combined Bomber Offensive, appeared to be the most effective way for the United States and Britain to hit at Germany, and also to demonstrate to Stalin that they were doing their utmost. At Casablanca, Britain and the United States agreed on the invasion and also on the offensive, with the

Americans bombing by daylight, which apparently offered greater precision, and the British by night. It was believed that the bombing should serve to destroy the German economic system and hit German popular morale so that the capacity for armed resistance would be fatally weakened. Thus, bombing would complement any invasion.

Although challenged by the significant strategic depth Germany enjoyed thanks to its conquests in 1940, and thus by more room for interception, strategic bombing was made more feasible for the Allies by four-engine bombers and, subsequently, by the deployment of long-range fighters, notably Mustangs and Thunderbolts, capable both to provide escorts and to engage with German fighters in separate operations. There was also a marked improvement in the operational effectiveness of Allied bombing in 1944.[10]

At the Trident conference in Washington, DC on 12–25 May 1943, the United States and Britain agreed their military strategy, including a landing in France on 1 May 1944. This was followed up by the Quadrant meeting of 17–24 August, which fixed the invasion site as Normandy. The British concession, on 19 May 1943, to the American wish may have been due in part to concern about American intentions. In particular, in 1942, the Americans had delivered fewer troops to Britain than had been anticipated.[11] In part, this was a reflection of the commitments of the Torch offensive. By 1944, in contrast, the number in Britain was massive.

Delaying the planned invasion of France (Operation Roundup) from late 1943 until 1944 also enabled the American and British to benefit from the serious problems that hit the Germans in Eastern Europe in 1943. Failure at Kursk and subsequent large-scale Soviet advances in Ukraine chewed up part of the German army and air force; despite the commitment in

Italy, there were not comparable British and American losses in this period. The movement of German armour from the Eastern to the Western Front prior to the offensive launched in the Battle of the Bulge in December 1944 was a warning of what could have happened earlier in the event of an Allied landing in France. Indeed, often bitter debates within the German command structure in 1943–4 about the location of units between the fronts reflected the possibility of moving them. Germany's central position made this possible, as did the effective use of the rail system, albeit with the latter affected by air attack, and notably so at bridges and marshalling yards. So also with the rapid movement of German forces into Vichy France and Tunisia in November 1942, and into Italy in August and September 1943.

As it was not feasible to invade France in 1943, the Americans finally agreed to the attack on Sicily, Operation Husky, which, with air and sea mastery, was successfully launched on the night of 9–10 July 1943. Admittedly with some difficulty, Sicily was rapidly conquered. However, from the outset, there was criticism of the decision to fight in Italy. Furthermore, this criticism continued when the invasion of Sicily was followed by that of mainland Italy in September 1943. Both Churchill and Roosevelt realised that, with no invasion of France due until 1944, it was necessary, in order to dispel, or at least lessen, criticism on that head, to continue conflict with the Germans after the fall of Sicily.

In *Newsweek*, significantly an American magazine, on 13 March 1944, J. F. C. Fuller, a retired British general, wrote: 'the strategy is execrable. We should never have embarked on this Italian adventure because it was unstrategic from the start.' Claiming, correctly, that the mountainous topography of Italy helped the defence, Fuller stated that Anglo-American forces should have been conserved for the Second Front in France. He frequently used strategy as a term in his writing, and sometimes in an inventive fashion, as in a piece he wrote for the *Sunday Pictorial* of 27 April 1941 in which he commented on the Germans driving back the British forces in North Africa: 'like a ladder in a girl's stocking, our splendid desert campaign is running backwards up our strategical leg from its ankle to its knee'.[12] Fuller had served in the First World War on the Western Front and, in part, his comments were his reflections on what he felt should have been learned from that conflict.

Churchill, in contrast, was anxious not only to advance in Italy, but also to use the Mediterranean as a staging post for large-scale amphibious operations into the Balkans. To the Americans, although the Mediterranean was certainly an opportunity,[13] operations into the Balkans were a distraction from defeating the Germans in France. They also threatened to be a logistical nightmare, as appeared to be the case in 1999 when NATO intervention against the Serbs in the Kosovo crisis was considered. To Churchill, however, the Balkans presented an opportunity not only to harry the Germans, but also to pre-empt Soviet advances, notably by advancing through the Ljubljana Gap from Trieste via Slovenia towards Vienna. In practice, this route would have provided the Germans with significant defensive opportunities as well as exposing the British to very grave problems with logistics and the weather.

In political terms, it was hoped that such an advance into the Balkans would influence Hungarian and, maybe, Romanian, Bulgarian and Turkish policies, as well as the intensity and direction of Resistance activity in Albania, Yugoslavia and Greece. This strategy reflected Churchill's suspicion of the Soviet Union, and his linked strategic insight that the war was only an episode in the history of the twentieth century, a formative stage, but one that would be succeeded by challenges and rivalries that had only been partly suspended during the conflict. This insight was a reminder of the variety of chronological scales and contexts in which strategy is conceived, pursued and analysed. Churchill, like Stalin but not Roosevelt, understood that the Second World War was in part a stage in the longstanding struggle over the ambitions and position of the Soviet Union.

At the same time, what was tried in the Dodecanese Islands campaign in the Aegean in September–November 1943, alongside the failure of the Gallipoli operation he had backed in 1915, suggests that Churchill's broader Balkan plans were misconceived. Moreover, the establishment in 1943 of garrisons on Leros, Cos and the other islands was not only ill-conceived, but also poorly resourced and badly executed. British failure in the face of German air power formed a striking contrast with American successes in the Pacific, where island targets were isolated prior to attack. This produced a poor augury for operations closer to major German concentrations of force, although the German reinforcement of Greece in June and July 1943 in the face of largely misplaced invasion concerns was part of the equation.

In practice, the rapid German response in mainland Italy in September 1943, followed by the strength of their resistance there, meant that Allied options for additional operations did not match many hopes. Whereas the Allies had to move by sea, the Germans could do so by rail and road, with neither system in Italy as yet seriously disturbed, then and until the end of the war, by bombing; and with a reasonable speed on both.

Churchill knew that he had to present his overall Mediterranean strategy as in part a matter of the diversion of German strength, which, indeed was an important aspect. Thus, with reference to the Anzio operation and characteristically using divisions as his unit of account, Churchill wrote to Stalin:

The battle in Italy has not gone as I hoped or planned. Although the landing was a brilliant piece of work and achieved complete surprise, the advantage was lost and now it is a question of hard-slogging. However, the enemy has brought five additional divisions to the south of Rome and we are now actively engaging seventeen. We have good hopes of a satisfactory outcome, and anyhow the front will be kept aflame from now on.[14]

The value of the Mediterranean was not simply a matter of amphibious operations. There were also important advantages in naval and air terms. The flexibility of Allied supply links was enhanced, as it was no longer necessary to face the choice of risking Axis interception or of sailing round South Africa, which was a very long route with heavier demands for fuel, as well as with requirements for protection against submarine attack. Instead, thanks to Allied dominance of the Mediterranean, the route between the North Atlantic and the Middle East was greatly shortened. Moreover, the movement, in the face of German air attack, of much of the Italian navy to Malta and Alexandria, in accordance with the Italian armistice, altered the naval balance and enabled the British to withdraw warships from the Mediterranean, so as to support the invasion of France and, eventually, in late 1944, for operations against Japan without lessening the availability of warships in the battle against German submarines. This was important, as naval dominance and British naval support was crucial for both the invasion and for the planned operations. The British provided 80 per cent of the naval vessels used at D-Day on 6 June, whereas the Americans dominated the naval war with Japan.

Once the Allies were established in southern Italy, they developed an impressive aerial capability and began new bombing attacks on the industrial cities of north Italy, principally Milan and Turin, and on Balkan targets, notably the heavily defended Romanian oilfields at Ploeşti. In response, however, Italian industries were moved into factories in tunnels near Lake Garda, and these produced a large quantity of munitions until April 1945, although without the degree of brutality seen in German underground factories. Moreover, the delivery of oil from Romania continued until the Romanian armistice of August 1944.

The delay in the invasion of France helped ensure that, for the United States and Britain, alongside much fighting against both Germany and Japan, 1943 was primarily a year of preparations, including training, which tends to be an underrated aspect of strategic capability. These preparations were both an aspect of strategy and contributed greatly to it. Part of the campaigning was in effect a form of training, but the more significant side for the American and British armies was that of preparation for the 1944 invasion. More Allied troops died rehearsing for the Normandy invasion than on 6 June itself and, by June 1944, 3 million Americans were stationed in the United Kingdom.

In practice, three major amphibious invasions were mounted in Europe that year: at Anzio in Italy, Normandy and on the French Riviera. The last two, Overlord and Dragoon, were designed to be simultaneous, thus handicapping Germany's defence of France by dividing its reserves. However, the serious problems that faced the Anzio operation led the British to seek to replace Dragoon by operations in Italy and/or the Balkans. Churchill saw advancing into the Rhône Valley after Dragoon as a strategic 'cul-de-sac'. Indeed, as a result of Dragoon, there was not going to be the hoped-for cutting off of German troops in south-western France because they fell back successfully. Moreover, the launching of Dragoon in mid-August ensured that it did not affect operations in Normandy.

Nevertheless, to the Americans Dragoon, which had been agreed at the Tehran Conference of 28 November–1 December 1943, represented an appropriate use of French troops from North Africa, a way to ease logistical burdens for the Allies in France by providing control over additional ports, notably Marseille, and part of the political, as well as military, strategy in the French campaign, not least forestalling a takeover by the Communists in the Resistance. So also with the American determination to ensure that an acceptable (to them) non-Communist government be established in Rome, an issue that concerned Churchill due to what he saw as the likely impact on the campaigning. Dragoon involved the use of 887 warships, including nine aircraft carriers, five battleships and 21 cruisers, 1370 landing craft and overwhelming air superiority.

The role of France in the war is one that is underplayed by considering it in terms of the Resistance, important as that was by 1944, because France remained a significant element throughout the war. A leading industrial, agricultural and coal producer, it was, perforce, a major economic partner of the Germans, who accumulated 160 billion francs worth of debt to France under compensation agreements for trade, and probably gained about 860 billion francs from France, as well as large numbers of forced labourers, and maybe 30,000 troops for the German army. There was also the major support provided by the willingness of Vichy forces to resist the British in 1940–2, in West Africa, the Middle East and Madagascar. Italy also played a continued role in the war, but that was somewhat diminished in impact and view in 1943–5 because, alongside the Italian effort on the Allied side, there was that for the Fascist Republic of Salò under Mussolini.

The changing fortune of war led to the German occupation of the Vichy zone in November 1942, an onerous occupation imposing further demands on German troop numbers. These changing fortunes of war helped increase German pressures on the civilian population of occupied areas, and these increased support for the French Resistance in 1943. So did the greater direction of Allied resources to that end: Resistance recruitment rose greatly, although it remained a minority of the French population. Resistance activities, notably by the French Forces of the Interior, increased the burden of occupation for the Germans and their collaborators, and directed attention to the future. The potential offered by France was to be differently shown in 1944–5 as the French contributed an appreciable share of the forces of the Western Allies: over 400,000 men in France and Germany and a corps in Italy.

SUMMIT DIPLOMACY

The Allies did not follow the imperial theme seen with Hitler's use of personal meetings. Factors of distance, time, politics and ideology ensured that the 'Big Three' (Roosevelt, Stalin and Churchill) did not meet in Washington. A Tsarist-era recreation hotspot, still charming today, Yalta in Crimea in 1945 was the closest they all got to Moscow. Under the threat of German air and later rocket (V-1 and V-2) attack, London was too danger-ous to suggest, and neither Roosevelt, who did not wish to be too closely associated with the British, nor Stalin would visit it. The three men did not meet until Tehran in November 1943, when the Soviets claimed that they thwarted Operation Long Jump, an alleged German assassination plot, although the exist-ence of this plot has been doubted. In practice, Allied confer-ences at Casablanca (1943), Cairo (1943), Tehran (1943) and Potsdam (1945) reflected the importance of intermediary loca-tions within the Allied ambit between London and Moscow.

At the same time, there was an emphasis on personal agreement among the leaders, rather than on formal diplomatic processes, and thus on their meeting. This emphasis reflected the conviction on the part of the leaders that they could change the world by personal diplomacy. This conviction proved misplaced. Nevertheless, this diplomacy helped to manage the issues at stake, including the transition of power from Britain to the United States as the former became more of a great power on terms, and with the terms increasingly set by the United States.

Summit diplomacy represented a continuation of pre-war practices, including of special diplomatic missions. It also stemmed from the determination of leaders to control the diplomatic process. As such, this diplomacy reflected the wish of leaders to circumvent the limitations and constraints of bureaucratic systems, one seen with all of the participants.

NORMANDY AND AFTER

The Second Front, finally launched on 6 June 1944 with the invasion of Normandy by American, British and Canadian forces, of which 156,115 men landed that day and 326,547 by 11 June, was part of an assemblage of Allied pressure that ended the war in Europe within a year. The Allied losses on 6 June were fewer than were feared, although the subsequent breakout from the invasion zone proved more difficult than had been anticipated. Nevertheless, the success of the invasion encouraged looking ahead to the strategic situation in the post-war world. However, for understandable reasons, strategic commentators did not always get it correct, not least because they could seriously misunderstand the politics of the campaign. Ever-willing to speculate, Fuller informed the readers of *Newsweek* on 10 July 1944:

Though the German High Command is faced with forces beyond its means to check, it doesn't necessarily follow that it is checkmated because utilization of these forces depends upon the circumstances in which they are placed . . . the Russians, being more war-worn than their Allies, are more likely to welcome speedy termination of the war . . . the Americans and the British also seek its speedy termination so that they may still be fresh when they in turn fall on Japan . . . if the war can be prolonged throughout next winter, by spring or summer of next year political circumstances may have so changed that the Allied powers will be willing to bring the war in the west to an end on terms more favourable to Germany than those of unconditional surrender . . . Time is the crucial factor not only strategically but also tactically; tactically for the Russians in order rapidly to beat their enemy; strategically for the Germans in order slowly to sell ground at high cost.

This view, which possibly in part reflected Fuller's pronounced right-wing tendencies, seriously underrated the resolve of the Allies to defeat Germany. Yet, this view also helps remind us of the uncertainties of contemporaries and of the continued need to relate military developments to political objectives. That point throws further light on the long-running discussion over whether the Allies, who captured Aachen, an important German city, on 21 October, followed the best strategy in the west in 1944. This discussion is often somewhat unhelpfully reduced to a debate over the virtues of the broad-front approach advocated by General Dwight Eisenhower, an American and the overall Allied commander in France, and the very different narrow-front attempt for a rapid advance beyond the Rhine advocated by

General Bernard Montgomery, the senior British field commander and, due to his self-confidence and lack of interpersonal skills, a difficult character. The clash over strategy was linked to Montgomery's unsuccessful pressure for his appointment, under Eisenhower, as a deputy entrusted with command over ground forces. There was also bitter rivalry between American commanders, indeed sometimes to a dysfunctional level, although that tends to be underplayed in order to focus on Montgomery.

The idea of a narrow-front advance presupposed a war of manoeuvre in which the initiative and tempo were dictated by the Allies. However, the German 'Bulge' offensive of December 1944, an offensive for which Hitler had called for plans on 19 August,[15] indicated the risk posed by this approach. An Allied advance across the Rhine in 1944, the basis indeed for the rash and unsuccessful Arnhem offensive, Operation Market Garden, would have been vulnerable to counterattack as the Germans had been building up a significant armoured force in northern Germany from September. An Allied advance would also have been dependent on a precarious supply route, one made more difficult by German damage to key ports, or retention of them, notably the demolition of harbour works at Cherbourg before its surrender and the damage to Brest, Le Havre and Saint-Malo before they fell to American forces. These ports became more important as Allied forces in France increased in number. It took from 7 August to 19 September 1944 for the Americans to capture Brest. Overstretched logistical lines were a problem for all powers in the war, including the well-resourced Western Allies whose advancing forces had major requirements for fuel and ammunition.

At the same time, the preference for a broad front helped the Germans withdraw without heavy casualties after their serious defeat at Falaise, where there was a failure to impose an encircle-ment on the Germans. Moreover, Eisenhower's caution greatly lessened the chance of cutting off German forces,[16] and contrasted with the operational means of the 'deep-battle' attacks the Soviets employed to sustain their strategy of advance across Eastern Europe. The Anglo-American broad-front approach in part reflected a 'come-as-you-are' approach, in the shape of moving forward troops from existing alignments in northern and south-ern France. This approach also lessened the burden on particular communication routes. More positively, a broad front was a reflection of the need to maintain superiority over the qualita-tively strong German forces which, alongside limited equipment, still retained considerable fighting ability. There was not the confidence in advance shown by the Germans in France in 1940.

At the same time, the Allied approach represented a needless anxiety about flanks and, in part related to this, a major diffu-sion of combat effectiveness, with no equivalent to what the Germans were to do initially on a narrow front in the Battle of the Bulge. Like the Allied invasion of mainland Italy in 1943, this strategy was also executed in a chaotic and improvised manner, with generals failing to display the necessary coopera-tion. Yet, that point was also true of German operations, which, in part, indicated the degradation of the German capability, alongside the need to respond to increasingly difficult circum-stances imposed by Allied attacks and resources.

Given the resilience of the German military, Allied hopes of victory in 1944 were misplaced. From that perspective, both Eisenhower's broad-front approach and Montgomery's usually methodical war making (which was not in evidence in the Arnhem offensive) were sensible options. Each weakened the German army. With Germany losing the multi-front war, as intended by the Allies, there were cumulative strains of note imposed on the Germans, as well as significant particular ones. Both were important. Thus, on 7 December 1944, Eisenhower 'emphasised the heavy rate of attrition they were forcing on the enemy, a rate very much greater than our own. He pointed out that the enemy could not afford losses on such a scale.'[17] Meanwhile, a combination of the Allied goal of unconditional surrender with the resolve of their opponents' leaderships, their grip over their populations, and the extent of territory still for the Allies to conquer, ensured that the war would not end in 1944, but would go on with great intensity in Europe and Asia.

The focus for 1944 is generally on Allied strategy, as the Allies tended to take the initiative, and notably so in Europe. This strategy involved coalition dynamics. These encompassed, on the one hand, both realism in the need for allies and the needs from them, not least in providing numbers and exerting pressure on opponents, and, on the other hand, responsibility in the bearing of burdens. So also with the overthrow of Napoleon in 1813–14 and 1815 by the Sixth and Seventh Coalitions. These coalition dynamics were most successful if differences and problems within them were not probed, but that was difficult given the need for realism and burden sharing. Competitive cooperation became more serious as the post-war world neared and the related issues were pushed to the fore.

Realism was very different as far as the public was concerned. The many problems of alliance politics were a subject kept well from the eyes of contemporaries. Instead, these politics were particularly prone to propaganda designed to make alliances appear natural and strong. This was especially so of Anglo-American propaganda about the value of alliance with the Soviet Union during 1941–5, and of German propaganda about the value of the alliance with Mussolini. The latter was an implausible claim at the best of times.

SOVIET ADVANCES

The Soviet winter counteroffensives of 1941–2 and 1942–3 indicated the incremental nature of success; as opposed to the earlier German focus on complete victory in one campaign, as had occurred from 1939 to early 1941. It was only possible in the 1941–2 and 1942–3 counteroffensives for Soviet forces to achieve so much before exhaustion, losses and supply difficulties had an impact and led to the slackening and then end of the offensive. It took a while for the Soviets to appreciate that offensives simultaneously mounted along the Eastern Front but at great distances from one another, as Stalin favoured, would not, in practice, automatically draw off German strength from one theatre to another, and thus provide mutual support. Instead, the offensives suffered from the lack of adequate coordination. Moreover, until 1945, there was to be no one-campaign end to the war as a whole, nor to that on the Eastern Front, which led to an emphasis on the strength necessary for attrition. Soviet operational art was linked to this attritional strategy. The Soviets deployed their forces along broad fronts, launching a number of frontal attacks designed to smash opposing forces and to maintain continual pressure.

To Stalin, the changing fortune of war offered opportunities, but also dangers. He feared both the consequences for Germany and those for the Western Allies. In the former perspective, Stalin was concerned that Hitler would seek peace with the Western Allies and focus, instead, on fighting the Soviet Union. Stalin's worry about change in Germany extended to the July 1944 Bomb Plot against Hitler, as he saw a German army takeover as even more clearly leading to this outcome. There were indeed some links between the plotters who sought this outcome and the Western Allies. The ability of the Western allies to do a deal with the Italian army in 1943 apparently underlined this threat to the Soviet Union; but there was no basis to it with the Germans in 1944 on the part of the American and British leaderships.

Moreover, from Stalin's perspective, whether or not the United States and Britain pursued this route, there was the risk that the concentration of German forces on the Eastern Front would ensure that the Western Allies could succeed rapidly in overrunning France and the Low Countries. This would place them closer to conquering Germany than Soviet forces which, as of mid-June 1944, were, due to the failure of the offensive launched the previous October, well to the east of Minsk. This situation encouraged Stalin to begin Operation Bagration on 22 June 1944, a summer date very much in contrast to that of the previous October when the terrain was reduced by rain to mud. At Tehran, Roosevelt had asked Stalin to launch a simultaneous attack with the D-Day landings, an attack intended to fix the German forces and make it difficult to move troops between fronts.

Stalin, in contrast, wanted the Western Allies to attack first, so that the German reserves had already gone west to face them. Moreover, he planned for a far deeper offensive than any launched so far. This reflected both his abiding competition with the Western Allies and his sense that the German counteroffensives on the Eastern Front, as were indeed attempted, would fail. Soviet strategy focused on the disorientation of the Germans by sequential operations designed to destroy their cohesion, and to achieve, and exploit, penetrations in depth. Stalin achieved this deep offensive and it put the Soviets into the equation to end the war in Europe the following year. By the close of 1944, they had advanced to within striking distance of Berlin.

Distrust of the West characterised Soviet policy, as with the Soviet response to Operation Frantic, which entailed American bombers using Soviet bases to refuel and rearm having bombed the Axis zone. This operation began on 2 June 1944 after over 200 American bombers that had attacked Debrecen in Hungary landed in Poltava, Ukraine. The Soviets were opposed to the possible impact of such an American presence in Ukraine. There were to be very few missions, and Stalin refused to accept that the aircraft could provide help to the Warsaw Rising against German control.[18]

CHINA

Jiang Jieshi and Roosevelt played up the role of China, whereas Churchill was contemptuous of the idea of China as a great power. American support for the *Guomindang* carried with it strategic commitments, notably of assistance, aircraft and advisers. These also involved questions of how best to provide this support. China received help by air 'over the hump', or Himalayas, from India. This was a difficult route, and that encouraged the United States and China to press for the reconquest of Upper (northern) Burma from Japan so as to improve ground routes. In contrast, Britain correctly saw this as a somewhat tangential and hard area for operations. Indeed, the British command in India clashed repeatedly with the Chinese over planning for operations there. The British preferred the idea of an amphibious invasion of Lower (southern) Burma, a course that would permit the use of their naval assets, which was a goal also seen in Churchill's abortive idea for seizing a base in northern Sumatra. In 1944, British and Chinese successes in Upper Burma opened up an improved ground route for moving supplies to China.

The Americans eventually came to be disillusioned with Jiang's conduct of the Chinese war effort. By 1944, there was serious tension, as Jiang resisted pressure for Joseph Stilwell, an American, to become commander of all Chinese forces, and also American demands that Jiang seek a coalition with the Communists in order to put pressure on the Japanese. In practice, Jiang could not mount a defensive front and could not switch to an offensive mode due to a lack of equipment, a weak senior officer corps (which for political and cultural reasons he could not significantly alter) and his heavy losses of professionals from 1937. The Americans were insufficiently attentive to this. The irascible Stilwell, moreover, could not get on with anyone.

The failure of American pressure in 1944, combined with major Japanese successes in the Ichi-Go offensive in southern China that year, ended American hopes of China as a key partner. Most of the large quantities of supplies the American Tenth Air Force had been flying into China were for the American air assault on the Japanese, and not munitions for the Chinese armies. However, from the summer of 1943, the Americans had also been planning for a Chinese advance on Guangzhou (Canton) to link up with an American advance, via Taiwan, to the Chinese coast. These advances were to be followed by joint operations to clear northern China and establish bases from which Japan itself could be attacked. Confident that an air assault on Japan could make a major difference to the war, the Americans sent the first B-29s to become operational to China. From there, they bombed targets in Japanese-occupied China, Korea and southern Japan; most of Japan was outside range from the Chinese bases. In practice, however, the strategy had weak fundamentals, not least as it relied on the coincidence of too many variables. In addition, Chinese military and logistical deficiencies were serious.

In the event, Japanese success in 1944 wrecked this strategy. It also created for Japan an alternative to being subjected to American naval success by allowing an overland route between central China and Indo-China; although this alternative was still limited in strategic, military and economic value in the face of American capabilities. In the event, there was no equivalent in China, for either Japan or the Americans, to the strategic possibilities increasingly available to the Americans in the Pacific. Moreover, these possibilities permitted the Americans to use their clear superiority in naval strength, amphibious capability and air power.

CAMPAIGNING AGAINST JAPAN

The Allied advance on Japan in 1943 continued in 1944, pushing to the fore questions of priority and organisation. The resources were increasingly present, although essentially for the Americans and not really so as to permit British independent action on the scale desired by Churchill. On 16 March 1944, General Hastings Ismay, Churchill's close military advisor, wrote to him:

> the war we have to wage against Japan is of an entirely new type. It is no mere clash of opposing fleets. Allied naval forces must be so strong in themselves, and so fully equipped to carry with them land and air forces, that they can overcome not only Japanese naval forces but also Japanese garrisons supported by shore-based air forces . . . the bigger the Allied fleet free to seek out the enemy, the better the chances of destroying the Japanese fleet.[19]

For both the United States and Britain, it was unclear how far to concentrate on the Japanese Home Islands or, in contrast, attack other targets first. The Mariana Islands of Saipan, Tinian and Guam, captured in a campaign from 15 June to 10 August

1944, provided valuable bases for further operations, including against the Home Islands, but, in the event, the Americans attacked the Philippines. This, the largest American offensive in the Pacific (as the planned invasion of Japan was never launched), began in October 1944 when the island of Leyte was invaded, and continued in January 1945 when a substantial force was landed on the largest island, Luzon.

All operations are also opportunities lost. In some respects, the Philippines, the focus of American operations in 1944, were a cul-de-sac for a strategy centred on the target of Japan. Tinian and Iwo Jima were a more important axis than the Philippines for providing airfields for the attack on Japan; although control of the central Philippines would increase the number of American air bases in the western Pacific. Control of the Philippines also provided naval advantages, including bases for attacking Japan and isolating South-east Asia. Moreover, the reasons for recapturing the Philippines were given added force by MacArthur's determination to reverse his flight from them in 1942. He insisted that the Americans had obligations to their Filipino supporters. It is also possible that Roosevelt wanted to keep a candidate for the Republican nomination as president committed to military operations.

Alternatively, the American seizure of Formosa (Taiwan) would have been more important so far as affecting the war in China was concerned and, crucially, helping to keep the pressurised and defeated *Guomindang* in the war, or, rather, able to launch attacks on the Japanese. However, the heavily defended Formosa would probably have only fallen after heavy American losses. It was also less vulnerable to American amphibious attack.

Furthermore, aware of the crucial significance of resources, the Japanese feared an attack on the oilfields in the Dutch East Indies, oilfields that were particularly important for the navy to continue operating. In the event, in 1945, Australian amphibious forces were launched against those in Borneo, while British carrier-based aircraft attacked the well-protected refining facilities on Sumatra.

Differences over strategy reflected and accentuated divisions in the American war machine that were already strong. In particular, service rivalries were significant. Major-General William Penney, a British officer who was then Director of Intelligence, South-East Asia Command, reported from Manila, where he was visiting MacArthur in April 1945:

> Theatre commanders are extremely independent and resentful of independence. This, as a matter of fact, extends through all US formations . . . Feuding between US Army and Navy, including Marines, is openly expressed. In the General's Mess at Manila I was astounded to listen to the scornful references to operations on Okinawa and other land battles fought under Naval or Marine command.[20]

Although the navy had to get the army to Leyte and Luzon, to supply it, to provide firepower and to support secondary operations on other islands, the Philippines became very much an army show, unlike Iwo Jima and Okinawa. Moreover, alongside the efforts made in the interwar period, the pre-First World War education of officers who were in command positions had offered little on combined operations or, indeed, logistics.

As critics of the campaign had feared, the invasion of the Philippines led to a delay in the operations planned against Iwo Jima and Okinawa. At the same time, the Philippines offered staging areas for an invasion of Japan, which was a formidable logistical task. Indeed, the strategical implications of logistical strain were significant. This was more so for the Americans advancing in

1943–5 than for the Japanese in 1941–2 because the requirements of American forces were far greater. That reflected an enhanced capability but, in turn, created significant needs. The invasion of the Philippines offers some parallels (as well as differences) with that of Italy in 1943, but is less contentious because it was an American operation and thus unlike that of Italy, which saw differences between the United States and Britain.

Alongside the serious divisions within the American military, there were others concerning Japan among the Allies, and notably over the occupation plans. At the same time, there was also a basic commonality of purpose stemming from Stalin's agreement at the Tehran Conference to declare war on Japan once the war with Germany was over. The date was settled at the Yalta Conference of 4–11 February 1945, and the Soviets rapidly conquered Manchuria that August.

1945

The sense of Axis defeat as inevitable had become far stronger in Allied capitals at the start of 1945 despite the fighting determination shown by their opponents and their refusal to surrender. The Battle of the Bulge was very much seen as the last throw by the Germans, and indeed it was followed by a failure on the part of Hitler to move forward any viable military or political plan. Hitler had run out of strategic options because the Allies were fighting to the finish, and doing so with increasing effectiveness. On 18 January 1945, Churchill told the House of Commons: 'I am clear that nothing should induce us to abandon the principle of unconditional surrender, or to enter into any form of negotiation with Germany or Japan, under whatever guise such suggestions may present themselves, until the act of unconditional surrender has been formally executed.'

Separately, what does not happen is always significant. In the case of Germany and its allies, the weakness of popular resistance once areas had been conquered by American and British forces was significant. In contrast, the Soviets faced nationalist resistance in some of the areas they had conquered, such as Poland, the Baltic republics and western Ukraine. This contrast is instructive for wider questions of strategy. States and regular forces tended to be ambivalent about Resistance activity as it seemed to them to be independent and disorganised. The Germans and Japanese did not make Resistance efforts comparable to those of the Allies, especially the Soviets. The window of opportunity for any Axis Resistance was far shorter but, at any rate, the military and political leaderships were unenthusiastic. A key element, as was the case also with insurgencies after 1945, was external support, notably the provision of arms. The Western Allies did not provide support against the Soviet advance to nationalist resistance until the Cold War really developed. This was a significant strategic choice, although Resistance divisions, popular war-weariness, and Soviet strength, determination and ruthlessness all left limited opportunities for any opposition, let alone assistance to it.

Meanwhile, the strategic players changed in 1945. Roosevelt's death brought the Vice President, Harry S. Truman, to power, while Churchill's sweeping defeat, in the first British general election since 1935, led to the first majority Labour government, with Clement Attlee, the former Deputy Prime Minister, as Prime Minister. Stalin, however, remained in absolute control of the Soviet Union.

On the Axis side, Japan remained in the war after Germany had rapidly surrendered following Hitler's suicide, only itself to surrender more than three months later, after the dropping of the atom bombs. Japan staying in the war indicated the degree to which the Second World War was a case of two separate wars linked by Anglo-American participation in both. The German–Japanese alliance never amounted to anything practical when it came to actual war. From that perspective, an attack by Japan on the Soviet Union in 1941 is a major counterfactual, as it might have made a big difference, not least to the very character of the war.

By late 1945, the leaders of the victorious Allies faced the grim task of trying to stabilise the world, much of which was in ruins, while at the same time confronting the prospect of the alliance collapsing, a prospect Stalin had always anticipated. The full-scale Cold War was already in prospect.

7

Strategies for the Post-war

This is not a question of fighting for Ddansk [Gdansk] or fighting for Poland. We are fighting to save the whole world from the pestilence of Nazi tyranny and in defence of all that is most sacred to man. This is no war for domination or imperial aggrandisement or material gain, no war to shut any country out of its sunlight and means of progress. It is a war, viewed in its inherent quality, to establish on impregnable rocks, the rights of the individual, and it is a war to establish and revive the stature of man.

> Winston Churchill, House of Commons,
> 3 September 1939

Seeking to mould the post-war world, or continue the pre-war situation, was important from the outset of the war and, indeed, alongside the pressures of the moment, a major reason for declaring it in 1939. This search therefore helped explain the purpose of the war. The lack of a settlement in 1940 directed more attention to the war making. Subsequently, the attempt to mould the post-war world, while always important, became more significant for the Allies during the war, notably from 1943 and, more particularly, from 1944. This ambition had an impact on tensions within alliances, although less so for the Axis as it did not have the degree of cooperation between near-equals seen with the Allies. Moreover, Hitler had failed in 1940 to maintain cooperation with the Soviet Union over Eastern Europe, and this was a prelude to the collapse of that alliance.

Turning to the Allies, there were major differences over goals and means, notably with the former in the case of contrasting views over Poland by Britain and the Soviet Union. Looking back to rivalry from the outset of the Soviet Union, Stalin informed Churchill that the Poles were 'incorrigible'.[1] He added, in March 1944, that there could not be 'normal relations' between the Soviet Union and the London-based Polish government in exile, and that the Polish view of the frontier was unacceptable. Churchill was willing to be helpful about the frontier, but offered a view on power that was very different to that of Stalin:

> Force can achieve much but force supported by the good will of the world can achieve more. I earnestly hope that you will not close the door finally to a working agreement with the Poles which will help the common cause during the war and give you all you require at the peace. If nothing can be arranged and you are unable to have any relations with the Polish Government, which we shall continue to recognise as the government of the ally for whom we declared war upon Hitler, I should be very sorry indeed. The War Cabinet ask me to say that they would share this regret.

The last point underlined that the stance was not solely that of Churchill.[2] In 1944, Soviet forces were not willing to continue their offensive to relieve German pressure on the Poles who had risen in Warsaw, mainly because Stalin did not wish to see Polish nationalists in control of their capital, but, rather, his own protégés. This issue took precedence, in explaining the failure to help, over the serious logistical problems arising from the Soviet extensive advance that had already occurred. Stalin did not want political options, then or on other occasions, set by logistics or, indeed, by military problems.

The competing strategies for the post-war world also affected discussion of wartime strategy in the shape of the direction and speed of Allied advances. For all powers, planning for the post-war in part involved a determination to insert forces into areas judged of particular significance. This strategic dimension drew on a wide range of concerns. The prospect of post-war conflict played a role.

So also did the pursuit of existing territorial interests, in the shape of the return of authority to areas that had been lost. Thus, in late 1944, Australian forces continued their campaign in New Guinea where they had had territory before the war, while the Americans comparably focused on the Philippines, although other factors played a role in both, not least the Americans seeking to satisfy MacArthur's ego and to separate Japan from the natural resources of the East Indies. MacArthur left the Australians only a limited role in this stage of the war.[3]

Similarly, the creation of the South-East Asia Command in October 1943 was designed to give effect to Churchill's wish to recapture Britain's lost colonies and, specifically, to use amphibious operations to strike at the Japanese perimeter. In March 1944, he instructed the Chiefs of Staff to delay sending naval help to the Americans in the Pacific:

It is in the interest of Britain to pursue what may be termed the 'Bay of Bengal Strategy' at any rate for the next twelve months . . . All preparations will be made for amphibious action across the Bay of Bengal against the Malay Peninsula and the various island outposts by which it is defended, the ultimate objective being the reconquest of Singapore. A powerful British fleet will be built up based on Ceylon, Adu Atoll and East India ports.[4]

Churchill, however, was not alone. In September 1944, Admiral Sir Geoffrey Layton, Commander-in-Chief, Ceylon, wrote of:

the vital importance of our recapturing those parts of the Empire as far as possible ourselves. I would specially mention the recapture of Burma and its culmination in the recovery of Singapore by force of arms and not by waiting for it to be surrendered as part of any peace treaty . . . the immense effect this will have on our prestige in the Far East in post-war years. This and only this in my opinion will restore us to our former level in the eyes of the native population in these parts.

Admiral Louis Mountbatten, Supreme Commander of South-East Asia Command, strongly agreed.[5] British anxieties about empire in part reflected a growing awareness of a relative decline of British influence compared to an increasingly assertive United States and the Soviet Union. Alan Brooke commented in August 1944:

the Americans now feel that they possess the major forces at sea, on land and in the air, in addition to all the vast financial and industrial advantages which they have had from the start. In addition, they now look upon themselves no longer as the apprentices at war, but on the contrary as full blown professionals. As a result of all this, they are determined to have an ever increasing share in the running of the war in all its aspects.[6]

In the event, the fall of Rangoon on 3 May 1945 to British amphibious forces was followed by just such an emphasis, rather than that of continuing to campaign overland into southern Burma or Thailand against the large Japanese forces in the region; or, alternatively, of focusing on the invasion of Japan. Operation Zipper, an amphibious attack on western Malaya designed to lead to the recapture of Singapore, was planned for 9 September 1945, but was rendered unnecessary by the Japanese surrender.

Alongside the need to consider demobilisation, which had strategic, military and domestic aspects,[7] there were also domestic dimensions to the attempt to mould the post-war world, as with British debates over social policy, for example the Beveridge Report of 1944 on social welfare. So also with the Butler Education Act of 1944. These measures reflected a sense that the 'new order' that came from the war had to be domestic as well as international. In part, there was a clear strategy, that of keeping the working class from communism.

The geopolitics of the post-war world were at issue while it continued. There was much discussion in particular of the future political settlement for Eastern Europe and Germany, and consideration of how this settlement might affect wider international relations. In December 1942, Anthony Eden, the British Foreign Secretary, told the Commons: 'It will be the first and imperative duty of the United Nations to establish such a settlement as will make it impossible for Germany to dominate her neighbours by force of arms. It would be sheer folly to allow some non-Nazi government to be set up and then trust to luck.'

Henry Morgenthau Jr, the US Secretary of the Treasury, proposed in 1944 that Germany should be divided into two and deindustrialised. Robert Chapin's map 'German Jigsaw', a larger version of one published in *Time* on 21 February 1944, similarly proposed a division. The south was to be a separate state, while Pomerania, Silesia and East Prussia went to Poland, and Denmark also made gains. The future of the Saar and the Ruhr were left unclear. As with ideas of partition at the end of the First World War, notably from the French, this approach was not pursued in full: Germany again was to lose territory to neighbouring powers but, with the exception of the reversal of the 1938 union with Austria, was not to be partitioned into separate German states.

Aside from the risk of German *revanche*, the British Chiefs of Staff were, from 1944, actively considering post-war threats to the British world. This consideration included concern about the Soviet Union and with reference to Chinese *Guomindang* pressure on British India. The Chiefs of Staff Post-Hostilities Staff, for example, produced a map in 1944 about projected Soviet lines of advance against India, a map that looked back to nineteenth-century British anxieties about a Russian advance there. This map was consistent with the view in British India, which was still a centre of strategic perception and planning, that Baluchistan (and the Herat–Kandahar–Khojak–Bolan route) formed India's 'front porch', as opposed to the side entrance via Kabul and Khyber Pass. To the British in 1944, western Afghanistan also formed a kind of pivot on which a Soviet force might turn towards southern Iran and, more particularly, the bottleneck of the narrow Strait of Hormuz to the entrance of the Gulf, an area that remains of geopolitical significance.

Western geopoliticians also looked to a new global order and, in particular, to the future roles of the Soviet Union and

Germany. Halford Mackinder, Britain's leading geopolitician, published an essay, 'The Round World and the Winning of the Peace', in the American journal *Foreign Affairs* in 1943. In this, the Soviet Union was seen as an ally against any German resurgence, which, on the basis of 1919–39, was a major concern and, indeed, was mentioned both during the war and subsequently. Germany was to be restrained by obliging it to face the certainty of war on two fronts: with the Soviet Union in the heartland and, secondly, with sea power based on the United States, with Britain as a forward stronghold for the latter (as during the Second World War) and France as the defensible bridgehead on the Continent. Mackinder also saw the development of China as a cooperative project for the United States and Britain.

In contrast, Nicholas Spykman, a Dutch immigrant to the United States, who was head of the Institute for International Studies at Yale, argued that a Europe dominated by the Soviet Union would be as dangerous as one run by Germany. Instead, rebutting the powerful American isolationism of the interwar years, he pressed for interventionism as a key American means to furthering a Europe in which the United States played a role, which was presented as a crucial American interest. In his *The Geography of the Peace* (1944), Spykman developed a 'rimland thesis' as a form of forward protection for the United States. Taking forward Mackinder's pre-First World War views, expressed most famously in 1904, this approach looked towards the post-war geopolitics of 'containment' of the Soviet Union and, from 1949, of American membership of NATO.

The Axis powers, their governments, commentators and domestic critics, also looked to the post-war world. There was a melange, contradictory and often incoherent, of ideas and policies focusing on geopolitics, ethnicity, economics and military considerations. New transport routes were part of the process, and both Germany and Japan sought to develop them, harshly using forced labour to that end. These routes were regarded as strategic enablers, as with the projected German DG IV road across Ukraine between Lvov (Lviv) and Stalino (Donetsk). Heinrich Himmler's personal involvement led to the road being called the 'Highway of the SS'. A spur of the DG IV was to cross Crimea and bridge the Strait of Kerch to its east. From there, the road would continue into the Caucasus to serve German strategic interests in the area, notably gaining control of oil production, and also enabling the deployment of German forces near Turkey and Persia (Iran). Japan's plans included new transport links, not least into Burma, that were designed to lessen the need to rely on maritime routes, which were inherently more vulnerable.

Defeat brought other plans. The failed 20 July 1944 Bomb Plot against Hitler was based on the idea that a Germany without Hitler could end the war with Britain and the United States while fighting on against the Soviet Union. This strategy was based on a misreading of that of the Allies. However, the idea of counterweighting was a general one in Axis circles as well as that of their domestic opponents. Facing defeat, the Japanese leadership sought in 1944 to bring the Chinese Communists into play as a post-war counterweight to the United States and the Soviet Union.

FEAR

The Axis powers were overcome in 1945 but, by then, the campaigning in part strongly looked towards the Cold War. The victorious Soviet advance in Manchuria and Korea that August, a major defeat for the Japanese army, in practice also greatly weakened the American position in East Asia and affected the future struggle between the Communists and the *Guomindang* in China. Already, in mid-1944, planners for the British Chiefs of Staff had suggested a post-war reform of Germany and Japan, so that they could play a role against a Soviet Union whose ambitions in Eastern Europe were arousing growing concern. By May 1945, the British Joint Planning Staff, anticipating that Soviet resilience would prevent a speedy end to any future war with the Soviet Union, and that the conflict could only be waged as a total war, envisaged a fully mobilised American war economy, as well as German support. That month, General Penney noted the claim that the United States and Britain wished to build up Japan as a bulwark against the Soviet Union with which they would be at war relatively soon.[8] At that stage, Japan had not yet surrendered.

In turn, Soviet ambitions were designed to provide the Soviet Union with yet more territory that would lessen the risk of any attack comparable to 1941 or those during the Russian Civil War. Indeed, the strategic overhang of recent years was to be important to strategies during the Cold War. Arguments about Hitler's inherent hostility to Britain and the United States are less convincing than noting Stalin's hostility to both. Stalin's assumption that the alliance with Britain and the United States could not be sustained after the war, itself almost the definition of a self-fulfilling prophecy, left him determined to extend the Soviet sphere of influence, as well as to obtain direct territorial control through annexations. Stalin, who was paranoid (although, instructively, not about Hitler in 1939–41), exaggerated British commitment to the cause of hostility to communism, indeed discussing in the autumn of 1942 whether Churchill wanted a separate peace with Germany so as to leave the latter free to oppose the Soviet Union.[9]

The purging of Soviet diplomats who did not support a firm Communist line ensured that the only advice received by Stalin was that which treated the Western allies critically and with suspicion. This was the sole advice he wished to obtain. This attitude was a serious weakness for the Soviet Union, and for the anti-German cause more generally. It was a weakness, both in the short term, notably with the failure to appreciate the threat from Germany in 1941, and over the long term. Stalin's paranoia increased as a result of Hitler's attack in June 1941.

Soviet expansionism was in part defensive in ethos and intention. However, other elements were involved, including acquiring strategic points from which further gains could be pursued. They were creating an Eastern European cordon sanitaire as their barrier. The second rank were the Soviet non-Russian union republics arced around the western and southern frontiers of that part of the Russian Soviet Federative Socialist Republic west of the Ural Mountains.

That defensiveness did not preclude more distant Soviet ambitions across Western Europe. Thus, Stalin sought a Communist role in France and Italy. For that reason, Stalin was disturbed by the separate surrender of the German forces in northern Italy on 2 May 1945. Engineered by the Americans, Stalin saw this as a means employed to thwart the Italian Communists in the Resistance. This was unwelcome to him but, at the same time, Stalin was well aware of the impact of geography on Soviet expansionism. This meant that the French and Italian Communists would be largely reliant on their own efforts. In 1944, Stalin told the Greek Communist Party that it had to face 'geopolitical realities' and cooperate with the British. So also, later, with the limited prospects for Soviet intervention in the Portuguese revolutionary crisis of 1974–5.

The Soviets also had ambitions for the Far East. They wished to further the Communist cause in China, a strategy pursued from the 1920s and to supplant Japan as much as possible as the Far East empire. This meant expansionism into Manchuria, Korea, southern Sakhalin and the Kuril Islands; the last still a point of contention for Japan which fruitlessly pursues a territorial revision. Stalin, moreover, was ambitious for a Soviet role in the future of Japan itself; although in that he was to be thwarted by the Americans. The attacks launched by the Soviets on the Japanese Empire in August 1945 were motivated by post-war goals, such that, to a degree, this was the first conflict of the Cold War.

Stalin's attitude to the post-war world was very much geopolitical. Control over territory was a key objective. He did not have a comparable interest in the 'maritime commons' of the oceans, which were to be more important to the alternative nexus of power, one in which the United States replaced Britain. Stalin had planned to increase the navy pre-war, but did not have the opportunity to persist with this scheme during the Second World War. Moreover, Stalin's moves were not on the scale of the Soviet naval build-up that followed the successful American naval interdiction of Soviet shipping approaching Cuba during the Cuban Missile Crisis of 1962.

Irrespective of the role of Stalin, although affected by it, the 'Cold War' was vigorous because rivalries in the Resistance between (as well as among) Communists and non-Communists became more significant as the war moved against the Axis. This was true in particular of China, Greece, Albania, Yugoslavia, Poland, Italy and France. Moreover, Resistance activity affected, or at least potentially affected, the options for advancing Allied regular forces.

The wide-ranging nature of what would become the Cold War, within the umbrella of the Second World War, was seen with its possible spread to Spain in 1944 after the German occupation of France ended. In addition to Republican soldiers hidden in the mountains after defeat in the Spanish Civil War in 1939, the Franco government faced guerrillas operating from the French border in the Pyrenees. In October 1944, an invasion by about 2500 men was launched through the Val d'Aran. The Spanish Republican flag was flown over captured places, but the Francoists were ready and the invasion failed. There had been strikes in Spain the previous month, but there was little support there for the insurrection. In 1944, anxious to focus on Germany, both the United States and Britain pressed the new French government not to let the situation in Spain get out of hand. The remaining Republican rebels were defeated by the Franco government in the late 1940s and early 1950s. In most states, the rivalry between Communists and non-Communists was far more bloody.

THE FUTURE OF EMPIRE

A replacement of the United States by Britain was not just a matter of relative power because there were fundamental divisions between Britain and the United States over the future of the empire. The Roosevelt administration was opposed to colonial rule (although not by the United States in the Pacific) and, instead, in favour of a system of 'trusteeship' as a prelude to independence. Prior to the war, the Americans had already promised to give the Philippines its independence, and were to do so in 1946.

Roosevelt pressed Churchill on the status of both Hong Kong (which he wanted returned to China) and India, and British officials were made aware of a fundamental contradiction in attitudes. In 1943, at the Tehran Conference, Roosevelt told Churchill that Britain had to adjust to a 'new period' in global history and turn its back on '400 years of acquisitive blood in your veins'.[10] That October, *Life* declared 'Of one thing we are sure. Americans are not fighting to protect the British Empire.' Churchill, in contrast, was at pains to emphasise his opposition to losses, writing to Roosevelt in March 1944:

> Thank you very much for your assurance about no sheep's eyes at our oil fields in Iran and Iraq. Let me reciprocate by giving you the fullest assurances that we have no thought of trying to horn in upon your interests or property in Saudi Arabia . . . Great Britain seeks no advantage, territorial or otherwise, as the result of the war. On the other hand she will not be deprived of anything which rightly belongs to her.[11]

In practice, the 'destroyers for bases' deal of 1940, under which British bases in the New World had been transferred for ninety-nine years to the United States in return for warships, represented just such a diminution, and was seen in that light.

Indeed, American opposition to imperial preference, the commercial adhesive of the British Empire, was a major challenge. Article seven of the Lend-Lease agreement of 1942 stipulated the eventual end of such preference, and this strategy of opening up the British Empire was followed up as a result of the financial loan from the United States that Britain was obliged to seek after the close of the war.

The two powers competed over Middle Eastern oil, with the United States successfully developing links with Saudi Arabia, and over economic interests elsewhere. There was also strong American support for a Jewish state in British-ruled Palestine, a policy opposed by Anthony Eden, the British Foreign Secretary, because of concern about Arab views, both there and elsewhere.

Roosevelt's opposition to key aspects of British policy was shared by significant advisers, such as Sumner Welles, Under Secretary of State from 1937 until 1943, and was also echoed in public, notably, but not only, by isolationist or quasi-isolationist opinion.

Indeed, American dominance of the Anglo-American alliance had important implications for the British Empire, as there was a marked increase in the American military presence in the dominions, the colonies and the areas of imperial influence. This presence was a matter not only of units and bases, but also of defence planning. There was tension, not least over the American role in the south-west Pacific, but the war ended with closer strategic relations between the United States and both Australia and Canada. At the same time, Britain only won security and success as part of an alliance system. In particular, the American 'Germany First' policy was of great value to Britain.

Roosevelt was certainly not keen on the British extending their empire, for example, as Churchill considered, at the expense of Thailand in the Kra Isthmus, which would have strengthened Malaya's northern defences, removing a problem encountered with repelling the Japanese attack in December 1941. Roosevelt's opposition to French and Dutch imperialism in Asia was also very strong. He mistrusted the French Empire even more than the British one, which was ironic as, by 1954, President Eisenhower was unsuccessfully pressing the French to stay in Indo-China in order to prevent a Communist takeover.

In Europe and the Mediterranean, territorial boundaries changed less in 1945 than in 1918–23 or 1940–1. Nevertheless, as a result of the war, Italy lost its overseas empire, and there was to be no real revanchist desire to regain this empire. There was, however, to be a large-scale ethnic transformation from

1945, with Germans, Italians, Poles and others forced to move in substantial numbers as frontiers were redrawn.

A NEW WORLD ORDER

American and British negotiators in the Arcadia Conference of 22 December 1941–14 January 1942, taking forward the Atlantic Charter of post-war goals agreed by Churchill and Roosevelt on 9–12 August 1941, drew up a statement of war aims called the United Nations Declaration. This agreement for joint support was the first official use of the term United Nations, which rapidly entered into common parlance. The Declaration was signed by the leading Allied powers, and in due course by other Allied nations. On 17 October–11 November 1943, a conference of Allied foreign ministers, meeting in Moscow, agreed to establish a European Advisory Council of senior officials, based in London, in order to begin serious post-war planning. The Soviet agreement to join the United Nations was important. So also, as an attempt to provide a more settled basis for international relations, was the decision to establish an international court and the reversal of German annexations. Reversal of Japanese annexations followed in the Sextant Conference on 22–6 November held in Cairo.

The foreign ministers at Moscow also signed a declaration committing their states to post-war cooperation. In practice, the world order being devised was increasingly seen in an American light. This was because of the work by the Americans on a system and infrastructure for a post-war world. Alongside what was to become the United Nations and aligned to discussions at the Bretton Woods Conference, there was work on what was to become the World Bank, the International Monetary Fund and the General Agreement on Trade and Tariffs. Agreeing with

Stalin that any crisis of capitalism was destabilising, although with very different conclusions, the Americans advocated a move beyond the economic remedies of the 1930s, namely protectionism and 'beggar-my-neighbour' currency devaluations, both of which challenged American economic interests.

The United Nations Conference on International Organization, held in San Francisco on 25 April–26 June 1945, was the inaugural meeting of the United Nations. Attended by delegates from fifty Allied states, the conference agreed a United Nations Security Charter. The Security Council, the executive of the United Nations, was to consist of five permanent (United States, Soviet Union, Britain, France and China) and six temporary members; its first meeting was held in London on 17 January 1946.

The San Francisco conference, however, also indicated serious tensions within the alliance, notably between the United States and the Soviet Union. The former was unwilling to accept the Soviet claim that the Moscow-supported Polish government was independent. As a result, the Polish seat was left vacant.

To an understandable degree, Germany was the central focus of plans for the new world order. In part, this reflected the cause of the war, with no comparison to the role of Austria-Hungary in 1914 that could lessen the focus on Germany. However, military circumstances were also crucial: the dominance of most of Eastern Europe by Soviet forces acted as a constraint, as did America's victory over Japan. More significantly, the Allied forces all occupied parts of Germany, and it was necessary to manage this relationship. In doing so, occupation, which had been agreed by the United States and Britain in the Octagon Conference of 12–16 September 1944, was seen as a way to transform Germany so that it ceased to be a threat to world peace.

The Yalta Conference in February 1945 agreed on four occupation zones in Germany, and these were delimited in the Potsdam Conference after the war in Germany ended. These zones did not simply reflect the consequences of the campaigning. In return for the United States, Britain and France gaining zones in what became the enclave of West Berlin, the Americans pulled back from territory occupied in what became the Soviet zone and eventually East Germany, for example Leipzig, which the Americans had seized on 19 April. So also in western Czechoslovakia, where the Americans had liberated Pilsen and could have pressed on for Prague. These withdrawals ensured that the Soviets would have less far to advance in the event of war with the Western powers, but the United States alone had the atomic bomb at this juncture.

At Potsdam, the 5Ds were also agreed for Germany: disarmament, denazification, decartelisation, democratisation and decentralisation. Moreover, the definition of Germany's external borders marked a major change in the situation in Eastern Europe, with Poland's frontiers moved far to the west, to the benefit of the Soviet Union and to the loss of Germany. Ironically, this led to a post-Soviet situation in which Ukraine, Belarus and Lithuania were larger than they would otherwise have been. This was an instance of the degree to which the long-term consequences of the peace settlement were often very different to the situation that had been anticipated; and the long-term was in play within a half-century of 1945.

8

Post-war Dissension
and Speculations

DISSENSION

Kurdish fighters 'didn't help us in the Second World War, they didn't help us with Normandy'. President Donald Trump's remark at a news conference on 10 October 2019 indicated how the war, accurately or misleadingly, serves as a lodestar of justification and identification. Indeed, the strategic choices, real, apparent or imagined, of the war played a major role in post-war politics. This was notably so during the Cold War from 1945 to 1989, when many from the wartime generation were active in politics, for example Charles de Gaulle, French President from 1958 to 1969, and George H. W. Bush, American President from 1989 to 1993. This political role has remained the case since, as the war has been employed as a theme and lesson in modern political identities. These choices also played a part in the related subjects of geopolitics and international relations.

The prominent role of the Second World War in the historical narratives of many modern states, and in the recovered memory of their publics, helps ensure that controversies over the war attract great and continuing attention. Indeed, the war played a central role in the public history of all the former combatants. Victors sought validation from accounts of this victory, although this validation had different meanings in a democracy such as Britain, where the war leader could be removed in an election, as Churchill was in 1945 (returning in 1951–5), compared to the Soviet Union where Stalin continued in murderous power until his death in 1953.

In Britain, the wars, and their strategic issues, were diffused, and defused, as a wider social memory with an emphasis on national cohesion, although what that meant in practice remained controversial. As late as October 2019, a British anti-EU group, Leave.eu, produced an image of Germany's Chancellor, Angela Merkel, on social media with the caption 'We didn't win two world wars to be pushed around by a Kraut' [German], only to apologise the following morning. From the other political direction, on 27 October 2019, the *Sunday Mirror* urged the public not to give in to Boris Johnson, the Conservative Prime Minister, just because it was tired of Brexit, claiming that it would be like saying in 1944 that 'we couldn't be bothered with D-Day because the Second World War was getting tiresome'. Johnson, a biographer of Churchill, was fond of making references to the war.

In contrast, in the Soviet Union, there was a more political focus on the role of the Communist state under Stalin in winning the 'Second Great Patriotic War', the first being that of 1812 against Napoleon in which the Soviet Union had not been involved. The Second World War was seen by the Soviet state and its supporters in the West as a vindication of the role of the Communist Party and a justification of its dictatorial control. On behalf of the post-Soviet Russian government, that tradition was to be continued under Vladimir Putin. The war, which has an almost religious role in Russian identity and memorialisation, was an iconic period of heroism for Putin, and Victory Day continues to be a major annual occasion, one in which modern weaponry is rolled out in Moscow to display sustained prowess.

Wartime alignments were a major cause of post-war controversy, as guilt and responsibility were contested. Thus, the 1939 Nazi–Soviet Pact became an aspect both of the propaganda of the Second World War and of that of the Cold War. After 1941, the pact was written out of the Soviet historical account, and that of Communist parties and leaders who had praised it, such as Mao Zedong of China. In so far as it was officially discussed, the pact was presented benignly as an opportunity to gain time and space to resist German attack, which was not, in fact, Stalin's prime intention when he negotiated it. Instead, he wanted to gain an opportunity for expansion.

In contrast, the pact was referred to by external and internal critics of the Soviet system. For example, the fortieth anniversary of the pact in 1989 was marked by opponents in the Baltic republics as it had provided the Soviet Union with the opportunity to seize these states in 1940. The pact has never had a resonance in the West comparable to the Munich agreement of 1938; and Appeasement and Munich have proven far more significant images and terms in public debate, both being part of an international lexicon of complaint. However, far from being a tactical consequence of Appeasement, the Nazi–Soviet Pact showed much about the logic, as well as the methods, of Soviet foreign policy. Moreover, there is no inherent reason why the pact should be regarded as less significant than the Munich agreement, which did not last for as long. The pact indeed was more important, since both sides took advantage of the result, which was not the case with the Munich agreement. This point underlines the active role of the Soviet Union in the early stages of the war, one that is underplayed because the Soviet invasion of Poland did not lead to Britain and France declaring war. The contrast in views also reflects the tension between Western and Eastern European views of the war, a tension that has been present from the outset, although with varying cross-currents.

The role of Soviet expansion in 1939–40 and anew in 1944–9 came to the fore as non-Communist Eastern European views were foregrounded after the fall of the Communist bloc and the end of the Soviet system in 1989–91. These views repeatedly presented the Soviets as akin to the Germans, and therefore offered distinctive views on the particular stages of the war. In particular, there was criticism about the eventual settlement. 'One of the greatest wrongs of history,' was President George W. Bush's 2005 description of the Yalta Conference and the allocation of Eastern Europe to the Soviets. At the time, however, the circumstances of the moment were crucial. 'I didn't say the result was good . . . it was the best I could do,' said Roosevelt after Yalta, a conference that took place five months before the atom bomb was even tested. American generals insisted that they needed Soviet help to invade Japan, and the Soviets anyway were in control of Eastern Europe.

Linked to this presentation of the Soviet Union, although not coterminous with it, there was the positive re-evaluation by some of those who had collaborated with the Third Reich, and notably so in Romania, Slovakia and Croatia. In contrast, from the Polish perspective, Poland was an ally betrayed by Britain and the United States in 1944–5 to the interests of the Soviet Union, as it had been betrayed by a lack of help from Britain and France in 1939–40; an approach that, as a tangential point, tended to overlook Poland's role in participating in the carve-up of Czechoslovakia as a result of Munich, gaining areas disputed after the First World War. Poland, however, was certainly an ally that it was difficult to assist in either 1939–40 or 1944–5. This was essentially due to Soviet policy and to distance. The latter was a key aspect of the limited Allied capability for action, but far from the only one.

There was also criticism of the Americans and British for handing over to the Soviets those they captured who had been Soviet nationals before the 1939 pact. This had been agreed at the Yalta Conference. Apart from the many killed at once, those handed over were sent to the *gulags*, described as traitors and counter-revolution activists, and as far as is known, nobody came out alive. They were usually sentenced to thirty years but many, subsequently, had that sentence increased. The criticism of the British and Americans also relates to their handing over former Soviet prisoners of war taken by the Germans and freed by the Western Allies; they too were sentenced to thirty years in the *gulags* (although many survived this) or killed. Those who served in the German army received the same punishment. As Alexander Solzhenitsyn later noted: 'this was wonderful in Stalin, this impartial equanimity, for both the innocent and the guilty were treated in the same way'.

The post-Soviet era re-evaluation was not accepted by all, and led to domestic and international contention. As a consequence, the strategic course of the war was reopened for debate across Eastern Europe. The extent to which this debate influenced wider perspectives of the war varied greatly and, again, politics as well as national perspectives played a role. The overall consequence was a marked lessening of any agreed view of the war as a whole. For example, the prominent essay in *The Times* of 14 September 2019, 'The two Britains that exasperate and enchant the rest of the world', by Neil MacGregor, a Germanophile, condemned Britain and the United States for exaggerating their role and downplaying that of the Soviet Union, without mentioning the Nazi–Soviet Pact or the Anglo-American role against Japan. Paradoxically, this approach implied that Britain should have done more to help Poland in 1939 and 1944, but without underlining that this would have entailed conflict with the Soviet Union, a point that tends to be neglected when there is critical discussion of Appeasement as widely practised.

A different account was offered by Baiba Braže, Latvian ambassador in London, in the September/October 2019 issue of the conservative British periodical *Standpoint*:

> two authoritarian regimes – Stalin's USSR and Hitler's Nazi Germany – concluded a pact dividing Europe thus set the stage for the Second World War. Soviet tanks rolled into my country annexing the Baltic States. The USSR invaded Finland and partitioned Poland with the Nazis.
>
> It is not enough to know the facts about the past; what matters is how we interpret them, and the meaning we give them today. They influence our decisions today and tomorrow. The Russian Foreign Ministry has lately renewed its efforts trying to justify Soviet collaboration with Nazi Germany. This cannot fail to cause alarm in the whole world.
>
> The Euroatlantic security space is indivisible. Aggression against one country threatens everyone who wants to live in peace.[1]

As with so much about the present discussion, there was a degree of misdirection here, because the Baltic republics suffered from a lack of unity in 1938–40. Moreover, Lithuania, threatened by Poland with invasion in 1938, turned to Germany, while, in 1939, Latvia also looked to Germany. Similarly, today, there is a lack of unity, and a habit of blaming outsiders, for the weakness in their response to the Soviet Union.

There has not been a comparable change in East Asia, as there has been no political revolution in the states there similar to that in the Soviet bloc in 1989–91. Thus, the war with Japan continues to be crucial to the legitimation pursued by the Communist Party in China as it emphasises its own success in opposing Japan, as opposed to the failure of the *Guomindang*.[2] This factor is also held up today as a reason why Taiwan and South Korea should follow the Chinese lead against Japan; and thus is an element in the cultural politics underlying the difficulties that the United States has in constructing an anti-Chinese security system that would incorporate these powers.

Controversies are far from simply over alignments and related strategy: they play a role in debates that involve other points at issue. This can be seen in the debates over bombing campaigns against Germany and Japan. Ethical issues were pushed to the fore in these controversies, and continue to be, alongside those tackling the question of the value of bombing to the war effort. The ethical aspect ensured that criticism of the wartime bombing drew energy from successive campaigns against bombing after 1945, notably at the time of the Vietnam War. Opposition to area bombing, and to bombing that involved civilian casualties, played a major role in this cultural shift. Linked to this shift came academic assessments initially suggesting that the wartime bombing had lacked effectiveness. This was notably the case with the British official history, including Charles Webster and Noble Frankland's *The Strategic Air Offensive against Germany, 1939–1945* (1961).

The strategic debate also became part of a German presentation of themselves as victims, one that sometimes coexisted with an acceptance of responsibility. A focus on the Allied bombing provided a way for Germans to offer what they saw as an acceptable history. Unfortunately, many (although not all) Germans are disinclined to consider Germany's wartime role in beginning terror bombing (and then crying foul when the other side used the same technique but more effectively), as well as Germany's willingness in 1944–5 to use rockets fired simply against civilian targets. The V-1s and V-2s were unguided terror weapons that had no military use, but were employed in order to spread terror in civilians. Nor does the vicious nature of the wartime German state always receive adequate attention, nor the extent to which it had enjoyed popular support.

The bombing can also be misleadingly presented as a form of equivalence by all the powers, as when I visited Dresden in September 2019. This approach ignores the wider context of the bombing,[3] and perpetuates the German attempt, prominently seen in 2014 with the centenary of the First World War, to sink the responsibility of one state beneath the general fault of all. There are parallels with German discussion of the forcible expulsion of German civilians from Eastern Europe in the last stages of the war and after its completion; as well as complaints about outrages by Soviet troops.

So also with the dropping of atom bombs on Japan in 1945. Critics, many on the American left, argued that this was an early stage in the Cold War, both to show the Soviet Union the extent of American strength – in particular a vital counter on Soviet numbers on land – and to ensure that Japan could be defeated without the Soviets playing a major role. This may have been a factor, although there is clearly a political agenda behind this criticism. However, there seems little doubt that the prime use of the bombs was to ensure a rapid surrender that obviated the need for a costly (and destructive) invasion of Japan and, linked to that, a lengthy continuation of the conflict. Such a surrender would include the large Japanese forces in China and South-east Asia, which otherwise would have been difficult to defeat.

Japanese complaints about the bombs serve to direct attention from wartime aggression and cruelty.

Other criticisms can be addressed. For example, the policy of unconditional surrender was to be condemned by some commentators as making it difficult to encourage German resistance to Hitler. This was seen as undermining the chance for a shorter war, as lessening the options for German resistance to Hitler, and as making difficult the resolution of the conflict in the shape of a post-war anti-Soviet alliance of the United States, Britain and Germany. This longstanding condemnation, however, is misplaced. Unconditional surrender was an accurate response to Allied strategic goals, and to the politics of German (and Japanese) power during the war. The Allies explicitly sought to destroy not only the Nazi regime and Nazism, but also Prussian militarism and the potential for Germany to cause trouble anew, with parallel goals as far as Japan was concerned. These aims, which contrasted with the far more limited Allied achievement in the aftermath of the First World War and drew on lessons from the subsequent rise of Hitler, were seen as requiring the occupation of all of Germany, the destruction of the Nazi regime and the dismantling of the German military; with again an equivalent for Japan. To ensure this outcome, unconditional surrender appeared necessary, and this conclusion still appears well-founded. The myths of German power propagated by Hitler had to be destroyed; as indeed they were, not only by the Allies, but also as a consequence of Hitler's actions, although there has recently been a disturbing revival of neo-Nazi arguments in Germany.

A separate established narrative was that European unification was a reaction against the horrors of the Second World War, and that this factor motivated a successful determination to ensure that there were no other wars. However, aside from underplaying the major role of NATO and the Soviet Union in preventing any subsequent German *revanche*, as well as war, that narrative led to a downplaying of the extent and impact of wartime cooperation within the new German empire, notably between Germany and Vichy France, but also with elements in the Benelux countries. Moreover, aside from that collaboration, other themes of European cooperation that played a role in the foundation and development of what became the European Union looked back to older twentieth-century movements, notably anti-communism, especially Catholic anti-communism, and the social welfarism of this policy with its attempt to win over the working class.

From this perspective, the war was simply a stage, albeit an increasingly important one, in the development of understandings and practices of European identity; a situation also seen, albeit differently, in Asia with anti-Western strategies. Advancing such understandings was an aspect of Axis wartime politics, with the key strategic dimension being that of winning support.

More generally, after 1945, the war became a keynote point of reference, one held up as a warning to the present, as by the journalist Bret Stephens in the *New York Times* on 30 August 2019 when castigating modern-day ideology and intolerance.[4] Yet, doing so underplayed the variety of lessons that could be drawn from the war. Indeed, the war was used to support every political and military strategy and lesson on offer. In part, there was a failure to note both this and the extent to which the course and consequences of the conflict helped determine these lessons.

COUNTERFACTUAL SPECULATIONS

Hypotheticals or counterfactuals, the 'what-ifs?' of history, frequently come into play for this war. Before, during and after the war, alternative outcomes played a major role in the discussion of strategy. These outcomes were both private and public, military and non-military. The private ones ranged from leaders, such as Hitler speculating in 1945 about the possible consequences of the death of Roosevelt, to the vast numbers, military and civilian, who made up the societies of the combatants and indeed occupied populations. Alternative outcomes, past, present and future, played a significant role in their grasp of the realities affecting them, in their consideration of options and in their discussion of these points in so far as that was possible, let alone prudent.

Concern about such speculations played a role in the commitment by governments to gauge public opinion and to influence it. Each process was pursued, not only for the state in question, but also for the evaluation of allies, opponents and neutrals. A belief in the significance of public opinion owed much to the defeat of Germany in 1918, which Hitler attributed to a collapse on the Home Front in part stemming from British propaganda. This belief in the role of public opinion was greatly enhanced by contemporary explanations of the sudden fall of France in 1940, an outcome so radically different to the experience of the previous world war that it led to speculation about a very different context.

Morale was not only a matter of the public. There was more particularly the morale of the governing group, as in France and, differently in the event, Britain in May–June 1940. How best to respond to failure, and in a rapidly changing context, invited the question of alternatives. Already dismayed by the unexpected start of Barbarossa, Stalin apparently had a nervous collapse of will on 28–30 June 1941, when the advancing Germans reached Minsk, and there was possibly consideration on his part of a settlement with Germany, similar to the Treaty of Brest-Litovsk accepted by Lenin in 1918. Indeed, this treaty might have been used to vindicate such an agreement, underlining the degree to which the past, or at least the presentation of the past, creates options that help define and explain later choices. As another turning point, there was also a panic in Moscow in mid-October 1941; but, although Stalin left for Kuibyshev, where he had a meeting with Sir Stafford Cripps, the British ambassador, on 23 October, the ruthless NKVD secret police were used to prevent anarchy and to restore order. This again invites counterfactual speculation. The stability of the Soviet regime was certainly a key element, but one that German strategy could not determine.

Placing counterfactualism in the context of morale helps ensure that it is not treated as a marginal, even foolish, speculation and activity. So also does a treatment of counterfactualism in light of the military planning of the period. There is a different chronology, and therefore perspective, at play compared to that of subsequently looking backwards; but the common theme is that of uncertainty and, in particular, of the non-linear character of developments and, therefore, history. This non-linear approach is valuable because it is a counterpart to that of suggesting that the tendency to focus on a quantitative analysis of the war, in the shape of the resources available to the two sides, is misleading. That tendency underplays qualitative factors at each level. These are varied and overlapped, but notable ones are unit cohesion at the tactical level; combined arms skill and leadership at the operational level; and an adroit reading of practicalities, and of the elements necessary to bridge the divide from goals to planning, at the strategic level. Indeed, counterfactualism is explicit in strategy because it entails choice between alternatives; and that process of choice involves assessing possible outcomes. So also at the operational and tactical levels.

The order in which counterfactuals are approached entails implicit judgements of significance. More appropriate at the outset is returning consideration to the counterfactuals that were envisaged by contemporaries. The meteorite that hit the western Pacific in December 1941, creating a tsunami destroying the Japanese fleet *en route* to Pearl Harbor, leading also to the abandonment of the other planned Japanese attacks, is not an impossible counterfactual, but was not considered at the time, and was so unlikely that it is not worth envisaging. It is more appropriate to consider a 'normal' alternative in the shape of the Japanese use of the northern route of Pearl Harbor. This route often had very bad weather and could easily have entailed the fleet running into a devastating storm, as happened to the Americans in 1945, but only after the war ended. As another counterfactual, an American submarine on picket duty might have spotted the Japanese invasion fleet on 6 December 1941. As far as storms are concerned, 18 June 1944 saw a terrible storm in the English Channel, which would have hit the Allied invasion of Normandy hard had it been mounted on 17 June, the next date that was judged convenient after 6 June, a date that itself was nearly postponed because of anxieties about the weather. The 18 June storm led to a closure of the Channel for three days.

The possibility that Japan would not attack the United States, with which there were negotiations, is worthy of attention because the range of options in 1941 was far from fixed. Indeed, the Japanese could have attacked the British and Dutch colonial empires without attacking America; and this option was considered, which is a key element in counterfactualism. Their ability to attack China without other powers intervening showed how the war could be sectionalised. So also with Japanese–Soviet neutrality. In part, therefore, counterfactualism is an exercise in assessing choices that were made by considering their causes, course and consequences in the light of other variables. So, for example, one may consider the possibility of war in 1938 over Czechoslovakia. The entire range of wartime activity is open to counterfactual speculation, and has launched many books and millions of conversations. All of such speculation is potentially of strategic significance because differing capabilities and outcomes, in terms of tactics, operational considerations and weaponry, could all have influenced strategic possibilities and, therefore, the causes, content and consequences of planning.

Discussion of equipment and weaponry, a key element of capability, risks adopting a potentially misleading 'magic bullet' account, as with the Anglo-American failure to develop signals interception by means of Enigma (Ultra) and Magic data, or the earlier development by Germany of jet fighters or improved submarines. Alongside an enthusiastic interest in new technology, notably aircraft, the Nazi engagement with the occult encouraged a sense that wonder weapons could offer a quasi-magical solution. At the same time, just such an outcome was seen with the American development and use in 1945 of nuclear bombs. These certainly totally altered equations of power and outcome routes. If, for example, the invasion of Normandy had failed in June 1944, then the first atom bomb could have been dropped on Berlin, decapitating the German system by killing Hitler.

This possibility opens up the issue of multiple, and thus interacting as well as conflicting, counterfactuals, and with varying timescales. In this perspective, counterfactuals can cascade down, although it is mistaken to vary an original event and then assume a fixed pattern of consequences. The invasion of Normandy was a risk, albeit far less of one by June 1944 than if mounted a year earlier, let alone in November 1942. Possession and use earlier of an atom bomb might have avoided the need for the risk. At the same time, a Germany still in control of most of Europe might well have responded to an atom bomb by going on fighting. So much would have depended on the number of available Allied bombs, which was low originally, and on whether the first had killed Hitler. The chance of the latter would have been lessened had he been, as he was for much of the period, in the Wolf's Lair, as that would have increased the distance necessary for any flight, and in a period prior to mid-air refuelling. There was also the serious problem posed by German aerial interception, which remained a major issue throughout the war and a serious problem until the spring of 1944. Thus, 'strategic counterfactuals', in the shape of the use of nuclear weaponry against Germany, rapidly became intertwined with operational, and even tactical, questions. There were also the attempts by Germany and Japan to produce their own nuclear bombs, although these lacked the resource support provided in the United States.

This intertwining with operational and even tactical questions is less necessarily the case if we are considering 'strategic counterfactuals' in the shape of the determination of the powers to fight on. The knowledge that all the major states still independent after June 1940 did so until total victory or defeat should not deter us from asking serious questions about persistence. The date June 1940 refers, of course, to the collapse of France. Its army was defeated and the country overrun; but the French navy and the second largest empire in the world were still free of German control, and France's ability to fight on in that respect was enhanced by alliance with Britain, which, albeit with its own army defeated in France, had the largest navy and empire in the world. However, there was a lack of sufficient shipping to evacuate the French army to Algiers, not least in the face of rapidly advancing German forces and complete German air superiority. The panic affecting millions of French civilians was also pertinent, as military personnel had families and going to North Africa would be damning relatives to what was then commonly believed to be a merciless enemy.

Without getting drawn for the moment on the prospect of France fighting on in 1940, as it had done, but only for several months, in 1870–1, its surrender underlined the unpredictable political consequences. So also did the fall of Mussolini in 1943. Thus, to assume that this would not definitely happen for other powers, if defeated, would have been unrealistic. Moreover, the 20 July Bomb Plot of 1944, like the earlier Hess mission in 1941, underlined the uncertainty of the situation at the very top in Germany. So also with the fall of Tōjō and, at a lesser scale, governmental changes in Hungary, Romania and Thailand, all in 1944.

None of this was seen with the 'Big Three' Allies, but the purges of 1937 indicated the potential instability of the Soviet Union, an instability that troubled a paranoid Stalin. Moreover, born in 1878, Stalin was not well, and his busy work schedule increased the pressure on him. Information about his health was classified, but he apparently suffered from neurasthenia and angina, as well as the after-effects of surgery in 1921. In 1944, he was particularly unwell. Churchill also had health problems, while those of Roosevelt, already an issue going into the 1944 presidential election, killed him soon after in early 1945. All three men smoked heavily.

To assume that a change at the top might not affect policy would have flown in the face of the suppositions of German, Japanese and, even, Soviet politics. The *führer* (leader) concept and practice of the Nazis encouraged a focus on the attitudes of other leaders, and on changing or persuading them.

In the case of Stalin, counterfactual speculation has addressed the likely consequences of his replacement, for example by

Levrentiy Beria or Georgy Malenkov. Leaving aside the uncertainty as to whom would have emerged, and also whether they would have been able to sustain their position (which proved a major issue in 1953–7 after Stalin's eventual death), and notably so in the difficult circumstances of wartime, the prospect of any successor changing policy would in part have depended on a German willingness to accept peace with the Soviet Union. Despite attempts to argue that Hitler was focused on enmity towards Britain and the United States, such a willingness does not appear plausible. Yet, such a peace was a possibility at the time, as the Western Allies knew, and this is not simply a counterfactual with the benefit of hindsight.

As far as a change in American policy was concerned, the earlier death of Roosevelt or his electoral defeat were both possible, but would probably not have affected strategy. The Republicans had moved beyond their isolationism in 1940, while there was no effective support within the Democrats for another line. 'Japan First' had not gathered traction. Although backed by some on the right, Douglas MacArthur, a candidate for the Republican nomination for President in 1944, failed to win much support. American successes in both Europe and the Pacific in mid-late 1944 encouraged a sense that both 'Germany First' and 'Japan First' could be pursued successfully, as was indeed the case in 1944–5. It is worth considering the changes that could have occurred, but there is nothing to suggest that they would have been substantial.

Churchill is a different case, because a contrasting tendency and strategy were on offer in 1940 as the Battle of France went totally wrong. At present, there is not much favour in academic circles for the 'Great Man' approach to history, and Churchill, notably over the Government of India Act in 1935, as well as over the Bengal Famine, has been strongly attacked. This is an aspect of a highly partisan approach to British history that can be seen as a central aspect of modern 'culture wars'. Yet, Churchill is an instance in which an individual clearly made a difference, and most especially so in May–July 1940. Both the man, and what he could be seen to represent, were significant, and they were important to the definition of a new strategy in 1940 and to the ability to sustain it, not least in the face of failure.[5]

Having been driven from the Continent, an experience that was outside the strategic experience of the British since the French had driven them out in 1796, Churchill had to devise a new approach that matched his political determination. The 'indirect approach' provided the opportunity, with campaigning against Vichy France and Italy, and calling on naval strength, amphibious capability and the support of the empire. This strategy could not defeat Germany, but it kept Britain in the war as an active participant, able, as with the successful air attack on the Italian warships in harbour in Taranto in November 1940, to provide morale-lifting victories.

As a consequence, it is reasonable to ask what would have happened had Churchill fallen or, indeed, not been chosen in the first place. American entry into the war would have been a different prospect had there not been a strong leader in Britain. The scenario of Churchill's fall possibly becomes of diminishing significance once the war had broadened out in December 1941 to include the United States, as that provided a clear possibility of success for any prime minister. Churchill's leadership was still under challenge, however, as was shown by the parliamentary and other criticisms of the summer and autumn of 1942. Had he fallen then, then it is unclear how strategy would have developed. The exigencies of Britain's position, notably in the Mediterranean, would certainly have encouraged campaigning there. At the same time, Churchill's misguided wish to advance into the Aegean and the Balkans, in order to thwart the Soviets, might not have been matched. A replacement for Churchill, whether Clement Attlee, the Labour leader and Deputy Prime Minister, Sir Stafford Cripps, the left-wing Leader of the House of Commons, or another Conservative, would not have had his prestige or influence with Roosevelt and Stalin; and this might well have affected both British views and Allied strategy as a whole. In practice, Attlee had a good relationship with Churchill.[6]

At the same time, Churchill's vigorous opposition to pressure from Roosevelt and Stalin for a Second Front in France in 1943 rested on objective considerations about preparedness and capability. Stalin was prepared to ignore those, not least because he did not really understand the impact on such an operation of considerations such as control of the Atlantic and of the air. However, Roosevelt was in a different position. The geography of air power, in the shape of fighter cover, defined the northward extent of the invasion zone considered possible for mainland Italy in September 1943, while, although Torch, Sicily, Salerno and Anzio all indicated the possibility of an earlier amphibious attack on France that was far larger in scale than the Dieppe operation, in each case, Normandy, the target in France, was far more exposed; and, even so, there were major difficulties in the Salerno and Anzio operations, and against opposition that was weaker than was to be deployed by the Germans in Normandy. This counterfactual about the timing of the Second Front has been, can be and will be batted back and forth. Churchill's survival was part of the equation, but his position was also convenient for Americans who had doubts about a Second Front in 1943 and, still more, 1942.

Churchill's death or his fall in 1944 or 1945, maybe in the event of the failure of D-Day, is another counterfactual. Hitler hoped for such a change, but there is scant evidence that it would have led to a significant alteration in British strategy. There might well have been differences, notably over the sequencing of operations against Japan, had Churchill died. However, Britain would have continued to fight, while the major drift towards an alliance in which Britain was the third most significant power was already underway.

Whatever the leadership, war involves conflict. The imponderables involved ensured that, in a fast-changing context, it was unclear how to measure strength and capability, and how to plan action accordingly. In general, the intervention of weaponry in strategic consideration was less decisive than it was in the case of aerial warfare. Hitler made much of wonder weapons, notably tanks and rockets, but most strategists focused on the use of existing systems, albeit with enhancements, rather than on transformations. That focus encouraged strategic assumptions about the value of reducing the output of enemy weaponry. These were particularly seen with the Allies as, alongside the threat to morale, they provided a logic to the use of strategic air power. Yet, the Axis also employed these assumptions, as when arguing for air and naval campaigns against Britain. Indeed, resource-based assessments of capability encouraged such considerations of strategic posture. As aircraft employed for one purpose, such as strategic bombing, could not be used at the same time for another, such as the defence of maritime trade – which was a trade-off in dispute in Britain in 1942–3 – the room for such speculation both came to the fore and was important in prioritisation.

During the war, speculation was employed to aid planning. Strategists, for example, were asked what damage might be inflicted upon the German economy if the Allies managed to knock out the entire German railway system, which, indeed, was hit hard.[7] So also with the bombing of German synthetic oil plants. Such discussion looked towards post-war debates about the overall effectiveness of the Allied air offensive. A relevant counterfactual relates to the major efforts the Germans devoted to anti-aircraft defence, notably fighter aircraft and anti-aircraft guns. These might otherwise have played a role on the front lines. Alongside fixed defences, many of the military assets employed by the Germans in air defence were readily transferable and, for that reason, their commitment to air defence was important. In part, this was a matter of protecting the German public, and thus an instance of a political strategy focused on morale on the Home Front.

The direction and timing of Allied attacks, issues in which leadership and a sense of practicality interacted, remain contentious to the present. Thus, the results of amphibious invasions lead to the question of whether air and sea operations were inadequate unless supported by an invasion. This is a question that arises with the German threat to Britain itself in 1940 and thereafter, with Axis pressure on Malta in 1941–2, with American 'island-hopping' in the Pacific in 1943–5, and with the American 'endgame' for Japan. Similar questions can be raised about areas that were not islands, but nevertheless were vulnerable to amphibious attack, notably mainland Italy and Yugoslavia in 1943–5.

In short, had a combination of naval pressure and air attack made the actual presence of invading troops less necessary or even redundant? This point then links to issues of strategic priority as with the necessity, or not, of the recapture of the Philippines as a stage prior to the invasion of Japan. Such hypotheticals, which, in part, reflected later arguments about what were then present (as well as past) options in terms of capability, doctrine and planning, are of value because many of them played a role in strategic debate at the time.

Implausible counterfactuals help to throw light on what occurred as the causes, course and context that explain the implausibility can be clarified. A frequently cited one, notably so by Poles, is the counterfactual in which Britain and France invade Germany on 4 September 1939, using every available soldier, while also continuing their build up. In practice, despite a lack of preparations, especially in terms of the location of British units, which took time to deploy in France, some advance could have been made but, as with the idea of sending the British fleet into the Baltic, the wisdom of such a step is highly questionable. The advance would have left an exposed front that would have been vulnerable to counterattack, as happened to the French in 1870. There would not have been the possibility in this resulting front of reliance on prepared fortifications in the shape of the Maginot Line. In facing Anglo-French attack, there was a buffer zone for the Germans in the sense of the area to the west of the Rhine and, in addition, it is unclear how the river could have been passed. There was also the political dimension that such an invasion might have strengthened support for Hitler.

So with the counterfactual that Hitler preserved an alliance with the Soviet Union, either through continuing an alliance with Stalin or by disposing of him. This thesis is implausible given Hitler's views. It demonstrates, nevertheless, how the list of counterfactuals can be readily expanded. They throw much light on the many possibilities for speculation that the war provides, but without necessarily offering plausible alternatives.

Grouping counterfactuals is instructive. Most of those covered so far relate to choices made at the time. There are also those focused on events. The key ones are obviously those of the war itself. A good example is the Battle of Midway which provides a key example for a 'Japanese-doing-better' counter-factual. The launching on time of a Japanese patrol aircraft might have led to the discovery of the American carriers with sufficient time for the Japanese to destroy them. Under major domestic political pressure, the Americans would then, irrespective of the real character of the Japanese threat, have had to concentrate resources on defending the West Coast and even more the Hawai'ian Islands, thereby deflecting resources from Operation Torch. The consequence might have been to leave the Axis defeat in North Africa in doubt and the Allied invasion of Italy indefinitely delayed. Cumulatively, this would have enabled the Germans to siphon off resources from the west and use them against the Soviets. A focus on the defence would have also lessened the chance of a Solomon Islands offensive. Thus, reasonable success for the Americans in the Pacific theatre was a precondition for sustaining both the eventual level of engagement in the European theatre and the eventual pace of Pacific advance. At Midway, Japan certainly had good equipment and better aircrew, and it is worth noting that the American 'intelligence' advantage requires a 'fist' to use the advantage.

At Midway, luck was a key American aid. It was also important in responding to Japanese attack at the Battle of Leyte Gulf in 1944, but, by that stage of the war, the Americans had greater fighting experience as well as superior resources.

Preceding events are important as well, and some are so in an unexpected fashion. For example, Republican victory in the Spanish Civil War (1936–9) would have had consequences both during the German–Soviet alignment in 1939–41 and in 1941, when this broke down, possibly leading then to a German invasion, maybe assisted by Italian and, even, Vichy forces. Spanish naval bases challenged British control of Atlantic trading routes.

As with most counterfactuals, the range of possible permutations, and over different timescales, means, however, that clear conclusions about likely trajectories cannot be readily drawn.

There is room for considerable discussion about the value of many counterfactuals. For example, any scenario about Japan fighting the United States without having to fight China, because the latter had been defeated or a peace negotiated, is implausible in light of the situation in China and the ethos of the Japanese army. In addition, had more Japanese troops been available, for example in the Philippines in 1944–5, then the Japanese would probably have had higher casualties, but without there being any difference to the outcome of the war. Again, the issue is problematic, but it does capture the contingencies faced by contemporaries.

Counterfactual practice is taken further in board games. These have a long presence. As a child, I played the Avalon Hill game Stalingrad (1963), which in fact was about the Eastern Front as a whole. It captured the strategic dilemma faced by the Germans in military terms,[8] but not really the issue of political resilience or the military one of surprise. Other Avalon Hill wargames included Afrika Korps (1963–4), Blitzkrieg (1963), Midway (1964) and Battle of the Bulge (1991 reissue). As part of the regrouping of the industry, the Avalon Hill label eventually acquired Axis and Allies (1981), originally published by Nova Game Designs, and later called Axis and Allies: Classic. The variations thereof has been highly successful, with the variants including Axis and Allies: Europe, Axis and Allies: Pacific, Axis and Allies: Revised, the 2009 anniversary edition, and more specific games including Guadalcanal Afrika Korps and Battle of the Bulge. The global interaction was offered in Axis and Allies 1942 (2009) not least with the note 'Axis and Allies Pacific 1940 can be combined with Axis and Allies Europe 1940 to create the

Axis and Allies experience to date.' In practice, moving pieces on such boards greatly reduces the necessary complexity of the discussion of possibilities. Moreover, this process is linked to a tendency to attribute success or failure to one factor at the expense of many. The complexity flowing from a focus on many factors is far more appropriate.[9]

9

Conclusions

The dates 25 July 1943 and 18 July 1944 saw strategy to the fore. On each of those days, governments fell as a result of military failure. Allied success in Sicily led to the arrest of Mussolini on 25 July, and to the formation of a new Italian government, backed by the army. The new Prime Minister signed, on 3 September, an armistice with the Allies without informing most of the cabinet, nor the three services Chiefs of Staff, nor the King, thus helping cause a disastrously confused and weak response to German intervention. This showed anew the significance of the military dimension.

The American capture of Saipan and Tinian in 1944, from which Japan could be bombed, led to the resignation of the Japanese cabinet on 18 July. Japan fought on, although without real governmental coherence or even direction. Each episode demonstrated the extent to which strategies were impacted in contexts of political cause and consequence, contexts that were ever present, even if not always to the fore publicly. Indeed, the need for success in order to strengthen, or at least maintain, political control was a constant.

The 20 July 1944 Bomb Plot in Germany further illustrated this point. Like the overthrow of Mussolini, it also indicated the significance of the military if opposition was to be possible, let alone successful. The role of the Emperor, however, prevented, or at least seriously lessened, any such resistance in Japan, although there was to be opposition in the Manchurian army in August 1945 to the instruction to surrender, and the Emperor had to intervene to ensure obedience. In the Soviet Union, the capacity for a different path was crushed by Stalin's pre-war purges. In Britain and the United States, despite frequent grumbles about politicians, for example in Britain in early 1940 and later directed against Churchill, the military accepted their position and the war did not lead to any change to it.

However, failure did have political consequences, which very much brings to the fore the strategic assumptions of the time, as well as some of the counterfactuals discussed in the previous chapter. In Britain in May 1940, Neville Chamberlain fell as Prime Minister. He was weakened by Conservative disquiet over the energy and style of his war leadership, harmed by poor man-management, and discredited by failure in Norway. His successor, Churchill, had backed a rash policy over Norway; but his reputation as a resolute opponent of Hitler helped ensure that he became Prime Minister on 10 May, although not leader of the Conservative Party, a position that Chamberlain continued to hold until ill health led to his retirement, after which Churchill replaced him. Failure in France soon after Churchill became Prime Minister challenged his position, with some politicians wanting to negotiate peace. Nevertheless, Churchill was able to see off the challenge, which lacked parliamentary traction. Moreover, there was no immediate German military follow-up to the Fall of France.

In 1942, failure in North Africa, where Tobruk fell to German and Italian forces on 20–1 June with the loss of most of the garrison, failure that Hitler misleadingly thought might result in

Britain turning to negotiations, led to a censure motion in the House of Commons on 1 July. Churchill easily survived this mishandled attack, but it reflected widespread political concern about military failure and his leadership. This concern continued in the autumn, with much criticism, intrigues by Sir Stafford Cripps, the left-wing Lord Privy Seal and Leader of the House of Commons, who wanted to replace him, and the call for his resignation from the pro-Soviet Labour MP Aneurin Bevan. Immediately after victory at El Alamein in November 1942, Churchill, whose political position had become far less vulnerable, was able to demote Cripps to Minister of Aircraft Production. Hitler's belief that military defeat would challenge governmental stability in Britain was not necessarily wrong, even though it was lessened by the coalition formed in 1940. There was also criticism of Churchill in the press. Lord Beaverbrook, a press magnate who was the Minister of Aircraft Production in 1940–1, used his newspapers to press for a Second Front at once. Moreover, he was a consistent supporter of Stalin. Thus, Beaverbrook claimed that the Soviets were entitled to annex the Baltic states and also defended Stalin in 1944 for refusing to help the Warsaw Rising.[1]

In the United States, there was no such wartime coalition, while national elections proceeded in wartime, as they did not in Britain where they were only held to fill vacancies. The American government did not take political blame for failure against Japan in the first months of the year. One of the 'might have beens' relates to what would have happened had failure continued; and there was no inherent reason why Midway on 4–5 June 1942 should have been an overwhelming triumph. The previous naval battle, Coral Sea, had been closer to a draw in terms of warships sunk. In contrast, the Americans were to be in a considerably better position at the time of the major naval battles of 1944.

In the event, the 1942 midterm elections, held on 3 November, took place against the background of the dramatic success at Midway, of no more Japanese advances and of the American counterattacks at Guadalcanal, which very much suggested a turning of the tide, although the last was not certain until January 1943. The Republicans gained seats in both houses of Congress, but the Democrats retained control of each; and Congress subsequently focused on domestic issues and not on challenging Roosevelt over the war. This proved a good background for him to win re-election as President on 7 November 1944, and with a continued dominance of Congress as a result of the elections that year. Internal domestic constraints were very different in Germany and the Soviet Union.

The failure of the powers that launched each world war to translate their initial victories into lasting political or military success helped to give an attritional character to each war, and at the strategic level as well as in the nature of fighting. In the Second World War, Allied attacks simultaneously on Germany from a number of directions proved more successful than they had done in the First World War when attempted each year in 1914–17. By late 1943, the cumulative pressure was more intense in the Second World War, in part due to the addition of large-scale air attack. Ironically, this pressure owed most to the total failure of Hitler's strategy bound up in the unsuccessful attack on his one-time Soviet ally in 1941. Having sought to impose sequential warfare and prioritisation on other powers, Hitler had simultaneous warfare and total commitment imposed on Germany. This was also the case for Japan in August 1945.

The parallel with Napoleon in 1812 was instructive, even if the ideological context of the two struggles was very different. That Napoleon was the key field commander of the army, a role Hitler, despite his micro-management, neither sought nor fulfilled, does not negate this comparison nor alter this verdict of total strategic failure in both cases. Whereas Germany in the First World War had eventually, in 1918, succeeded in its goal of turning a two-front war begun in 1914 into a one-front one, Hitler, in 1941, went from a one-front to a two-front one. Like Napoleon in 1812 (but not 1805 or 1808), this proved disastrous, although Napoleon in 1812 at least had the advantage of the outbreak of a diversionary war between Britain and the United States that he had helped to cause.

For both Napoleon and Hitler, the broadening out of the war was not so much military adventurism, although that doubtless played a role, but, instead, a totally flawed reading of the international situation. In particular, there was a failure to understand the political situation within Russia or the Soviet Union, namely the ability and, crucially, willingness there to continue fighting despite facing defeats. Depending on the definition of strategy, Napoleon and Hitler lost the war because they should have chosen the strategy of continued peace with Russia/the Soviet Union; a conclusion amplified by Napoleon failing to respond adequately in negotiations with Austria in 1813 and 1814, and by Hitler's declaration of war on the United States later in 1941. However, such a choice would not have been in accordance with their ideology, nature or regime. In particular, it is unclear that a rational actor model can be applied, or certainly narrowly applied, to the Germans in either world war and the Japanese in the Second World War, or indeed to Napoleon who was also inherently bellicose.

The inadequacies of Axis strategy alone do not explain Allied victory. Indeed, analysing the strategies of the Axis and Allies is not enough to explain the war's outcomes. Positing outcomes at one level of war, or mostly at one level, is too deterministic. Instead, Allied victory rested on a number of factors, and the weight placed on them is significant to the issue of the appropriateness of the strategic choices of both sides. In a repetition of analysis of the First World War, there is a tension between emphasis on the battlefield and that on the Home Front, the latter focused for the Second World War on the struggle for production. The United States and the Soviet Union were certainly wedded to tactical, operational and strategic concepts that were founded upon a significant advantage over their opponents in resources and industrial capability, as (eventually) with the use of American aircraft carriers in the Pacific. The Allies deliberately used their superior resources in the sure knowledge of history, in the shape of the previous world war. Resources and, crucially, their deployment and employment were an important aspect of the strategic dynamic. This use, of course, had to relate to the military environment. Thus, carriers were far more significant in the Pacific than in European waters where, in contrast, there was a vulnerability to land-based air power, and notably so in the Mediterranean.

Such general points, however, did not determine the success of more particular strategies. Linked to this, Soviet operational art and, even more, American and British war making also reflected a determination not to be limited to attritional methods. The Americans and British knew that the size of their armies did not permit such an approach.

Moreover, moving away from a resource-focused explanation of the Second World War, with the determinism that implies, or can imply, not least with German and Japanese arguments about losing only due to being 'out-resourced', leads to a recovery of pre-war and wartime uncertainties, and of the political and military conjunctures and contingencies of wartime. That recovery results in a greater emphasis on the choices made, and that is an appropriate approach to the subject. It means that the focus on mass and attrition has to be qualified.[2]

The choices made were strategic, not just in the choice of areas for attacking and in the sequencing involved, but also with reference to the procurement and use of specific weapon systems, and, in particular, their integration into combined arms practices and doctrine. Moreover, the latter had to develop in response to choices made by opponents, choices at the strategic, operational and tactical levels. The quantity of military resources as well as their transformation in the shape of new capability have to be understood in interaction with tasking: the goals set and envisaged.

New capability was a matter of qualitative as well as quantitative advances, and on land, sea and air. As Fuller pointed out, in the *Sunday Pictorial* of 1 October 1944, this involved changes in doctrine, tactics and operational method as well as technology. Writing of D-Day, Fuller noted the need no longer to capture a port:

> had our sea power remained what it had been, solely a weapon to command the sea, the garrison Germany established in France almost certainly would have proved sufficient. It was a change in the conception of naval power which sealed the doom of that great fortress. Hitherto in all overseas invasions the invading forces had been fitted to ships. Now ships were fitted to the invading forces ... how to land the invading forces in battle order ... this difficulty has been overcome by building various types of special landing boats and pre-fabricated landing stages.

Complicating the strategic dimension was the extent to which, in part due to the dynamics of international alignments, goals were neither predictable nor readily quantifiable. Moreover, the interaction was a two-way process, in that capability can greatly help shape tasking and, moreover, affect the underlying assumptions referred to as strategic culture. At the same time, the choice of words is deliberate: 'help' and 'affect' are not the same as determine.

Strategy involved an effective use of information. The Allies eventually proved to be better than the Axis at understanding the areas in which they were fighting and the resources that could be deployed, and in planning accordingly. In contrast, improvisation strongly characterised Axis planning and responses, and did so in the case of Germany, Italy and Japan. Moreover, this situation did not improve as the war continued. Instead, it deteriorated. Repeatedly, Hitler's emphasis was on the socio-economic and political conditions he wished to see, and not on those that existed. Linked to this, in planning and campaigning, the Axis stress was often on the value of superior will, rather than on the realities of climate, terrain and logistics. The constraints posed by the last three were ignored, for example, in the totally unsuccessful Japanese offensive against the British on the India–Burma (Myanmar) border in 1944.

Constraints operated in many ways, whether in terms of the resources available or in their successful use. Thus, in March 1944, the British Chiefs of Staff responded to pressure from Churchill that they plan for a year's campaigning to restore British power in Malaya and Singapore, before British forces were switched to join the Americans in the Pacific in attacking Japan:

This assumes a flexibility which would not, we fear, prove practicable. The administrative preparations for whatever operations may be decided upon, whether in the East or in the West, will be on a vast scale, if indeed not beyond our power, to make these preparations in both areas. There is thus no question of retaining indefinitely an option in this matter. It is essential to make a decision within the next three months as to which policy is to be adopted, and to adhere to it.[3]

They were also convinced of the need to focus on the Pacific in order to bring the war to a speedy conclusion.

Instructively, the Axis poverty of strategic understanding is difficult to capture in maps, both those produced at the time and subsequently, since assumptions about willpower were not really subject to cartographic depiction. At the same time, there were clear contrasts between availability and use of information due to countries' differing cartographic capabilities – for example, the much greater American one as opposed to that of Japan. This was symptomatic of a more general contrast in information capability. With this, as with other aspects and in other conflicts, it can be too easy to attribute to winners all the skills of vision, strategic know-how, preparation and back-up; whereas there is a tendency to imply that losers lose because they lack these skills. The skill set just enumerated was clearly significant, but it also interacted with multiple contingencies including the dynamics of alliance relations and the results of operational moves.

Evaluations vary considerably. Stalin was a winner from the war, and therefore his strategy deserves attention. In practice, however, this strategy hit major problems, notably through failing to understand Hitler's intentions. Instead, alliance with Hitler in 1939–41 helped ensure that the latter was able to strengthen his position greatly by defeating other powers so that most German land forces could focus in 1941 on fighting the Soviet Union; while Hitler, like Napoleon in 1812, could also call on an extensive alliance, as he would not have been able to do in 1939 or, even so clearly, 1940. In another context, and facing powers with different values, the Soviet Union from the early 1970s faced a much more difficult strategic situation because the Sino-Soviet split of the 1960s became militarily more of a threat due to China's rapprochement with the United States. China, in the 1950s, had built up its strength with Soviet support.

The surprise German attack on the Soviet Union in June 1941 was also a serious failure for the Soviets, not least as it forced Stalin to seek help from his former opponent, Britain. Subsequently, Soviet strategy also hit problems in that Stalin's timetable for help from Britain and the United States in the shape of the Second Front was unrealistic, and put pressure on the alliance. Moreover, Stalin's victories were won at a heavy cost for the Soviet Union, notably in human life. Nevertheless, prior to the war, during it, and in the peace settlement and aftermath, Stalin did expand the Soviet empire greatly.

The other Allied powers might appear as losers which had to spend lives and resources to maintain at least elements of the status quo before the war. While very much the case with Britain, France and China, this was not the case with the United States. It did not represent nor really support the status quo. Instead, the United States transformed the situation in Europe and East Asia by becoming a power in both, which matched the Soviet increase in range in both. Added to this, the United States, as the world's only nuclear power in 1945, possessed the clear strategic advantage of being alone at the cutting edge of military technology, and thus having both a known and an unknowable capability advantage. The Americans by 1945 were also the world's leading naval power and had an unrivalled amphibious strength. With Britain, the United States had the only viable long-range bomber force, while the Soviets had developed none of these capabilities.

Indeed, while the Soviets did best at benefiting from the collapse of Germany and its East European allies, they had to share with the Americans the benefit from the collapse of Japan. Initially, this was very much to the advantage of the Americans. In essence, the Soviet Union got southern Sakhalin, the Kuriles and the potential offered by Manchuria and North Korea, as well as clear dominance over Mongolia. In contrast, the United States gained control of Japan and its Pacific possessions, and its allies were able in 1945 to establish themselves in China (bar Manchuria), South Korea and their former colonies, albeit with a degree of precariousness. This precariousness, indeed, translated into the revival of the Chinese Civil War (1946–9), which ended in a Communist victory, as well as the developing crises of the British, French and Dutch empires in Asia. From the latter, the Communists were to benefit, but the Americans even more.

How far wartime strategy can be linked to these post-war developments is open to debate. Yet, planning for the post-war was a continual aspect of wartime activity, and any assessment of wartime strategy has to take note of this point.

Strategy, throughout, emerges as a crucial tool not only for contemporaries conducting the war, but also for subsequent consideration of it, and notably so in the contested field of public history. A broad definition of strategy captures the ways in which it was considered by contemporaries and then subsequently.

Notes

ABBREVIATIONS

ADD	Additional Manuscripts
AWM	Australian War Memorial
BL	Department of Manuscripts, British Library, London
CAB	Cabinet Office papers, London
Churchill Papers	Churchill papers, Churchill College, Cambridge
Kremlin Letters	D. Reynolds and V. Pechatnov (eds), *The Kremlin Letters: Stalin's Wartime Correspondence with Churchill and Roosevelt* (New Haven, CT, 2018)
LH	Liddell Hart Centre for Military Archives, King's College, London
NA	National Archives, London
NAA	National Archives of Australia, Canberra

CHAPTER 1

1 Committee of Imperial Defence, Defence Requirements Sub-Committee Report, 28 February 1934, NA, CAB. 16/109 fol. 15.
2 General Staff, 'The future reorganisation of the British Army', 9 September 1935, NA, WO, 32/4612.
3 K. Roy, *Battle for Malaya. The Indian Army in Defeat, 1941–1942* (Bloomington, IN, 2019), p. 20.
4 Memorandum by Sir Victor Wellesley, 1 February 1932, NA, CAB, 24/228 fol. 66.

5   B. A. Wintermute and D. J. Ulbrich (eds), *Race and Gender in Modern Western Warfare* (Boston, MA, 2019), pp. 187–231.
6   'The Present Sino-Japanese Military Situation', report by Chiefs of Staff, 9 December 1939, NA, CAB, 66/4/2, p. 16.
7   S. C. M. Paine, *The Japanese Empire: Grand Strategy from the Meiji Restoration to the Pacific War* (Cambridge, 2017).
8   LH, Alanbrooke papers 6/3/6.

CHAPTER 2

1   B. W. Blouet, *Halford Mackinder* (College Station, TX, 1987), p. 174.
2   Summary of Evidence in regard to the Progress of German Rearmament, NA, CAB, 24/250 fols 123–5.
3   D. Bakić, *Britain and Interwar Danubian Europe: Foreign Policy and Security Challenges, 1919–1936* (London, 2017).
4   M. Shiavon, *Corap: Bouc émissaire de la défaite de 1940* (Paris, 2017).
5   LH, Adam 2/3, pp. 2–3.
6   NA, CAB, 24/84 fol. 285.
7   G. T. Clews, *Churchill's Phoney War: A Study in Folly and Frustration* (Annapolis, MD, 2019).
8   A. Lambert, 'The Only British Advantage: Sea Power and Strategy, September 1939–June 1940', in M. H. Clemmesen and M. S. Faulkner (eds), *Northern European Overture to War, 1939–1941. From Memel to Barbarossa* (Leiden, 2013), p. 73.
9   Strategic review for regional commanders, 16 August 1941, AWM, 3 DRL/6643, 1/27.
10 E. Maudsley, *The War for the Seas: A Maritime History of World War II* (New Haven, CT, 2019), p. 79.
11 D. Showalter, J. P. Robinson and J. A. Robinson, *The German Failure in Belgium, August 1914* (Jefferson, NC, 2019).
12 C. Hartmann, *Halder: Generalstabschef Hitlers 1938–1942* (Paderborn, 2010).
13 G. P. Megaree, *Inside Hitler's High Command* (Lawrence, KS, 2000), p. 235; R. Hutchinson, *German Foreign Intelligence from Hitler's War to the Cold War: Flawed Assumptions and Faulty Analysis* (Lawrence, KS, 2019); V. Ullrich, *Hitler: Downfall 1939–45* (London, 2020). p. 626.
14 B. Simms, *Hitler: Only the World Was Enough* (London, 2019).
15 R. M. Citino, *The German Way of War: From the Thirty Years War to the Third Reich* (Lawrence, KS, 2005).

CHAPTER 3

1 R. Bassett, *Hitler's Spy Chief: The Wilhelm Canaris Mystery* (London, 2005).
2 Wavell to Lieutenant General Sir Thomas Blamey, 25 June 1940, AWM, 3 DRL/6643 1/27.
3 C. Goeschel, *Mussolini and Hitler: The Forging of the Fascist Alliance* (New Haven, CT, 2018).
4 G. Sloan, 'The Royal Navy and Organizational Learning: the Western Approaches Tactical Unit and the Battle of the Atlantic', *Naval War College Review*, vol. 72, no. 4 (2019), p. 129.
5 D. C. Watt, *Russia. War, Peace and Diplomacy* (London, 2004), pp. 276–86.
6 J. Harris and R. Wilbourn, *Rudolf Hess* (London, 2019).
7 A. Toprani, *Oil and the Great Powers: Britain and Germany, 1914–1945* (Oxford, 2019), p. 251.
8 R. F. Wetterhahn, *The Early Air War in the Pacific: Ten Months that Changed the Course of World War II* (Jefferson, NC, 2019).
9 J. D'Angelo, *Victory at Midway: The Battle that Changed the Course of World War II* (Jefferson, NC, 2018).
10 E. Cernuschi and V. P. O'Hara, 'The Italian Navy and the Pacific War', *World War II Quarterly* (2006), pp. 14–19.
11 Strategic Review for Regional Commanders, 16 August 1941, AWM, 3 DRL/6643.
12 Field Marshal Lord Alanbrooke, *War Diaries, 1939–1945* (London, 2001), pp. 245–7.
13 P. Tuunainen, 'The Finnish Army at War: Operations and Soldiers, 1939–45', in T. Kinnunen and V. Kivimäki (eds), *Finland in World War II* (Leiden, 2012), pp. 158–9.
14 J. Gooch, *Mussolini's War: Fascist Italy from Triumph to Collapse, 1935–1943* (London, 2020).
15 D. Motadel, 'The Global Authoritarian Moment and the Revolt against Empire', *American Historical Review*, no. 124 (2019), pp. 843–77.
16 R. Dale, '"For What and for Whom Were We Fighting?" Red Army Soldiers, Combat Motivation and Survival Strategies on the Eastern Front in the Second World War', in C. Pennell and F. Ribeiro de Meneses (eds), *A World at War, 1911–1949: Explorations in the Cultural History of War* (Leiden, 2019), p. 158.
17 B. Shepherd, *War in the Wild East: The German Army and Soviet Partisans* (Cambridge, MA, 2004).
18 E. Mark, *Japan's Occupation of Java in the Second World War: A Transnational History* (London, 2018).
19 Wilson to Blamey, 19 April 1941, AWM, 3 DRL/6643, 1/3.
20 Menzies to Blamey, 21 June 1941, AWM. 3DRL/6643, 1/1.

CHAPTER 4

1 C. L. Symonds, *World War II at Sea: A Global History* (Oxford, 2018), pp. 180–1.
2 W. T. Johnsen, *The Origins of the Grand Alliance: Anglo-American Military Collaboration from the Panny Incident to Pearl Harbor* (Lexington, KY, 2016).
3 C. E. Kirkpatrick, *An Unknown Future and a Doubtful Present: Writing the Victory Plan of 1941* (Washington, DC, 1992), p. 128.
4 D. M. Glantz, *Kharkov 1942: Anatomy of a Military Disaster Through Soviet Eyes* (Rockville, NY, 1998).
5 P. Chasseaud, *Mapping the Second World War* (Glasgow, 2015).
6 Kirkpatrick, *An Unknown Future and a Doubtful Present*, p. 128.
7 A. Toprani, 'The First War for Oil: The Caucasus, German Strategy, and the Turning Point of the War on the Eastern Front, 1942', *Journal of Military History*, no. 80 (2016), pp. 815–54.

CHAPTER 5

1 Gooch, *Mussolini's War*.
2 D. M. Glantz, *Battle for Belorussia: The Red Army's Forgotten Campaign of October 1943–April 1944* (Lawrence, KS, 2016).
3 H. Boog, G. Krebs and D. Vogel (eds), *Germany and the Second World War VII: The Strategic Air War in Europe and the War in the West and East Asia 1943–1945* (Oxford, 2006).
4 D. W. Wildermuth, '"I am fully aware of my guilt . . .": Insights from a Soviet Military Tribunal's Investigation of the German Army's 35th Division, 1946–47', *Journal of Military History*, no. 83 (2019), pp. 1189–212.
5 B. H. Shepherd, *Hitler's Soldiers: The German Army in the Third Reich* (New Haven, CT, 2016).
6 J. P. Duffy, *Target: America. Hitler's Plan to Attack the United States* (Westport, CT, 2004).
7 D. K. Yelton, 'Older German Officers and National Socialist Activism: Evidence from the German *Volkssturm*', *Journal of Military History*, no. 83 (2019), pp. 455–85.
8 J. A. Yellen, *The Greater Fast Asia Co-Prosperity Sphere: When Total Empire Met Total War* (Berlin, 2018).
9 T. J. Cutler, *The Battle of Leyte Gulf at 75: A Retrospective* (Annapolis, MD, 2019).

CHAPTER 6

1 M. A. Stoler, *Allies and Adversaries: The Joint Chiefs of Staff, the Grand Alliance, and US Strategy in World War II* (Chapel Hill, NC, 2000).

2 W. Heinrichs and M. Gallicchio, *Implacable Foes: War in the Pacific, 1944–1945* (Oxford, 2017), p. 430.

3 A. Danchev, 'Great Britain: The Indirect Strategy', in D. Reynolds *et al.* (eds), *Allies at War* (New York, 1994), pp. 1–26.

4 A. Jackson, *Persian Gulf Command: A History of the Second World War in Iran and Iraq* (New Haven, CT, 2018), p. 345.

5 Information from Enrico Cernuschi.

6 Churchill to Stalin, 24 January, Stalin to Churchill, 29 January 1944, *Kremlin Letters*, pp. 364, 369–70.

7 *Kremlin Letters*, p. 232.

8 G. Bailey, *The Arsenal of Democracy: Aircraft Supply and the Anglo-American Alliance, 1938–1942* (Edinburgh, 2013).

9 C. Symonds, 'For Want of a Nail: The Impact of Shipping on Grand Strategy in World War II', *Journal of Military History*, no. 81 (2017), pp. 657–66.

10 W. A. Jacobs, 'Royal Air Force Bomber Command, the "Overlord Air Diversion", and "Precision" Bombing at Night', *Journal of Military History*, no. 83 (2019), pp. 1161–88.

11 P. Caddick-Adams, *Sand and Steel: A New History of D-Day* (London, 2019), p. 118.

12 Rutgers University Library, New Brunswick, New Jersey, Fuller papers, Scrapbooks vol. 6.

13 A. Buchanan, *American Grand Strategy in the Mediterranean during World War II* (Cambridge, 2014).

14 Churchill to Stalin, 8 February 1944, *Kremlin Letters*, p. 376.

15 Megaree, *Inside Hitler's High Command*, p. 217.

16 C. J. Dick, *From Victory to Stalemate: The Western Front, Summer 1944* (Lawrence, KS, 2016).

17 LH, Alanbrooke papers 6/2/35.

18 S. Plokhy, *Forgotten Bastards of the Eastern Front: An Untold Story of World War Two* (London, 2019).

19 LH, Alanbrooke papers 6/3/8.

20 Penney to Major-General John Sinclair, Director of Military Intelligence, War Office, 2 May 1945, LH, Penney 5/1.

CHAPTER 7

1 Stalin to Churchill, 7 January 1944, *Kremlin Letters*, p. 358.
2 Stalin to Churchill, 3 March, Churchill to Stalin, 7 March 1944, *Kremlin Letters*, pp. 387, 393.
3 D. M. Horner, *High Command: Australia and Allied Strategy, 1939–1945* (Canberra, 1982); P. J. Dean, *MacArthur's Coalition: US and Australian Military Operations in the Southwest Pacific Area, 1942–1945* (Lawrence, KS, 2018).
4 Churchill to Sir Alan Brooke, 20 March 1944, LH, Alanbrooke papers 6/3/8.
5 Layton to First Sea Lord, 13 September, Mountbatten to Layton, 15 September 1944, BL, Add. 74796.
6 Brooke to Sir Henry Maitland Wilson, 2 August 1944, LH, Alanbrooke 6/3/6.
7 F. A. Blazich, 'Neptune's Oracle: Admiral Harry Yarnell's Wartime Planning, 1918–20 and 1943–44', *Naval War College Review*, vol. 73, no. 1 (winter 2020), pp. 120–6.
8 Penney to Major-General John Sinclair, Director of Military Intelligence, 2 May 1945, LH, Penney 5/1.
9 J. Haslam, 'Stalin's Fears of a Separate Peace, 1942', *Intelligence and National Security*, vol. 8, no. 4 (1993), pp. 97–9.
10 N. Smith, *American Empire: Roosevelt's Geographer and the Prelude to Globalization* (Berkeley, CA, 2003), p. 360.
11 F. L. Loewenheim *et al.* (eds), *Roosevelt and Churchill: Their Secret Wartime Correspondence* (New York, 1975), p. 459.

CHAPTER 8

1 Letter, *Standpoint*, no. 114 (September/October 2019), p. 7.
2 B. T. Wakabayashi (ed.), *The Nanking Atrocity, 1937–1938: Complicating the Picture* (2nd edn, New York, 2017).
3 T. D. Briddle, 'Dresden 1945: Reality, History, and Memory', and 'On the Crest of Fear: V-Weapons, the Battle of the Bulge, and the Last Stages of World War II in Europe', *Journal of Military History*, no. 72 (2008), pp. 413–49, and no. 83 (2019), pp. 157–94.
4 B. Stephens, 'WWII and the Ingredients of Slaughter', *New York Times* (30 August 2019).
5 For the dangerous consequences for the United States of the fall of Britain, A. Roberts, *Leadership in War* (London, 2019), p. 65.
6 L. McKinstry, *Attlee and Churchill: Allies in War, Adversaries in Peace* (London, 2019).

7 A. Mierzejewski, *The Collapse of the German War Economy 1944–1945: Allied Air Power and the German National Railway* (Chapel Hill, NC, 1988).

8 L. Pulsipher, 'Stalingrad', in J. Lowder (ed.), *Hobby Games: The 100 Best* (Seattle, WA, 2007), pp. 291–4.

9 C. Stockings and E. Hancock (eds), *Swastika over the Acropolis: Re-interpreting the Nazi Invasion of Greece in World War II* (Leiden, 2013), p. 535.

CHAPTER 9

1 C. Williams, *Max Beaverbrook: Not Quite a Gentleman* (London, 2019).

2 R. Smith, *The Utility of Force: The Art of War in the Modern World* (2nd edn, London, 2019), p. 142.

3 Chiefs of Staff to Churchill, 28 March 1944, LH, Alanbrooke 6/3/9.

Selected Further Reading

There is a mass of relevant literature, and at many levels of discussion and scales of coverage. Moreover, a large number of relevant works appears all the time, and in all the languages of the combatants. As the readers of this work will primarily use English, I restrict myself to a selection of recent relevant books. Earlier studies can be approached through their bibliographies, while new research can best be approached through the *Journal of Military History*. The significant cartographic dimension is best considered through *The Times Atlas of the Second World War* (London, 1989), edited by John Keegan, and my own *A History of the Second World War in 100 Maps* (London, 2020). Jean Lopez *et al.*, *World War II: Infographics* (New York, 2019) uses the latest graphic design.

Ball, Simon, *The Bitter Sea: The Struggle for Mastery in the Mediterranean, 1935–1949* (London, 2009).

Black, Jeremy, *Tank Warfare* (Bloomington, IN, 2020).

Buchanan, Andrew, *American Grand Strategy in the Mediterranean during World War II* (Cambridge, 2014).

—, *World War II in Global Perspective, 1931–1953: A Short History* (Oxford, 2019).

Citino, Robert, *The Wehrmacht's Last Stand: The German Campaigns of 1944–1945* (Lawrence, KS, 2017).

Deletant, Dennis, *Hitler's Forgotten Ally: Ion Antonescu and His Regime, Romania 1940–1944* (Basingstoke, 2006).

Edgerton, David, *Britain's War Machine: Weapons, Resources, and Experts in the Second World War* (Oxford, 2011).

Fritz, Stephen, *The First Soldier: Hitler as Military Leader* (New Haven, CT, 2018).

Goeschel, Christian, *Mussolini and Hitler: The Forging of the Fascist Alliance* (New Haven, CT, 2018).

Gooch, John, *Mussolini's War: Fascist Italy from Triumph to Collapse, 1935–1943* (London, 2020).

Grier, Howard, *Hitler, Dönitz and the Baltic Sea: The Third Reich's Last Hope, 1944–5* (Annapolis, MD, 2007).

Imlay, Talbot, *Facing the Second World War: Strategy, Politics, and Economics in Britain and France, 1938–40* (Oxford, 2003).

Johnson, William, *The Origins of the Grand Alliance: Anglo-American Military Collaboration from the Pannay Incident to Pearl Harbor* (Lexington, KY, 2016).

Kaiser, David, *No End Save Victory: How FDR Led the Nation into War* (New York, 2014).

Kershaw, Ian, *Fateful Choices; Ten Decisions that Changed the World, 1940–1941* (London, 2008).

Kiesling, Eugenia, *Arming against Hitler: France and the Limits of Military Planning* (Lawrence, KS, 1996).

Kiszely, John, *Anatomy of a Campaign: The British Fiasco in Norway, 1940* (Cambridge, 2017).

Koshiro, Y., *Imperial Eclipse: Japan's Strategic Thinking about Continental Asia before August 1945* (Ithaca, NY, 2013).

Lewis, Julian, *Changing Direction: British Military Planning for Post-War Strategic Defence, 1942–47* (2nd edn, London, 2001).

Maiolo, Joe, *Cry Havoc: The Arms Race and the Second World War, 1931–1941* (London, 2010).

Maudsley, Evan, *The War for the Seas: A Maritime History of World War II* (New Haven, CT, 2019).

Megargee, Geoffrey, *Inside Hitler's High Command* (Lawrence, KS, 2000).

Moorhouse, Roger, *The Devils' Alliance: Hitler's Pact with Stalin, 1939–1941* (New York, 2014).

—, *First to Fight: The Polish War 1939* (London, 2019).

Müller, Rolf-Dieter, *Enemy in the East: Hitler's Secret Plans to Invade the Soviet Union* (London, 2015).

Neiberg, Michael, *Potsdam: The End of World War II and the Remaking of Europe* (New York, 2015).

O'Brien, Philips P., *How the War Was Won: Air-Sea Power and Allied Victory in World War Two* (Cambridge, 2015).

O'Hara, Vincent, *Torch: North Africa and the Allied Path to Victory* (Annapolis, MD, 2015).

Paine, Sally, *The Japanese Empire: Grand Strategy from the Meiji Restoration to the Pacific War* (Cambridge, 2017).

Peattie, Mark, Edward Drea and Hans van de Ven (eds), *The Battle for China: Essays on the Military History of the Sino-Japanese War of 1937–1945* (Stanford, CA, 2010).

Pinkus, Oscar, *The War Aims and Strategies of Adolf Hitler* (Jefferson, NC, 2005).

Raack, Richard, *Stalin's Drive to the West, 1938–1945* (Stanford, CA, 1995).

Reynolds, David and Vladimir Pechatnov, *The Kremlin Letters: Stalin's Wartime Correspondence with Churchill and Roosevelt* (New Haven, CT, 2018).

Rieber, Alfred, *Stalin and the Struggle for Supremacy in Eurasia* (New York, 2015).

Salmon, Patrick, *Deadlock and Diversion: Scandinavia in British Strategy during the Twilight War, 1939–1940* (Bremerhaven, 2012).

Stahel, David, *Operation Barbarossa and Germany's Defeat in the East* (Cambridge, 2009).

Stewart, Andrew, *The First Victory: The Second World War and the East Africa Campaign* (New Haven, CT, 2016).

—, *A Very British Experience: Coalition, Defence and Strategy in the Second World War* (Brighton, 2012).

Taylor, Jay, *The Generalissimo: Chiang Kai-shek and the Struggle for Modern China* (Cambridge, MA, 2009).

Tooze, Adam, *The Wages of Destruction: The Making and Breaking of the Nazi Economy* (London, 2006).

Ullrich, Volker, *Hitler: Downfall 1939–45* (London, 2020).

Index